AT THE LIMITS OF MEMORY

Legacies of Slavery in the Francophone World

FRANCOPHONE POSTCOLONIAL STUDIES

The annual publication of the Society for Francophone Postcolonial Studies

New Series, Vol. 6

Francophone Postcolonial Studies

The annual publication of the Society for Francophone Postcolonial Studies

The Society for Francophone Postcolonial Studies (SFPS) is an international association which exists in order to promote, facilitate and otherwise support the work of all scholars and researchers working on colonial/postcolonial studies in the French-speaking world. SFPS was created in 2002 with the aim of continuing and developing the pioneering work of its predecessor organization, the Association for the Study of Caribbean and African Literature in French (ASCALF). SFPS does not seek to impose a monolithic understanding of the 'postcolonial' and it consciously aims to appeal to as diverse a range of members as possible, in order to engage in wide-ranging debate on the nature and legacy of colonialism in and beyond the French-speaking world. SFPS encourages work of a transcultural, transhistorical, comparative and interdisciplinary nature. It implicitly seeks to decolonize the term 'Francophone', emphasizing that it should refer to all cultures where French is spoken (including, of course, France itself), and it encourages a critical reflection on the nature of the cognate disciplines of French studies, on the one hand, and Anglophone postcolonial studies, on the other.

Our vision for this new publication with Liverpool University Press is that each volume will constitute a sort of *état present* on a significant topic, embracing various expressions of Francophone postcolonial cultures (e.g. literature, film, music, history), in relation to pertinent geographical areas (e.g. France/Belgium, the Caribbean, Africa, the Indian Ocean, Asia, Polynesia) and different periods (slavery, colonialism, the postcolonial era, etc.): above all, we are looking to publish research that will help to set new research agendas across our field. The editorial board of *Francophone Postcolonial Studies* invites proposals for edited volumes touching on any of the areas listed above; proposals should be sent to Dr Charlotte Baker (c.baker@lancaster.ac.uk). For further details, visit www.sfps.ac.uk.

AT THE LIMITS OF MEMORY

Legacies of Slavery in the Francophone World

Edited by
Nicola Frith
and
Kate Hodgson

Liverpool University Press

First published 2015 by
Liverpool University Press
4 Cambridge Street
Liverpool
L69 7ZU

British Library Cataloguing-in-Publication data
A British Library CIP record is available

ISBN 978-1-78138-159-5 cased

Typeset by Carnegie Book Production, Lancaster
Printed and bound in the United States of America

Contents

**Beyond the Abolitionist Moment:
Memories and Counter-Memories of Labour Exploitation**

Illustrations

Slavery and Its Legacies: Remembering Labour Exploitation in the Francophone World

Nicola Frith and Kate Hodgson

Over the past decade, the field of memory studies has given rise to a growing body of literature that has responded to the recent boom in memories of slavery and the slave trade. The proliferation of memorial sites relating to Europe's slaving past has largely coincided with two key commemorative dates relating to abolitionism: the Abolition of the Slave Trade in 1807 (UK) and the Abolition of Slavery in 1848 (France). The accompanying literature – not least of which are the extensive studies conducted by Christine Chivallon and Françoise Vergès which bookend the current volume[1] – has served to enrich our understanding of this boom within both Francophone and Anglophone spheres. Within the particular socio-political context of the French Republic, research to date has tended to focus on the so-called *guerre de mémoires* ['memory war'] and its relevance to slavery studies, as well as on the (competing) forms of memory work that are taking place within and across distinct regions of the Republic as compared with other nation-states.[2] Yet until now there has been no collective study dedicated

[1] Their latest contributions include Chivallon's study of memories of slavery in the French Caribbean (2012) and Vergès's investigation into the continuation of predatory economics and its connections to slavery (2011).

[2] The list of possible references is too lengthy to be exhaustive here, but many can be found throughout this volume. Of particular note, in terms of France's memory war, are the works of Blanchard and Veyrat-Masson (2010) and Stora

to considering how these memorialization processes are operating across multiple Francophone contexts, or rather within and between countries that have a historical connection to France and its former colonial empire. While this volume cannot hope to be exhaustive in its scope, it nonetheless provides an important intervention that foregrounds the multiplicity of memories of slavery within the Francophone world, while also moving beyond slavery and, importantly, towards memories of other forms of colonial labour exploitation that took place in the post-abolition period of the nineteenth and twentieth centuries.

As is clearly revealed by the contributions presented here, memories of slavery and its colonial aftermath continue to represent a highly contentious subject of debate and have created complex matrices for the formation of national, regional and transnational identities. Chapters focusing on the French Caribbean and Haiti, West and North Africa, the Indian Ocean and metropolitan France do not simply showcase the breadth of memory work within the Francophone world, but additionally draw out important historical and discursive specificities that relate to the legacies of French-led slavery and labour exploitation. Divided into two parts, this volume highlights the blind spots that have marked public memories of slavery and slavery commemorations in all their many forms. It simultaneously engages with the (lack of) remembrance of other slave trades and other forms of labour exploitation that took place within and beyond the Atlantic triangle, including histories of domestic slavery in Francophone countries and the relationship between slavery and patterns of indenture and forced labour that followed the legal abolition of slavery in France's colonies in 1848. Part one – 'The Limits of Memorialization: Commemoration, Musealization and Patrimony' – focuses on nation-centred patrimonial processes and considers alternative forms of citizen-led resistance that are responding to state-centred imaginings of the past, while additionally exploring future memorial projects, such as Mémorial ACTe in Guadeloupe. In contrast, part two – 'Beyond the Abolitionist Moment: Memories and Counter-Memories of Labour Exploitation' – moves the debate beyond abolitionism, as the title suggests, by engaging with the complex legacies of other forms of labour exploitation in France's former empire post-1848 and by investigating some of the creative responses to the hegemony of western-centric and nation-centred abolitionist iconographies.

As will be explained in more depth below, these chapters serve collectively to problematize the much-celebrated abolitionist moment. They highlight the importance of transcending nation-centred configurations of memory and

(2011), whereas useful studies on slavery and its relation to memory include Bongie (2008), Vergès (2006), Miller (2008), Hourcade (2014) and Chivallon (2012).

teleological historiographies that have disconnected slavery from its pre- and post-abolitionist mutations. As such, they reveal the limitations of the ways in which the colonial past has been understood whenever it becomes locked into particular terminologies, iconicities and chronologies. In drawing from the fields of memory studies and postcolonial studies, it has thus been our intention to explore the eclectic forms of memory work being undertaken across France and its former empire. This ranges from memory work within nation-states, which is here explored to expose the workings of patrimonial discourses, to that which explodes the national narrative by reaching for a more complex, transnational and transhistorical understanding of the slave past and its meaning for society today.

Before providing an overview of the motifs that recur throughout this volume, it is worth outlining some of the historical and contemporary specificities relating to France's history of colonial slavery and abolition. This will provide the context for a more extensive understanding of the three key themes developed in individual chapters and which underpin the contents of this volume, namely: the need to find a broader definition of slavery and its relation to subsequent forms of labour exploitation; the instrumentalization of memories of slavery by state discourses and their use of particular iconographies, in contrast to 'guerrilla' or counter-forms of memorialization; and the more general need to move beyond the fixation on memory within national boundaries by moving out towards a more transnational approach to scholarship in slavery studies, while recognizing and exploring specific places and moments shaped by the history of French-led slavery and its contemporary legacies.

Historical Complexities, Complex Terminologies: Defining Slavery and Forced Labour

France's history of slavery and its subsequent construction of a public memory are atypical in many respects. The only European power to re-establish colonial slavery after having abolished it, France consequently lost the heart of its empire and its most valuable possession, Saint Domingue. Haiti, as it became known, was the first independent country in Latin America and the Caribbean, and the only black republic to have been founded by former slaves. In addition to the former losses of Canada and India to the British at the end of the Seven Years War (1754–63), the fundamental loss of Haiti and the subsequent attempts to forget it, notably by building a new colonial empire across Africa and Asia in the nineteenth and twentieth centuries, are central to understanding how slavery has been both of vital importance to and completely obscured within French national history. Importantly, this process of forgetting has, in recent years, seen a turning point. France has become the first, and indeed the only, European country to recognize slavery and the slave trade as crimes against humanity with the passing of the Taubira law on 10 May 2001.

In many other respects, however, the history of France's slave past can be compared to that of other European powers. As the third most prolific slave-trading nation of Europe (after Portugal and Britain), France was responsible for an estimated total of nearly 1.4 million slaves transported across the Atlantic over the course of three and a half centuries.[3] Like Britain, France developed a tradition of abolitionism, which saw major intellectual and political figures engaging with the problem of slavery in the eighteenth and nineteenth centuries. This historical legacy has dominated contemporary initiatives to commemorate slavery on a state-led level: while Britain saw the 'Wilberfest' of white abolitionist sentiment perpetuated in the bicentenary year of 2007, France's public memory of slavery during the 150th anniversary of the 1848 Abolition Act has equally been dominated by metropolitan abolitionism and particularly by the key figure of Victor Schœlcher (1804–93). Abolitionism, as part of a nation-centred narrative, has overshadowed the various international forms of black resistance that were so prominent and central to the history of the colonial and postcolonial francophone world, and has done so despite widespread acknowledgement among contemporary scholars of the fundamental significance of major historical events, like the Haitian revolution, in marking the beginning of the end of transatlantic slavery and heralding the modern postcolonial and neo-colonial era (Geggus, 2001; Nesbitt, 2005; Bongie, 2008).

We turn now to the first of our three themes — that is, the need for definitions that acknowledge the full complexity of French colonial labour exploitation before and after the supposed turning point of 1848. Like many other European imperial powers, France's colonial legacies were characterized by a complex combination of different forms of slavery and unfree labour that continued beyond the moment of abolition. These included the institutionalized practice of authorities turning a blind eye to entrenched generational servitude and debt bondage, as well as forced labour imposed by the state on colonized populations. The 1929 ILO report on global forced labour practices, published as France reached the apex of imperial ambition, revealed that the *corvée* (the system of unpaid labour for the state that was imposed by the colonial government) was widely employed across the French empire, although its administration was left to the governor of each individual

3 See Eltis and Richardson (2010), as well as the Trans-Atlantic Slave Trade Database, available online at www.slavevoyages.org.

colony. Similar systems were in operation throughout the British Empire and the colonies of other European countries, including the Belgian Congo. The report concluded that the strict regulation of compulsory labour in colonial situations was needed to avoid it becoming 'a more or less disguised form of slavery' (International Labour Conference, 1929: 9).

Defining slavery in the face of these multiple, fragmented and interconnected memories, which attest to the multiple forms of labour exploitation imposed during the period of French colonialism, is necessary, but also problematic. Historically, definitions of chattel slavery have been focused on the question of property and legal rights: a slave's right to dispose of his or her own person is removed upon legally becoming the property of another. The 1926 UN Slavery Convention, which considered slavery, servitude, forced labour and similar institutions and practices, defined the slave as a person over whom 'the powers attaching to the right of ownership are exercised'. This legal definition has subsequently been nuanced by social theorists, such as Orlando Patterson (1982), who views the slave's status as one based on alienation, violence and the fundamental imbalance of power to the extent that the 'social death' of the subject results. Ownership and power are thus key elements in defining slave status. Other characteristics that have contributed towards a shared definition of slavery include a system of inheritance, where the status of both master and slave is passed down from generation to generation, and caste, where slavery is an inescapably permanent state attached to a subordinated social group.

The process of alienation implicit in enslavement is thus based on the differentiation of the enslaved person from the dominant strata of society within which he or she exists, particularly through ethnic and/or racial distinction or other violent forms of othering. The absolute nature of the social alienation imposed on the slave was fundamental to the construction of the European Atlantic empires from the fifteenth century onwards. Spain, Portugal, Britain and France repeatedly justified their appropriation of the labour of indigenous peoples and imported Africans by staking their claims to a higher 'civilization' based upon race, culture and religion. The social alienation of the enslaved was also key in many parts of West Africa. In this context, ethnic identity and religion were determining factors in defining slaves' status and their suitability to be sold either to the domestic market or to the transatlantic trade (Lovejoy, 2009: 150). Once removed from his or her own social group and transported into an unfamiliar context, the slave is vulnerable to alienation and 'social death' – his or her descendants likewise becoming vulnerable to inheriting slave status.

Chattel slavery was not the sole form of labour appropriation practised in the colonies of the European powers, yet it quickly constituted the dominant and most sought-after workforce on the plantation. The majority of those who arrived as migrants in the Americas (forced or otherwise) prior to 1820 were enslaved Africans, as this was a labour force in particularly high demand among the European colonists of the time (Eltis, 2007). It was widely believed by the colonists that sub-Saharan Africans were constitutionally suited to hard labour in tropical climates. Despite the risks and expenses of procuring slaves from Africa, the transatlantic trade thrived, reaching its high point in the second half of the eighteenth century with nearly four million forcibly embarked upon the Middle Passage in a period of just fifty years (Eltis and Richardson, 2010). In the Francophone Atlantic context, the lion's share of slave imports went to Saint Domingue, generally considered to be the most prosperous and successful colony in the world. The other French Caribbean colonies of Guadeloupe and Martinique also received substantial numbers of imported and enslaved Africans. The very few slaves not consumed by the booming Antillean market sometimes made it to Louisiana and French Guiana, where demand was equally high, but purchasing power was weaker (Hall, 1992).

Early systems of indenture constituted another important source of labour, especially in the early years of the development of colonial plantations in the Americas. Before the transatlantic trade hit its peak, European workers, known as *engagés* or *trente-six mois* (three years commonly being the length of their period of servitude), were taken on by plantation owners desperate for labour. The nineteenth-century Haitian historian Thomas Madiou explained this phenomenon in the context of the colonial society of Saint Domingue, drawing clear distinctions between the fundamental and permanent alienation from the dominant colonial society experienced by the largely African-born enslaved population and the temporary legalized appropriation of labour or alienation to which European indentured labourers were subject: 'L'Africain arraché de son pays, par ruse ou par violence, était soumis à une éternelle servitude lui et sa postérité [...] Quant à l'engagé européen, il aliénait volontairement sa liberté pour trente-six mois seulement. A l'expiration de son contrat, il devenait l'égal de son ancien patron, flibustier comme lui, grand seigneur, et atteignait souvent au premier rang de la société coloniale' (Madiou, 1847: 16).[4]

[4] 'The African forced to leave his country, either by ruse or by violence, was subjected to eternal servitude for himself and his progeny [...] As for the European indentured labourer, he voluntarily alienated himself for a period of 36 months only. At the end of his contract, he became the social equal of his former employer; a buccaneer like him, or a powerful landowner, and was often able to reach the highest ranks of colonial society.' This and all subsequent quotations

The proximity of white and black labourers in the colonies, however, soon prompted concerns among the colonists. Despite the fundamental differences between the situations of slaves and indentured labourers, as outlined by Madiou, it was feared that the sight of white men labouring on the plantation would in itself undermine the established racial hierarchy, which served to institutionalize slavery through the violent alienation of the enslaved. The larger the black and mixed race population became, the more crucial the colonial plantocracy perceived it to be that black slaves should not witness white men carrying out hard labour. In the Indian Ocean colony of La Réunion, while white indentured labourers were still working alongside black slaves in the mid-nineteenth century, this was opposed by many who saw this labour as a shameful reflection upon their own colour. According to Victor Schœlcher's notes on slavery in the Mascarene Islands on the eve of abolition, indenture or forced labour on plantations by indigent white settlers was perceived as the 'new slavery'. As rumours of abolition spread via the press, the reaction among the white population of La Réunion was one of horror. An article in the popular journal *Le Cri Public*, cited by Schœlcher, conveys the message that the labour of the 'black slave' on the plantation was vital in creating racialized distinctions between the inhabitants of the colony: 'Certes, nous sommes loin, bien loin, de vouloir nous faire les panégyristes de l'aristocratie de la peau [...] mais de là [...] à l'assimilation complète du prolétaire blanc avec le noir esclave, il y a une distance immense, distance que n'a pu combler que l'ignorance la plus profonde et la plus dangereuse des choses coloniales' (*Le Cri Public*, 1847).[5] Indeed, questions of colonial labour and race would remain at the heart of the French imperial project long after 1848.

Despite fears of assimilation and white slavery, it is clear that in France's Caribbean and Indian Ocean plantation colonies, 'slave', 'black' and 'African' had become almost synonymous by the nineteenth century, as the widespread substitution in the French language of the term *nègre* for 'slave' and *traite négrière* for 'slave trade' testifies. The great wealth of some free mixed-race planter families did not permit them to access the upper echelons of colonial society, which remained restricted to the administrative elite and white landowning families. The social hierarchies of skin colour in France's colonies

---

from this source and others were translated by the author of this article, unless otherwise stated.

[5] Translation: 'Far be it from us to sing the praises of the aristocracy of skin colour [...] but it is a large step [...] from there to the complete assimilation of the white proletariat with the black slave; an immense distance that only a profound and dangerous ignorance of the colonial situation could traverse'.

in the nineteenth and twentieth centuries, which saw darker-skinned individuals positioned as inferior, were also deeply rooted in the racialized legacies of slavery (Cottias, 2007).

While slavery legally ceased to exist in France and its overseas territories from 1848, the abolition decree was not applied with equal vigour throughout the French empire. In sugar colonies such as Martinique, Guadeloupe, French Guiana, La Réunion and Mayotte, the labour of the former slaves was largely replaced by that of newly imported indentured labourers. Seen by many contemporaries as another form of enslavement, the practice of indenture was characterized by significant levels of coercion and duplicity in the recruitment stages, as well as high mortality levels and the harsh enforcement of discipline on the plantations. French efforts to recruit labourers in India and China for the plantations of La Réunion were supplemented by a 'thinly disguised continuation of the slave trade' from Madagascar and East Africa (Northrup, 1995: 26). In addition, a population of 79,000 Indian indentured labourers, along with smaller numbers of Chinese indentured labourers and 'recaptured' Africans from the illegal slave trade, were recruited to the plantations of the French Caribbean in the second half of the nineteenth century. France's colonies in Africa, Indochina and India, meanwhile, saw the continuation of forms of domestic slavery, often with the full knowledge and tacit acceptance of French traders and the colonial authorities, who were unwilling to disrupt fragile alliances with local elites (Klein, 1998; Campbell, 2004).

While abolitionist public opinion in metropolitan France during this period called for action against continued slave trading and slavery across the empire, colonial authorities often failed to confront, and even exacerbated, forms of domestic slavery where they encountered them, as well as instituting new systems of labour exploitation. The *corvée* (forced recruitment of labourers) and *prestations* (labour dues payable to the colonial authorities) were just two methods used to extract labour and profit from the indigenous inhabitants of the territories occupied by France. Railways, ports and roads were built by forced labourers on the *corvée*, and local people were compulsorily recruited to act as porters throughout the French empire, from West Africa to Indochina. As Inès Mrad Dali shows in her chapter in this volume, the French protectorate authorities in Tunisia at the end of the nineteenth century profited from indigenous forms of slavery, as well as from the exploitation of forced labour for the colonial state. The overall picture of slavery and forced labour in the Francophone world was thus increasingly complicated and blurred after the 1848 declaration of abolition, as French imperialism targeted new areas of global expansion, and encountered and/or instituted various forms of slave and forced labour. The legacies of colonial labour exploitation have had an ongoing impact in post-slave and postcolonial societies across the globe. They make themselves felt in unequal access to land, resources, employment and facilities such as healthcare and education, as Vergès notes in chapter twelve of this volume.

In contemporary postcolonial Africa, the surviving status of the slave descendant is often experienced as a form of shameful social exclusion, as chapters nine and ten by Omuku and Dali both suggest. In these contexts, a family history of slavery is not something to be commemorated, but acts instead as a stigma to be concealed wherever possible, or is used as a weapon to shame a rival, as in the historical epic of Bamana Segou of Mali, analysed by Omuku. In many Francophone countries, the impact of past and contemporary forms of slavery and descent-based discrimination thus continue to make themselves felt. For example, in contemporary Benin – a member of the International Organization of La Francophonie (OIF), which recently registered as the seventh country worldwide with the highest prevalence of modern-day slavery (Global Slavery Index, 2013) – the legacies of domestic slavery are omnipresent in daily life, presenting a 'most paradoxical mixture of sound and silence' (Hahonou and Pelckmans, 2012: 92). Inherited slave status is not openly discussed, but it is well known and still affects the public reputation and prospects of those concerned.

These findings are echoed across the Atlantic and in the Caribbean. In chapter three, Reinhardt examines the legacies of slavery in contemporary French Caribbean society, where the slave past was until recently viewed as something shameful, to be forgotten or obscured. As Frith notes in chapter four, this (in)voluntary forgetting has a clear echo in the 1848 abolition of slavery by France, which carried with it an injunction to move on and forget the past. Implicit in the new citizenship of the former slaves was the forced renunciation of centuries of humiliations, violence and injustice. Similarly, descendants of slaves in North and West Africa (as in the cases examined in this collection of Tunisia and the epics of Mali and Senegal) find themselves caught in a double bind of a compulsion to remember, combined with strategic interest to forget or conceal their slave origins. The descendants of slaves thus remain, even today, paradoxically caught between remembering and forgetting. The problematic complexities that surround scholarly attempts to define slavery and other forms of forced labour only reinforce these issues of memory – where no commonly agreed-upon terminology relating to a given situation of exploitation exists, how can language bridge this gap and support the transmission of the memories and legacies of slavery into the present? Addressing the question of terminology related to slavery and forced labour is thus a central concern of this volume, and a key point addressed in individual chapters.

Memory and the Limits of State Memorialization

Like its descendants, memories of slavery are also caught within the paradox of what Paul Ricœur (2000) has described as not enough memory on the one hand and then too much memory on the other – or rather, as Chivallon argues in chapter two, too much memory of the wrong kind. Indeed, memorialization processes have tended to eclipse the multiple legacies of colonial labour exploitation by focusing almost exclusively on the European transatlantic slave trade and its system of plantation slavery, and even more particularly on the celebration of their abolitions. As briefly noted already, this was particularly the case during the 1998 and 2007 anniversaries of the French and British abolition decrees (Vergès, 2006; Wood, 2010). In addition to challenging and expanding the meaning of the term 'slavery' by placing it within a far longer history of what Vergès (2011) terms 'predatory economics' (see also chapter twelve), this volume addresses a second key theme: namely, the limitations imposed upon memorialization whenever it is co-opted into patrimonial or national discourses and forced to grapple with nation-centred concepts of collective memory. As Chivallon poignantly argues in chapter two, the subjectification of slavery to state discourses governed by national interests results in a recognition that paradoxically fails to recognize slavery and its complex meanings for society today. This is not a concern that is limited solely to France, of course. As Hodgson explores in chapter six, the Haitian state's celebration of the Revolution, which led to the creation of the first black republic in 1804, has resulted in the history of French plantation slavery on Saint Domingue, as well as historical forced labour practices, being obscured.

While recognizing that the politicization of memory is common to many domestic situations (Araujo, 2012), the chapters presented in this volume are broadly connected by a shared socio-political context that is unique in a number of respects. Notably, in part one, what emerges is the specificity of France's history of colonialism and the ideological underpinnings of French republicanism, which provide the historical and discursive frames of reference in which memories of slavery are being constructed. These historical and ideological particularities include, among others, French abolitionism, which abolished slavery in 1794 under the radical Jacobin government of Robespierre, only to have it reinstated in 1802 under Napoleon Bonaparte (Drescher, 1991; Bangou, 1998); France's history of colonization under the Second Empire and Third Republic, and the importance of its 'mission civilisatrice' and assimilationist policies (Bancel, Blanchard and Vergès, 2003; Frith, 2014); decolonization and the process of 'departmentalization', where France's former colonies in the Caribbean (Guadeloupe,

Martinique and French Guyana) and the Indian Ocean (La Réunion) were transformed into overseas departments and thus became part of France following the 1946 law; and the ideological underpinnings of French republicanism, which rejects multicultural models by favouring strict neutrality before all forms of communitarianism and group identity (including those that see themselves as 'descendants of' particular histories connected with French colonial expansion, such as slavery).

It is in the concluding chapter of this volume that Vergès merges these multiple themes. In theory, she notes, demands to remember France's history of slavery, which historically connects metropolitan France to its overseas departments, should have gone hand in hand with social justice to mitigate the social and economic discrepancies that continue to exist between the metropole and its former colonies beyond the moment of decolonization. Vergès maps the ways in which memorial radicalism – once linked to the re-appropriation of black identity within the context of the anti-colonial and independence movements of the mid-twentieth century – has gradually become de-politicized in the wake of the 1946 departmentalization law. That these demands have not led to greater equality leads her to question the thwarted potential of memorialization and to challenge its capacity to contribute effectively to what might be seen as a suspended process of reparative justice.

This suggests that reparative justice is an essential reference point for the global boom in public memories of slavery and the slave trade, as Hamilton, Hodgson and Quirk usefully remind us by pointing to the recent proliferation of truth and reconciliation commissions following the collapse of the apartheid regime in South Africa (2012: 3). It is also useful, therefore, as Araujo states (2012: 2), to situate these memories within the historical aftermath of major world events that, over the past century, have been shaping the language of human rights, including the Second World War, the aftermath of decolonization and the rise of civil rights movements in the US. This broad setting provides a global framework in which activists operating at national and regional levels can assert their claims for official forms of recognition to acknowledge 'the contributions of the populations of African descent to the building of societies in Europe and the Americas' (Araujo, 2012: 2). Supported by a rights-based discourse rooted in defining crimes against humanity, demands for the former slave-owning and slave-trading nations to recognize their part in slavery consequently form part of a global language that seeks to find a shared understanding of what it is to be human in the wake of major human rights abuses.

While human rights provide the linguistic, legal and ethical framework in which society today may look back and judge its historical involvement in colonial slavery, it is also a language that is more symbolic than practical where 'national' memories of colonial slavery are concerned. There remains a wide chasm between the truth and reconciliation committees set up to deal with recent human trauma and the kinds of symbolic reparations that have responded to historical slavery within nation-states. As Darcy notes, truth and reconciliation committees have emerged as the 'common mechanism used in post-conflict or transitional societies' (2011: 1), with around thirty to forty committees held over the past few decades in an attempt to promote communal healing and social reconstruction following trauma. This is a formalized process that often works in conjunction with criminal trials and aims to create an accurate historical record of events by listening to the confessions of perpetrators, recording the experiences of victims and providing recommendations relating to reparations (Darcy, 2011: 1–4). It is not, therefore, a mechanism that can easily be transferred to the slave past, since there are no surviving actors or victims who can stand trial for or formally bear witness to this history. The absence of formalized mechanisms for 'working through' the past at official or state levels is compounded by the longstanding history of silence concerning the slave past. For example, in France, the abolition decree amounted to an amnesty for former slavers who were, in a number of cases, offered financial reparations for the loss of their human labour (Garraway, 2008).

This situation has resulted in the belated search for alternative, often inadequate and largely ad hoc actions led by subsequent generations of descendants, or what Terray calls 'victimes indirectes' ['indirect victims'] (2006: 22). These processes might be seen as a substitute for a more concrete framework of reparative justice. The subject of reparations – which might, for example, be recommended by a truth and reconciliation committee in instances where perpetrators and victims are still alive to bear witness – is typically glossed over, or simply removed from, debates concerning the legacies of slavery. While this does not mean that demands for reparation have been quashed, as the recent calls by the Caribbean Community (CARICOM) indicate, it does point to the absence of a legal framework in which to situate these post-generational claims. There is a sense that this situation might be set to change. The awarding of financial compensation to the Kenyan Mau Mau in 2013 by the British government has triggered renewed hopes among CARICOM's Reparations Commission that its eight member states can now legitimately demand that the former slave-owning nations of Europe 'engage Caribbean governments in reparatory dialogue to address the living legacies of these crimes' (CARICOM, 2013). Yet this only highlights a further particularity when dealing with a French national context, and that is that, unlike the former slave colonies that make up CARICOM, France's former slave colonies – with the major exception of Haiti, which is acting in concert with CARICOM and Suriname in demanding reparations from the British, French and Dutch governments – continue to belong to the French Republic as part of its overseas regions and are thus not free to act as independent states. That does not mean that reparations cannot be demanded, of course.[6] Rather, it means that the French state is in a different socio-political relationship with its former slave colonies of Martinique, Guadeloupe, French Guiana and La Réunion. Despite these legal differences, memories of slavery and other forms of labour exploitation nonetheless share an international context whereby reparative or restorative justice has yet to take place, resulting in an open-ended process of 'working through' that has not found an adequate legal, social and political framework in which to achieve recognition, reparation and reconciliation.

This lack of an adequate legal framework has led to major disagreements over how best to deal with the legacies of slavery and, indeed, colonialism. As is commonly cited, the 2005 'loi du 23 février', which proposed the need to emphasize 'le rôle positif' ['the positive role'] of French colonialism, 'notamment en Afrique du Nord' ['notably in North Africa'], represents the peak of French national disagreements over how to remember its colonial past.[7] But where memories of slavery are concerned, as the chapters by Chivallon, Frith and Hourcade collectively recall, the potential difficulties of remembering a shameful national past have largely been overcome by locating a unified discourse around the 'thinly' shared and celebratory narrative of abolitionism.[8] Like the UK (Wood, 2010), France's national narratives have favoured abolitionist memories to the detriment of memories of the transatlantic slave trade. But as Chivallon explores in chapter two, this situation is no longer tenable. Driven by a desire for social cohesion, the

---

[6] In 2013, France's remembrance day for slavery, the slave trade and their abolitions (10 May) was overshadowed by calls for a debate on reparations led by the president of a France-based association, the Conseil représentatif des associations noires [Representative Council for Black Associations] (see also Tin, 2013). Tin's call was based on the extensive work of Mouvement International pour les réparations (MIR), which has a growing network of groups based in the Antilles and the French metropole, and which has been actively demanding reparations from the French state since 2005.

[7] See in particular Stora's exploration of France's *guerre des mémoires* ['memory war'] around this law (2011).

[8] In Laborde's article on French republicanism and multiculturalism, she concludes by promoting the idea of 'a thin but genuinely common national culture', one that works 'for the purposes of democratic communication and social democracy' (2001: 731).

Franco-centric 'myth' of abolitionism structured upon the figure of Victor Schœlcher has long since lost its credibility as pressure has mounted over the past two decades for the state to recognize the role of slaves in their own emancipation and give explicit, as opposed to tacit, consideration to the nation's historical involvement in slavery.

Calls to revisit France's long history of colonialism and engage more critically with its historiography have led to dynamic shifts in the national memorial landscape that have coincided with a crisis in national identity and the meaning of French universalism (Schor, 2001). Barcellini summarizes this transformation as a movement away from heroism, or the celebration of 'les héros "morts pour la France"' ['the heroes who "died for France"'], and towards victimhood, or 'les victimes mortes à cause de la France' ['victims who died because of France'] (2010: 216). The result is a more fractured sense of national identity and collective memory that ushers in nostalgia for a past when France was perceived as a prominent leader in human rights and when colonialism was connected with a 'civilizing' mission.

In response, as Barcellini notes, the state has attempted to 'reconquérir un espace de liberté en favorisant l'émergence de héros compatibles avec les victimes', notably by nationalizing historical figures (such as Victor Schœlcher for slavery) or the unsung heroes of the Résistance (namely 'les Justes' ['the Righteous']).[9] It is perhaps worth noting, however, that, more often than not, those who have militated for remembering the victims of slavery, namely citizen-led associations (see in particular chapters four by Frith and five by Hourcade), have wanted not to victimize the figure of the slave, but rather to rehabilitate the slave 'victim' as a hero who ought to be recognized by the state and placed on an equal footing to that of the Republic's heroes (Forsdick, 2012). As such, memorialization, whether led by the state working separately or in conjunction with citizen-led associations, is often linked to the celebratory commemorative constructs of the nation-state. This suggests the limited number of signs in which the western imagination has been able to think slavery and abolition, hemmed in as it is by nostalgic concepts of the French nation that are resistant to deconstruction. It is thus a largely sanitized, reassuring and teleological narrative that allows us to live with the past, or as LaCapra notes in reference to memories of the Holocaust in Germany, to produce 'harmonizing modes of narration' (1998: 50), in this case through the narrative of abolitionism.

---

9 Translation: 'to re-conquer an area of freedom by favouring the emergence of heroes who are compatible with the victims'.

Beyond the Nation, Beyond Abolition

In France, official recognition of the abuses committed by the nation in trading and appropriating the labour of enslaved Africans, as opposed to the restitution of liberty through the passing of abolition laws, can therefore only be said to have begun with the Taubira law (10 May 2001). As mentioned earlier, this law is unique in Europe, although it has since been echoed in Senegal, but would not have been possible without recourse to a well-established legal context relating to human rights and the imprescriptible nature of crimes against humanity outlined in the Declaration of Human Rights.[10] The purposes of these symbolic laws are not, however, to enable a complementary trial of slave owners and former traders, but rather to support a complementary programme of commemorative efforts that intend to communicate the memory and history of slavery to the nation, and therefore 'repair' through cultural forms of memory. In the French context, that has meant establishing a national day for remembering slavery, the slave trade and their abolitions, which has taken place each year on 10 May since 2006 and has been accompanied by the inauguration of various new *lieux de mémoire* located in Nantes, Bordeaux, Paris and the Antilles, as chapters by Chivallon, Reinhardt, Frith and Hourcade explore.

The law's remit, however, remains limited. While it recognizes that slavery was not simply perpetrated against Africans, but also against Amerindians and Malagasy and Indian peoples, it does not recognize the subsequent human rights abuses that continued once slavery had been officially abolished in 1848 in the form of indentured and forced labour under the colonial empires of the Second Empire (1852–70) and Third Republic (1870–1940). The purpose of the law is not therefore to speak to the whole of colonial history, but rather to function as a symbolic form of reparation with specific reference to institutionalized chattel slavery in the French colonies prior to 1848. As a symbolic gesture, it thus plays a diplomatic role in negotiating relationships between divided communities in the present and can be seen as similar in intention, although certainly not in scope, to the role of a truth and reconciliation committee. As explored by Chivallon and Reinhardt in

10 While France's act remains unique in Europe, at a national level the Taubira law is only one of several 'lois historico-mémorielles' ['historical memory laws'] (Michel, 2010: 198) and was preceded by other laws, including the 'Loi Gayssot' (1990), which guards against acts of anti-Semitism and xenophobia, the 'Loi du 18 octobre' (1999), which renamed the process of Algerian decolonization a war, and the 'Loi du 29 janvier' (2001), which acknowledged the Armenian genocide of 1915.

chapters two and three, which consider memories of slavery in the French Antilles, the state's instrumentalization of memory in the wake of the Taubira law has led to a deep suspicion of memorialization processes, while opening up blind spots in terms of the Republic's ongoing refusal to engage with racial discrimination and the wanton lack of an educational strategy for effectively communicating the history of slavery.

The result of this former silence, which has now been 'filled' by the state's usurpation and exploitation of memory, is that a number of alternative memorial practices and forms of memory-making have emerged or are emerging to challenge national discourses and/or to offer alternative engagements with the slave past, be it through activist or artistic work. In her chapter on the recent inauguration of the Memorial to the Abolition of Slavery in Nantes, Frith examines the strategies by which engagement with black identity is erased from official discourses, while also noting the ways in which it remains embedded in the very architecture of the memorial space. The state's rejection of black identity has led, as Hourcade's chapter on Nantes's response to the national day for remembering slavery, the slave trade and their abolitions (10 May) suggests, to the production of alternative, 'guerrilla' practices that operate within and beyond national borderlines and that call into question the Republic's strict colour-blind policy specifically by foregrounding ethnicity.[11] Indeed, unlike in the multicultural models that dominate Britain and the US, where identity can be structured around adhesion to group identity (including ethnic identity), memories of slavery and the slave trade in the French context are always required to negotiate republican neutrality. This places descendants living in the Antilles, the Indian Ocean or the French metropole in a rather unique position. While they are able to challenge nation-centred narratives that have long ignored the histories of colonial slavery, and to question the continued existence of inequalities and racial thinking that underpin French society and culture, they must do so from within a united republican national space.

Until recently, demands from those sectors of society affected by slavery and other forms of labour exploitation have sought not financial reparation, but rather the creation of an expanded idea of republican identity in which their histories form part of the national narrative. Perhaps, as many of the chapters seem to suggest, this situation is due to change under increasing pressure for French republicanism to provide a more adequate response to

---

11 The term 'guerrilla memorialization' belongs to Alan Rice and refers to the way in which 'individual diasporan African stories live and breath' through 'political action', or 'a signal intervention into a landscape that has traditionally elided their presence' (Rice and Kardux, 2012: 252).

racial discrimination. This then forms the final theme of this volume, which relates not only to ways in which alternative memorial practices can serve to deconstruct national discourses, but also how remembering other histories of colonial labour exploitation, as well as forms of domestic slavery such as those foregrounded by Dali and Omuku, can move us beyond patrimonial discourses and the nation-centredness of the abolitionist movement.

Indeed, recent moves are now challenging the definitional limitations at the heart of the Taubira law. In 2014, the Conseil représentatif des associations noires [Representative Council for Black Associations] called for the definition of slavery as a crime against humanity to be expanded to include the abuses committed during the post-1848 colonial era. The principal case brought by the CRAN against the French state and several private enterprises was the construction by forced labourers of the Congo-Ocean railway from Brazzaville to Pointe-Noire in the 1920s and 30s, which brought about at least 17,000 deaths.[12]

While the focus in this introduction has predominantly been on the specifics of the French national context, the collection as a whole traces a gradual shift away from these blind spots within a French national context and towards more dynamic and transnational conceptualizations of memory. Chapter seven by Charles Forsdick, which opens part two of this volume, looks at the iconicity of Gorée Island in Senegal not just as a key site for slavery-related thanatourism and roots tourism, but also as a site of memory that has acquired an important symbolic existence within the international space of the Black Atlantic. By examining the wide range of cultural and political usages to which the island has been put, Forsdick explores the slippage between the historical functions of Gorée and the memorial functions it has subsequently played. Chapter eight by Ravi explores the literature of another island space, Mauritius, which offers a microcosm of multiple colonial heritages and competing memories. Encapsulated within this island space are multiple memories of labour exploitation that have produced complex memorial registers and have shaped Mauritian identities in the present. The result is a divided populace, split between different ethnic groups who are connected historically to the successive free and forced migrations from Africa and Asia. Yet, new works of literary memorialization

[12] See the website of the CRAN: http://le-cran.fr/communiques-cran-associations-noires-de-france_lire_affaire-du-congo-ocean—le-cran-porte-plainte-contre-l-etat-et-plusieurs-entreprises-francaises-pour-crime-contre-l-humanite_140_0_0.html. On the Congo-Ocean railway controversy, which was cited in the 1929 Forced Labour Report and discussed in the French parliament at the time, see Ieme van der Poel (2006).

are now protesting these divisions by subverting the idea of memory as a form of 'ethnic containment' that delimits particular groups, and moving towards a more transnational approach to memory-making. Likewise, chapter eleven by Claire Griffiths explores the potential of transnational iconographies of slavery with reference to West African art forms. By crossing between historic and contemporary forms of slavery, an alternative historiography of Atlantic slavery is being created that challenges the legal declaration of abolitionism and asks important questions about the continuation of slavery in the present.

Finally then, the importance of this volume lies in its attempt to challenge and move beyond all forms of territorialized memories, or, as Vergès forcefully argues in the conclusion to this volume, all forms of 'mutilated cartographies'. It does this by visiting sites within France's former empire such as Tunisia, Mauritius, West Africa and Haiti whose post-slavery legacies often go unexplored, and placing them in dialogue with metropolitan France and its remaining overseas territories of Martinique, Guadeloupe and La Réunion. It also challenges territorialized thinking on slavery by exploring the limitations of memory that have become locked into national borders and placing these discourses in dialogue with the multiplicity and complexity of alternative forms of memory work. It is only by locating new sites and emergent cartographies of resistance that we will be able to draw memory away from its domestication and back towards the radicalism of anti-slavery activism and politics.

Works Cited

Araujo, Ana Lucia (ed.). 2012. *Politics of Memory: Making Slavery Visible in the Public Sphere*. New York and London: Routledge.

Bancel, Nicolas, Pascal Blanchard and Françoise Vergès. 2003. *La République coloniale*. Paris: Albin Michel.

Bangou, Henri. 1998. *A propos du cent cinquantenaire de l'abolition de l'esclavage*. Kourou, French Guiana: Ibis Rouge.

Barcellini, Serge. 2010. 'L'État républicain, acteur de mémoire: des morts *pour* la France aux morts *à cause* de la France'. In Pascal Blanchard and Isabelle Veyrat-Masson (eds), *Les guerres de mémoires: La France et son histoire. Enjeux politiques, controverses historiques, stratégies médiatiques*. Paris: La Découverte: 209–19.

Blanchard, Pascal, and Isabelle Veyrat-Masson (eds). 2010. *Les guerres de mémoires: La France et son histoire. Enjeux politiques, controverses historiques, stratégies médiatiques*. Paris: La Découverte.

Bongie, Chris. 2008. *Friends and Enemies: The Scribal Politics of Post/Colonial Literature*. Liverpool: Liverpool University Press.

Campbell, Gwyn (ed.). 2004. *The Structure of Slavery in Indian Ocean Africa and Asia*. London: Frank Cass.

CARICOM. 2013. 'CARICOM Reparations Commission Press Statement'. 10 December. Available at http://caricom.org/jsp/pressreleases/press_releases_2013/pres285_13.jsp (consulted on 26 March 2014).

Chivallon, Christine. 2012. *L'esclavage, du souvenir à la mémoire: contribution à une anthropologie de la Caraïbe*. Paris: Karthala.

Cottias, Myriam. 2007. *La Question noire: Histoire d'une construction coloniale*. Paris: Bayard.

Darcy, Shane. 2011. 'Truth Commissions, the European Union and Reparations from Business'. In Faria Medjouba (ed.), *Building Peace in Post-Conflict Situations*. British Institute of International and Comparative Law: 43–60.

Drescher, Seymour. 1991. 'British Way, French Way: Opinion Building and Revolution in the Second French Slave Emancipation'. *The American Historical Review* 96: 709–34.

Eltis, David. 2007. 'A Brief Overview of the Trans-Atlantic Slave Trade'. Available at http://www.slavevoyages.org/tast/assessment/essays-intro-01.faces (consulted on 25 March 2014).

Eltis, David, and David Richardson. 2010. *Atlas of the Transatlantic Slave Trade*. New Haven: Yale University Press.

Forsdick, Charles. 2012. 'The Panthéon's Empty Plinth: Commemoration Slavery in Contemporary France'. *Atlantic Studies: Global Currents* 9.3: 279–97.

Frith, Nicola. 2014. *The French Colonial Imagination: Writing the Indian Uprisings, 1857–1858, From Second Empire to Third Republic*. Lanham, MD: Lexington Books.

Garraway, Doris L. 2008. 'Memory as Reparation? The Politics of Remembering Slavery in France from Abolition to the Taubira Law (2001)'. *International Journal of Francophone Studies* 11: 365–86.

Geggus, David (ed.). 2001. *The Impact of the Haitian Revolution in the Atlantic World*. Columbia: University of South Carolina Press.

Global Slavery Index. 2013. Available at http://www.globalslaveryindex.org/ (consulted on 25 March 2014).

Hahonou, Eric, and Lotte Pelckmans. 2012. '"History Must Be Re-Written!" Revisionist Ambitions among West African Slave Descendants'. In Douglas Hamilton, Kate Hodgson and Joel Quirk (eds), *Slavery, Memory and Identity: National Representations and Global Legacies*. London: Pickering & Chatto: 91–104.

Hall, Gwendolyn. 1992. *Africans in Colonial Louisiana: The Development of Afro-Creole Culture in the Eighteenth Century*. Baton Rouge: Louisiana State University Press.

Hamilton, Douglas, Kate Hodgson and Joel Quirk. 2012. 'Introduction: Slavery,

Memory and Identity: National Representations and Global Legacies'. In Hamilton, Douglas, Kate Hodgson and Joel Quirk (eds), *Slavery, Memory and Identity: National Representations and Global Legacies*. London: Pickering & Chatto: 1–13.

Hourcade, Renaud. 2014. *Les ports négriers face à leur histoire: Politiques de la mémoire à Nantes, Bordeaux et Liverpool*. Paris: Dalloz.

International Labour Conference, Twelfth Session, Geneva. 1929. *Forced Labour Report and Draft Questionnaire*. Geneva: International Labour Office. Available at http://www.ilo.org/public/libdoc/ilo/1929/29B09_10_engl.pdf (consulted on 13 August 2014).

Klein, Martin. 1998. *Slavery and Colonial Rule in French West Africa*. Cambridge: Cambridge University Press.

Laborde, Cécile. 2001. 'The Culture(s) of the Republic: Nationalism and Multiculturalism in French Political Thought'. *Political Theory* 29: 716–35.

LaCapra, Dominick. 1998. *History and Memory after Auschwitz*. New York: Cornell University Press.

Le Cri Public. 1847. In *Collection de documents contemporains réunis par Victor Schoelcher sur le regime et l'administration des Colonies françaises*. Réunion, Inde Française et Cochinchine. NAF 3635, vol. VII. Paris: BNF (Richelieu).

Loi no. 2005-158 du 23 février 2005 portant reconnaissance de la Nation et contribution nationale en faveur des Français rapatriés. Available at http://www.legifrance.gouv.fr/affichTexte.do?cidTexte=JORFTEXT000000444898&categorieLien=id (consulted on 21 February 2014).

Lovejoy, Paul. 2009. 'The Slave Trade as Enforced Migration in the Central Sudan of West Africa'. In Claudia Haake and Richard Bessel (eds), *Removing Peoples: Forced Removal in the Modern World*. London: German Historical Institute: 149–66.

Madiou, Thomas. 1847. *Histoire d'Haïti*. Vol. I. Port-au-Prince: J. Courtois.

Michel, Johann. 2010. *Gouverner les mémoires: Les politiques mémorielles en France*. Paris: Presses Universitaires de France.

Miller, Christopher L. 2008. *The French Atlantic Triangle: Literature and Culture of the Slave Trade*. Durham, NC: Duke University Press.

Mouvement international pour les réparations. Available at http://mirmartinique.com/crbst_19.html (consulted on 1 July 2014).

Nesbitt, Nick. 2005. 'The Idea of 1804'. *Yale French Studies* 107: 6–38.

Northrup, David. 1995. *Indentured Labour in the Age of Imperialism, 1834–1922*. Cambridge: Cambridge University Press.

Patterson, Orlando. 1982. *Slavery and Social Death: A Comparative Study*. Cambridge, MA: Harvard University Press.

Poel, Ieme van der. 2006. *Congo-Océan: un chemin de fer colonial controversé* (2 vols). Paris: L'Harmattan.

Rice, Alan and Johanna C. Kardux. 2012. 'Confronting the Ghostly Legacies of Slavery: The Politics of Black Bodies, Embodied Memories and Memorial Landscapes'. *Atlantic Studies* 9: 245–72.

Ricœur, Paul. 2000. *Le Mémoire, l'histoire et l'oubli*. Paris: Éditions du Seuil.

Schor, Naomi. 2001. 'The Crisis of French Universalism'. *Yale French Studies* 100: 43–64.

Stora, Benjamin. 2011. *La Guerre des mémoires: La France face à son passé colonial*. La Tour d'Aigues: Éditions de l'Aube.

Terray, Emmanuel. 2006. *Face aux abus de mémoire*. Paris: Actes Sud.

Tin, Louis-George. 2013. *Esclavage et réparations: Comment faire face aux crimes de l'histoire*. Paris: Stock.

UNESCO. 1926. 'Slavery Convention'. Available at http://www.unesco.org/new/en/culture/themes/dialogue/the-slave-route/spotlight/standard-setting-instruments/1-slavery-convention-1926/ (consulted on 25 March 2014).

Vergès, Françoise. 2006. *La Mémoire enchaîné: Questions sur l'esclavage*. Paris: Hachette.

—. 2011. *L'Homme prédateur: Ce que nous enseigne l'esclavage sur notre temps*. Paris: Albin Michel.

Wood, Marcus. 2010. *The Horrible Gift of Freedom: Atlantic Slavery and the Representation of Emancipation*. Athens: University of Georgia Press.

The Limits of Memorialization: Commemoration, Musealization and Patrimony

Representing the Slave Past: The Limits of Museographical and Patrimonial Discourses[1]

Christine Chivallon

This chapter is concerned with the development of new patrimonial and museographical practices relating to transatlantic slavery in France and its far-flung overseas departments in the Caribbean.[2] From the outset, it is worth recalling that these departments consist of micro-societies that were born out of slavery and whose historical trajectory has yet to find its rightful place within that of the French nation. What follows may therefore appear surprising since the proposed analysis chimes a dissonant note amid the increasing clamour for action at a museal level for the creation of places to collect, remember and honour the memory of slaves. Instead, this chapter takes an opposite approach by questioning the meaning of these new patrimonial practices within France's politico-memorial field through a critical investigation that reflects upon attempts to represent slavery. Starting with concrete experiences of the diverse scenographies of slavery – most of which will be museographical – this chapter will draw out the questions that emerge from the desire to make slavery visible, or rather the desire to

[1] This text has been adapted from a conference paper presented at an international colloquium, 'Exposer l'esclavage: méthodologies et pratiques', organized by Françoise Vergès in Paris (11–13 May 2011) at the Musée du Quai Branly in honour of Edouard Glissant.

[2] This chapter has been translated from French by Nicola Frith. Unless otherwise stated, all translations are the translator's own.

voice slavery through the language of patrimony. My intention here is based on previous works dedicated to the more general question of memories of slavery today and how they are associated with, or disconnected from, the racial categories that were constructed during slavery, and notably race and racism. To summarize, this previous work has been concerned with the ways in which society's conceptions today continue to be propped up by similar processes inherited from those that formed the foundations of colonialism and slavery (Chivallon, 2012).

Before beginning this analysis of patrimonial discourses, it must be stated that museographical practices relating to slavery expose practitioners to a situation where they are no longer dealing with an historical event that is reassuringly distant (temporally speaking) from the present day and has only to enter the museum. The museography of slavery is entirely subject to contemporaneous social relations and to the political governance that authorizes memory policy. In order to consider the discursive strategies that enable the slave past to become visible through the medium of museography, we must return to the conditions in which slavery is first able to enter a patrimonial space destined for public use. As will be shown, these contextual conditions inflect the museographical strategies that intend to voice the slave past. Not only do they force slavery to conform to circumstantial political demands, but they also shape the museum narrative itself, such that we might question the extent to which the museum can ever provide adequate knowledge about, and recognition for, the human experience of slavery.

In other words, on the one hand, there is the widespread and recent recourse to museal and patrimonial practices that locate their raison d'être in the political context in which memories of slavery have emerged. On the other, there remain gaps, contradictions and inadequacies relating to the relationship between the patrimonial and museographical language used to voice slavery, and the actual referent – the human experience of slavery – that ought to be conveyed to the public through the medium of this language. For this reason, and by way of a preamble, this chapter will first describe the context in which the patrimonial practices relating to slavery have emerged in order to then try to understand the extent to which this language fails to communicate what it wishes to say, before focusing on an examination of the patrimonial discourse itself. This chapter will therefore be divided into two parts. The first part will concentrate on the memorial context and on the issues that are at stake when recovering the slave past. The second part will demonstrate differences in museal and patrimonial experiences, with some found to be at odds with the social universe they are supposed to encapsulate (but which remains beyond reach), while others continue to feed into age-old divides inherited from the slave past.

Contemporary Patrimonial Practices and Politico-Memorial Contexts

Any consideration of recent patrimonial practices relating to the remembrance of slavery requires understanding the extent to which demands to remember are associated with a time where 'silencing the past' formed the dominant 'narrative' (Trouillot, 1995). I have often used Paul Ricœur's conceptualization of 'instrumentalized memory' (Ricœur, 1998, 2000), which he sees at work whenever one of two typical situations arises: either there is 'pas assez de mémoire' ['not enough memory'] or 'trop de mémoire' ['too much memory'] (see Chivallon, 2001, 2002, 2005). These situations are thought to be symptomatic of 'wounded' memories that are unable to complete a process of mourning by verbalizing those traumas experienced collectively, before arriving at a peaceful state of remembrance. Indeed, the evolution of the discursive field in which slavery has been recalled can be divided into two successive periods: a period of silence that was superseded by a period of visibility, or even hyper-visibility, where 'not enough' memory gave way to 'too much' memory. The point of transition can be located in the 1990s, with the primary reference point being the launching of the 1994 UNESCO project 'The Slave Route'. This acted as the precursor for what would happen in France and elsewhere, with a project that set out 'to break the silence surrounding the slave trade and slavery'.

At the beginning of the 1990s, the historian Carlos Célius completed a survey of museums dedicated to slavery. In this inventory, he identified an unequivocal absence of memory. He associated this absence with 'un refoulement' ['a repression'] of slavery, which had never succeeded in gaining a sufficiently significant, or indeed autonomous, space within museums (1998: 251). It is not a question here of creating an inventory, akin to that of Célius, of all the museal and patrimonial actions undertaken in the last twenty years. Rather, by drawing from a number of studies on familiar sites in Bordeaux, Bristol, the French Antilles and Jamaica, I will posit that there has been an undeniable transition towards an 'explosion' of memory (Chivallon, 2002, 2005). In France, this memorial boom followed the 150th anniversary of the abolition of slavery in 1998 and the promulgation of the Taubira law in 2001, which recognized slavery and the slave trade as 'crimes against humanity'. The term 'explosion' might appear shocking, given that arguably much remains to be done, or remains to be done differently, to ensure that the slave past is no longer silenced or subject to 'the differential exercise of power that makes some narratives possible and silences others' (Trouillot, 1995: 25). To assert the existence of this memorial frenzy does not appear to me to be contradictory to, or at odds with, the intention to work towards a just memory. For an overview of this frenzy, we need look no further than the impressive list compiled by the Comité pour la mémoire de l'esclavage [Committee for the Memory of Slavery] (2007), which attests to the number of actions undertaken within France's cultural, educational and academic domains.

Rather than recycling the canonical definition of patrimony as the intention to 'reconnaître, de défendre et de faire fructifier un ou des héritages communs' (Le Goff, 1998: 9), I prefer to speak of patrimony as a form of 'memory-making' (*fabrique mémorielle*) or even as a 'memory machine' (*machine de souvenir*) when describing its recent deployment in the realm of memories of slavery.[3] These expressions seem to translate more accurately the recent political drive 'to exhibit' (*to show, to make visible, to display, to demonstrate*) the extent to which politics has responded to public demands over the past two decades, but without any guaranties that a shared and mutual recognition has taken place, or will take place. Underpinning this process of 'memory-making' is a tried and tested economy of signs relating to the construction of patrimony. These signs set out to chart a route that begins with the present day and defines the past by selecting only those traces that are deemed valuable for today. It is the invention of what Claude Rivière (1995: 51) calls 'rites profanes' ['profane rituals'], whereby the act of commemoration – which interacts symbiotically with certain museographical modes of operation – becomes the centrepiece of a mechanism that intends to unify the social body through emotional impact and transcend society's hierarchies, while avoiding its schisms and ruptures. What underpins my assertion that there has been a shift towards 'too much' memory is not a desire to criticize all of these signs of recognition as worthless and illegitimate. Rather, I am concerned with identifying the extent to which these acts fall wide of the mark – they do not achieve what is desired of them because they remain bound by strategies that are concerned with social cohesion, and not remembrance. To continue with Ricœur, this process suggests a 'culte de la mémoire pour la mémoire' ['cult of memory for the sake of memory'], which tends to produce a 'mémoire répétition' ['repetition-memory'] that acts as a substitute for the act of remembering itself 'par lequel le présent serait réconcilié avec le passé' (Ricœur, 2000: 105, 96; 2004: 86, 79).[4]

In a similar vein, a previous comparison that I conducted between two former slave-trading ports – Bristol in the UK and Bordeaux in France – sees

[3] Translation: 'recognize, defend and encourage the proliferation of one or more common heritages'.

[4] Translation: 'by which the present would be reconciled with the past' (Ricœur, 2000: 79).

political remembrance as dependent upon models of social cohesion, with multiculturalism on one side and assimilation on the other (Chivallon, 2002). Other studies have recently confirmed the country-specific distinctiveness of these public policies (Hourcade, 2012). Indeed, the remembrance system relating to slavery has quickly found itself linked to the need to demonstrate the capacity of political institutions to integrate cultural diversity, and has thus found itself transformed into a method for managing inter-communal relations. This was very clear in Bristol, where the museographical and commemorative strategies put in place were born out of demands emanating from the city's Caribbean (and largely Jamaican) communities. These demands were voiced just as the city was getting ready to celebrate its maritime heritage, and was doing so without any mention of the city's long-standing links to the slave trade. This was in 1996, on the occasion of the 500th anniversary of the expedition undertaken by the navigator John Cabot, which left from Bristol. Immediately following protests from the city's most segregated groups, the 'memory machine' clicked effortlessly into motion, revealing the adeptness of multicultural political models at integrating difference. Yet, in authorizing the recovery of this hidden past, the political treatment of a cultural question also authorized the concealment of other social questions. The memory of the inner-city riots during the previous decade made it all the more pressing to demonstrate the acceptance and recognition of difference, without actually engaging with questions concerning social inequality. Similarly, in Martinique, the cultural sector and patrimonial projects have become vectors of an authorized identity that directs its own particular memory. As the sociologist Michel Giraud has observed, this has re-orientated 'l'observance rigide de la doctrine "républicaine"' towards 'la reconnaissance obligée de la diversité de traditions' (1999: 377).[5] Or, as the political scientist Frédéric Constant comments, this has seen the transition away from 'un pluralisme culturel nié' ['a denied cultural pluralism'] and towards 'un pluralisme culturel encadré' ['a plural cultural framework'] (cited in Giraud, 1999: 378).

The same could be said of the French Hexagon, where memory is deployed as a way of managing the crisis confronting the republican model. While I share in no way Jean-Loup Amselle's analysis of postcolonialism (2008), I nevertheless agree with him that recourse to a pluralist model of remembrance arises as a consequence of this crisis. Memory comes to the rescue of the discredited narrative of assimilation. Likewise, the Schœlcherian myth of the nation of equals, founded by the 1848 Abolition Act, has lost its potential

[5] Translation: 'the rigid observance of the republican doctrine'; 'an obligation to recognize the diversity of traditions'.

for credibility. The need to take into account different historical trajectories has become essential. With demands for visibility among minority groups becoming increasingly intense, the French state (within a few years of Great Britain) has managed to demonstrate a somewhat surprising capacity to develop a certain expertise that is characteristic of the multicultural model. However, the creation of this authorized memorial space remains closely dependent on certain compromises and agreements. The response provided notably by the museum strategy must ensure that the former narrative structure is not weakened. As will be discussed, unlike the former period of silence, the determined incorporation of slavery occurs only by keeping it within a limited spatial temporality.

If one overriding factor had to be maintained to explain this sudden increase in memorialization – which, let us recall, responds to demands first formed by civil society – it would be the change in referent in both power relations and the political critique of the social positions inherited from the colonial period. As several analyses have served to demonstrate, demands to remember arise from a political mobilization that has supplanted the former struggle against colonialism and its aftermath (see also Vergès's chapter in this collection). In the US, Martin and Yaquinto (2004) suggest that the recent reparations movement demonstrates a rise in anti-establishment arguments that are no longer rooted in class warfare, anti-colonialism and third-worldism, but in the language of justice and ethics. The two authors note that the resuscitation of this movement surfaced at precisely the moment when the Cold War and the East–West conflict was coming to an end, while minority rights and the question of North–South divides were becoming key preoccupations in global affairs. Similarly, Alec Hargreaves has stated that postcolonialism constitutes 'à bien des égards un substitut au marxisme, discrédité par l'effondrement de l'Union soviétique' (2007: 25).[6] For Martinique, Michel Giraud has noted that claims to identity, which remain anchored in demands for recovering memory, tend to subsume 'le tout de la revendication anticoloniale, ne laissant exister d'expression politique antillaise que la revendication culturelle' (1999: 380).[7]

These changes in referent in the power relations between groups whose paths are affected by colonial history can be found at all sites concerned with claims to remember the slave and colonial pasts. The identification of these changes is, to my mind, essential to understanding the context in

---

6 Translation: 'in many ways a substitute for Marxism, discredited by the collapse of the Soviet Union'.

7 Translation: 'all anticolonial claims, leaving only the existence of cultural claims within the political language of the Antilles'.

which patrimonial practices have developed. In effect, these practices are dependent no longer simply upon the need to recover the hidden past, but also upon power relations in which current social relations are played out over questions of social disparity, racial inequality and the unequal access to symbolic resources that permit the production of representations of the social body. It is these issues that give the field of memory its paradoxical nature. This outpouring of memory is testament to a mutilated process of recognition that, despite an ever-increasing abundance of expressions, struggles to produce a shared understanding because it remains embedded within socio-racial divides. We might consider that the slave has entered the museum, yet the memory carried by his or her descendant has arguably been left at the door and, with it, the very pressing concern to resolve questions of freedom and justice. The messages left in the visitor book of the new rooms dedicated to slavery at the Musée d'Aquitaine in Bordeaux bear witness, to some extent, to this phenomenon. Among the messages of praise can be found those that attest to this missing dialogue or this missed encounter. As one visitor wrote, 'Descendante d'esclaves, la douleur brûle mes veines lors de cette visite. La page sera complètement tournée quand les Bordelais auront entamé un véritable échange avec les Antilles' (cited in Rousset, 2009).[8] Similarly, in Bristol, one of my Jamaican interlocutors explained to me that, despite the deployment of an entire memorial arsenal, what remained lacking was the emotional content. The 'memory machine', in its use of 'repetition-memory' and of programmed, mediatized, authorized and spectacular forms of memory, risks swallowing up the possibility of genuine exchange and, therefore, the potential to reach out to the experiences of what the sociologist Eyerman calls (in reference to African-Americans) 'an identity-formation' in which 'the recollection of slavery was articulated as cultural trauma' (2008: 16).

The recourse to an operative language that aims to demonstrate the recognition of memory through hyper-visibility and display suggests that public recognition of the suffering caused by slavery remains weak and is unable to achieve legitimacy and unanimity. Indeed, slavery, as Achille Mbembe notes, poses first and foremost the question of the 'status of suffering in history' (2001: 24). Yet the memorial machinery only acts 'as if' this suffering were acknowledged, without that acknowledgement genuinely taking place. The surest sign of the paradoxical nature of this frenzy, where the pain of the

---

[8] An account by Adrienne cited in an article by J. Rousset and published in the local newspaper *Sud-Ouest*. Translation: 'Slave descendant, the pain was burning in my veins throughout this visit. The page will be completely turned when the people of Bordeaux have begun a real dialogue with those from the Antilles.'

past can be spoken without actually being legitimized, is the constant calling into question of the 2001 Taubira law. Recent attacks have labelled it as 'une honte' ['a disgrace'] for the country and as a 'loi anti-française' ['anti-French law'], and have given rise to a number of repellent incidents on Twitter.[9] The violent and overtly racists attacks against Christiane Taubira following the 2013 law (known as the 'Mariage pour tous' ['Marriage for all'] law), which she defended and brought before the parliament as Minister for Justice, dramatically amplify the fact that recognition is far from being attained for those living in the subaltern realities inherited from the French colonial past.

The positions of France's most celebrated historians have likewise contributed to this constant process of de-legitimation. This is the case for Pierre Nora, whose chapter, 'Malaise dans l'identité historique' attempts to dispute the quality of collective memories by setting up a hierarchy between those that encourage 'l'avènement heureux de la dimension mémorielle' ['the happy coming of memory'] and those, on the contrary, whose aim is essentially harmful and regressive (2008: 15–18). The latter, Nora associates with new minorities – 'les fils et filles de descendants d'esclaves' (2008: 13)[10] – who have opened up the way to a widespread abuse of the notion of a crime against humanity. Nora considers this 'mémoire un peu énigmatique' ['rather enigmatic memory'] of slavery and the slave trade as demonstrative of 'le potentiel particulièrement destructeur de la récente remontée du refoulé colonial' (2008: 22).[11] He speaks resolutely of 'humanités incomparables à la nôtre' ['incomparable humanities to our own'] (ibid.: 19), thereby creating a new and barely disguised ethno-racial differential, which might otherwise be called racism.

In this way, the space in which memories of slavery are being recovered is locked into an 'économie morale du soupçon' ['moral economy of suspicion'] (Chivallon, 2012: 62). Just as Didier Fassin noted for racial discrimination, slavery has undergone a transition from a state of denial (*déni*) to a state of disallowance (*dénégation*) – in other words, to a reality that is 'nommée publiquement tout en étant réfutée dans son interprétation' (Fassin, 2006:

---

[9] See, for example, the words by the UMP minister Christian Vanneste (2011), as well as the Tweet in response to the Parisian street riots on 12–13 May 2013 written by another UMP minister, Jean-Sébastien Vialatte: 'les casseurs sont sûrement des descendants d'esclaves. Taubira va leur donner une compensation' ['the hooligans are undoubtedly descendants of slaves. Taubira will no doubt compensate them'] (Gensse, 2013).

[10] Translation: 'the sons and daughters of the descendants of slaves'.

[11] Translation: 'the particularly destructive potential of the recent return of the repressed colonial past'.

149).[12] Continuing with Fassin, it could be said that 'l'économie moral de l'intolérable' ['the moral economy of the intolerable'], in its current form, is selective in its treatment of human suffering (Fassin, 2005: 47). It is this that lies behind the symptoms of memorial excess. It is this that helps us to translate a political game that sets out to construct a narrative of social cohesion on the basis of unresolved discriminations. It is also this that helps us to interpret the intensification of signs that mean to satisfy (and perhaps also silence) those voices that are articulated (and exploited) through the memory machine. Paradoxically, however, in giving increasing voice and scope to these demands, the memory machine reaches an audience that remains uninterested in listening to what those voices have to say about the experience of slavery and its consequences.

The Disharmony of Patrimonial Accounts of Slavery

In such a context where memorial strategizing triumphs over the need for a just memory, it is perhaps not surprising that patrimonial practices also give voice to discursive strategies that aim to serve political models of governance, and often do so despite the best intentions of practitioners working in the field of memory policy.[13] Yet, if this context deliberately shapes patrimonial practices, these same practices also serve to intensify the impact of discourses that, by their very nature (as the language of a historically situated and 'modern' narrative), are truncated. It must be stated from the outset that we cannot conceive of a museum, any more than any other patrimonial action, as a tool capable of attaining, through the magic of its scenography, some clear-sighted truth about the past. The process of selection inherent to patrimonial practices always testifies to a particular strategy for writing the past, which then serves the present-day projects of those who conceptualize the strategy. Through museographical language, 'the past is what the present needs to legitimize, naturalize and sustain itself; in and by museography, the past becomes a monument in the present' (Preziosi, 2004 [1996]: 76). Taking a few examples, I would therefore like to

---

12 Translation: 'publically named, yet remains discredited in its interpretation'.

13 Hourcade's work considers the interplay of interactions between different stakeholders who have different aims, or what he terms 'la conjonction d'une multitude de micro-pouvoirs' ['the convergence of a multitude of micro-powers'], that underpin memorial policy making (Hourcade, 2012: 614). Yet this 'convergence' of competing identities nonetheless operates within a process of subjectification and 'reste subordonné à la "construction étatique des esprits"' ['remains subordinated to a "state-centred construction"'] (ibid.: 623).

demonstrate that the kind of museographical and monumental language that has been forcefully deployed over the course of this memorial frenzy is not appropriate for communicating the social experiences born out of slavery. These experiences are eluded or re-silenced by patrimonial strategies that either erase entire social histories of pressing concern to contemporary society or endorse a representational system that remains closely linked to the specificities of societies still fractured by their colonial pasts. I will consider in turn four discursive strategies, including historical periodization, the national narrative, the witness site and, finally, the monumentality of the memorial. These strategies are not mutually exclusive, but are representative of those that are dominant and whose discourses serve to create particular imaginings of the slave past through their processes of selection and exclusion.

The Periodization Strategy

This strategy is undoubtedly the most common and widespread amongst museums that tackle the subject of slavery. In Bristol, just as in Bordeaux and also in Martinique, slavery is exhibited as a historical inventory. This strategy is used notably in response to memorial demands that are dictated by a concern to create history by following a path deemed to be historically rigorous in its connection to fact-based archivist methodologies. The museum presents itself as a site of education, in accordance with the normative definition provided by the International Council of Museums (ICOM). It is an institution at the service of society and its development, 'which acquires, conserves, researches, communicates and exhibits the tangible and intangible heritage of humanity and its environment for the purposes of education, study and enjoyment'.

In Martinique, the narrative thread, in drawing from classical models of historical periodization, provides a limited treatment of slavery by positioning it as one period amongst many so that it becomes circumscribed temporally. This is true of many museums that have marked the recent emergence of slave memories since the 1990s. In a survey of Martiniquais museums that I conducted in 2002 (and from which I will only draw a few elements here), I investigated the extent to which these sites, either because of their thematic interest or because of their location (as former plantations), were in a position to refer explicitly to the experience of slavery. At the time of the study, twenty-five out of the forty-two museums were identified as matching this criterion, which represented a sevenfold increase from 1986 to 2001 as a direct result of the intensification in patrimonial efforts (Chivallon, 2006, 2009).

From this, two categories of museums can be identified: those that make slavery visible and those that render it invisible. Against all expectations, given both the frenzy of memorialization and the location of these sites in the very heart of slavery, only five museums fell into the first category. If patrimonial action claims to be a way of reinforcing a memory that has, until now, been 'weakened' – as stated in one of the museum catalogues[14] – it is clear that its approach remains conventional. Its practice does not break with those practices used at the kinds of conservation sites that distance the past, and that name and classify their objects according to 'encyclopaedic strategies' rooted in the museal traditions of western modernism (Findlen, 2004 [1989]: 28). It is for this reason that the rigorous restoration of the history of slavery finds itself boxed into a single time period, and consequently into a single glass display. It is integrated into a classical language that belongs to modern historical categorization and its top-down approach to history – one that looks back from afar at that which is no longer supposed to exist. Surrounded by other distinct historical periods, slavery becomes just one of the many temporalities without any impact or subsequent consequences. The message that is presented finds itself trapped within the fabric of a museographical language that acts as an obstacle to attempts to sensitize the public to the realities of slavery and its after-effects. This conceptualization is almost identical to what Preziosi identifies as

> a 'centering device' and in fact a whole optical instrumentally for the positioning, the siting (and the sighting, the rendering visible, the framing) of modern(ized) populations in and for a history that was itself deployed, both museographically and historiographically, as the unfolding of transcendent truth [...]. If the museum is the veritable house of opticality, of vision, it is at the same time, and consequently, a place of blindness and masquerade, where what is visible is also invisible. (2004 [1996]: 80)

In these museums, where several time periods are covered, this invisibility is rendered all the more obvious through what might be called slips of the tongue, or unintentional gaps in the language, or even Freudian slips, which mean that the intention to voice slavery fails. The goal of rendering the slave past visible within the museum results in the object being submerged by 'something else'. Examples include the excessive emphasis on technologies relating to sugar production; the distinctive living conditions of the mixed-race bourgeoisie, where, in the midst of a reconstruction of a grandiose natural scene, a mannequin with white skin plays the role of

---

[14] This is according to the terms used by the Martiniquais politician, Alfred Marie-Jeanne, in the introduction to the catalogue, *Écomusée de la Martinique. Histoire vivante d'une culture et d'une communauté*, Écomusée de Rivière-Pilote (1995).

servant to the mulatto masters; the indigenous presence of the Amerindian population that promotes an archaeological and pre-slavery past over the slave past; the centrality of a historical figure such as Père Labat, a slave preacher, presented as an 'homme d'exception' ['exceptional man'], while accounts of his cruelty towards slaves hide in the shadows; and the polarization of the post-abolitionist period, which is linked to the freedom of the 'peasants'. These recurring deviations, or perhaps falsifications, skew the way that people see slavery, altering its constituent parts and ultimately creating a form of visibility that is an optical illusion (see Chivallon 2006, 2009).

In these museums, the violence of slavery is barely mentioned, as if it ought to be passed over as quickly as possible. This elision was noted by the anthropologist Richard Price (2001) following an exhibition in Martinique that took place during the 150th anniversary of abolition. As he commented, it is possible to speak of slavery without really speaking about it, 'as if the exhibition were designed to commemorate "a crime against humanity" that indeed happened, but that happened "somewhere else"' (Price, 2001: 59–60).

The National Narrative Strategy

According to Benedict Anderson (1996), museums hold a prime position within the construction of the nation by erecting genealogies of sameness and difference. As we have seen, museum scenography is rooted in western traditions or conservation practices that serve, as Marc Guillaume suggests, as a 'réservoir pour alimenter les fictions d'histoire que l'on construit à propos du passé' (1990: 18).[15] This is because all of these practices separate the past from the present by placing it at a distance, while attributing to it both a chronological temporality and a role that could be seen as operating in the name of western modernity and its desire to validate the national imaginary. The practice of separating the past from the present is, to continue with Guillaume, 'le mythe fondateur de la modernité' ['the founding myth of modernity'] (ibid.: 16). From the moment we select and organize historical traces (which are meant to capture the past) into a clear account of a collective trajectory, we are dealing with an approach that serves identity claims. In fact, the national narrative strategy is nearly always supported by chronology.

This national narrative can be found in museums where slavery is now displayed, without compromising the glorious, grand narrative of the nation-state. The study of one of the very first museographical interventions into slavery – the exhibition entitled 'A Respectable Trade?' at the Bristol Museum in 1999 – revealed that the recovery of this reality, when attuned to a

15 Translation: 'reservoir to feed the historical fictions that we create about the past'.

multicultural national model, did not prevent British identity from being reinvigorated and its moral values elevated (Chivallon, 2001). In France, the task is made even easier thanks to a historical shift from slavery to abolition that does not compromise the triumphalist republican configuration. The examples of the Musée d'Aquitaine in Bordeaux and the Musée des ducs de Bretagne in Nantes are notable on this point (Hourcade, 2012; Valognes, 2013). The opening of the four permanent rooms in Bordeaux (May 2009), before the state's most senior representatives, broke with the city's former memorial regime, which was considered, up until then, to have prohibited memories of slavery. These rooms evidently mark a clear rupture with the more bowdlerized tone of the previous exhibition on the Antilles in 2001. The curators at the time had stated that it was not a question of talking about slavery, although a few had battled to include a room dedicated to the slave trade. These same dedicated few had, ten years earlier, been censured during the exhibition 'Bordeaux, le rhum et les Antilles' ['Bordeaux, rum and the Caribbean'] for having wanted to cite Fanon and Césaire in the catalogue. The mayor at that time, Jacques Chaban-Delmas, stated what would be impossible to declare now: 'Bordeaux, ce port au milieu des terres, a attiré ou donné naissance à des hommes qui, armateurs, affréteurs, négociants, eurent l'audace et réussirent [...]. Nous leur devons sous l'impulsion des Intendants, un urbanisme qui, encore aujourd'hui, donne la mesure de sa puissance financière' (exhibition catalogue, 1981–82: 20).[16]

Contemporary museum rhetoric has definitively shifted us away from this historical denial by envisaging the human tragedy of slavery through an approach that lays claim to its historical rigour. These preliminary steps towards the slave era remain, however, entirely compatible with the recovery of the nationalist project. And Bordeaux is no exception. As with many other sites and patrimonial actions, it is always a question of following a narrative thread that makes full use of the abolitionist moment, which (as we know only too well) has been transformed into a founding act of republicanism. The visitor to Bordeaux's museum is invited to follow a museographical route through four rooms whose names alone demonstrate that the exhibition is not simply about reducing Bordeaux's history to a crime against humanity: 'La fierté d'une ville de pierre' ['The pride of a city made of stone'] (a description of Bordeaux in the eighteenth century); 'Bordeaux porte océane' ['Bordeaux, gateway to the ocean'] (a description of Atlantic commerce and

---

[16] Translation: 'The port of Bordeaux, situated in the middle of the country, has attracted and given birth to men who were ship-owners, charterers and merchants, and who succeeded with courage. [...] We owe to their stewardship a city that continues to display the extent of its financial power'.

the slave trade); 'L'Eldorado des Aquitains' ['The Eldorado of the People of Aquitaine'] (a description of the living conditions on the plantations); and 'Héritages' ['Heritages'] (a description of the aftermath of abolitionism). It is in this last room that it becomes possible to bring together the crime, which is clearly denounced, and the humanist values of the Republic. After all, these are the traditions that are associated with the Republic, and are represented in a room that brings the journey to an end with a 'Mur de la diversité' ['Wall of Diversity'], comparable to that of the 'Black Achievers' wall at the International Slavery Museum in Liverpool (Hourcade, 2012: 610–11). These largely congenial heritages speak of music, literature, creolization, *métissage* and even of an identity that, according to an article in the municipal review, has been 'recomposée et réconciliée avec son histoire' ['reconstructed and reconciled with its history'] (Anonymous, 2009: 16–19).

This museal display shows the extent to which the use of historical chronology is useful for narrativizing the national narrative, and therefore the extent to which it can also block our understanding of the complex cultural universe of slavery. Édouard Glissant pointed to the impossibility of reducing Antillean cultures to a decoupage, or a cardboard cut-out, modelled on the history of France, or what he described as a 'leurre chronologique' ['chronological ruse'] (1981: 27, 155). In one of the last interviews that he gave, he formulated the idea of history as the continuity of an uninterrupted chaos: 'Je ne me sens pas un post-colonialiste, parce que je suis dans une histoire qui ne s'arrête pas [...]. Il n'y a pas une période post-colonialiste de l'histoire de la Caraïbe [...]. Il y a un discontinuum qui pèse encore sur nous' (Glissant, 2010: 65).[17] The narrative break that allows the French nation to promote a social body that is detached from its slave background, having recovered its glorious identity, undoubtedly explains the ease with which the Republic has been able to invest itself in the memory of slavery without rocking its foundations. All that was required was to replace a policy of forgetting with the myth of Schœlcher. If the reality of slavery was to be recovered, it would only be as a pre-abolitionist reality attributable to the *Ancien Régime*, rendering the republican act of abolition all the more sacred.

The recourse to this narrative strategy, which makes the ignominy of the slave past visible only so that its glorious defeat can be all the more celebrated, is not just a characteristic of French republicanism. The same process can be found amongst independentist and nationalist movements in

[17] Translation: 'I do not consider myself to be a postcolonialist because I am living in a history that has yet to end [...]. There is no postcolonial period in the history of the Caribbean [...]. There is only a discontinuum that still weighs heavily upon us'.

Martinique. In this case, it is the revolt of the slaves that is privileged, and notably the revolt of 22 May 1848, which forced the immediate proclamation of the Abolition Act before its official arrival on the island. The fixation on the birth of this revolutionary act seems to absorb the past to such an extent that some of Martinique's historians, such as Édouard de Lépine, consider that the island's history has been impoverished as a result, being reduced to only two tropes that symbolize the conquest (and not the bestowal) of freedom: the Maroon (*Nègre marron*) and 22 May (1999: 154, 197). Even more than in museums preoccupied by painstaking and limited periodizations, these commemorative rituals, with their proliferation of sculpted representations of the Maroon and/or of broken chains, permit nationalist rhetoric to reach its fullest expression. This is no doubt the reason why in Martinique, where local society does not need to employ museographical strategies to demonstrate its acceptance of difference (unlike in the metropole), slavery only appears with a light touch in the museums, which themselves remain faithful to chronological and classificatory processes that swallow up its temporality. But in both cases, there figures a narrative thread that begins with the very worst and works towards something better, creating a sort of success story where the force of painful memories and the continuation of former systems into contemporary life do not really feature.

The Witness-Site Strategy

The witness-site strategy can be found in Bristol, where the first memorial action quickly developed around the idea of a guided city walk available from the tourist office (see Bristol City Council and Bristol Museums & Art Gallery). This trail traces across the city many of the sites associated with the slave trade. Its logic is based on a desire to expose, or unveil, the city's shameful past and thereby demonstrate its public assumption. This 'Slave Trade Trail' inspired an association of activists in Bordeaux, called 'Fondation du Mémorial de la Traite des Noirs' ['Foundation for the Memorial to the Black Slave Trade'], who are highly visible in the politico-media sphere. They offer regular guided tours around what they term 'Le Bordeaux Nègre' ['Negro Bordeaux'].

Unlike the above strategies, which force a shift in perspective, whereby cities with a slave past are transformed into witness sites that map the locations in which the slave trade took place, witness sites in the Antilles are found instead in plantation museums. Ever since Derek Walcott's poem on the 'absence of ruins' (1962: 12–13), it has been commonplace to approach the creation of Caribbean society by starting with the absence of material traces, and especially of those capable of communicating self-conscious collective memories freed from the matrices of the slave past. Walcott developed the idea of a country 'without monuments' and 'without heroic palaces'. As he would later state, '[t]he sigh of History rises over ruins, not over landscapes, and in the Antilles there are few ruins to sigh over, apart from the ruins of sugar estates and abandoned forts' (Walcott, 1992).

It is therefore those preserved remains of plantations today that we might expect to bear witness to the enclosure and violence of the system of slavery. Yet nothing could be further removed from this idea than the patrimonialization of the plantations. In Martinique, these plantations form the second group of museums cited above, and are by far the largest group in their capacity to render slavery invisible in the very heart of where slavery was once practised (Chivallon, 2006, 2009). As territories of the *béké* population (the descendants of the slave masters) par excellence, as well as the mixed-race bourgeoisie, these plantations, or so-called *habitations*, are often not ruins, but structures that are still inhabited, or buildings that remain active as rum distilleries set up with the tourist trade in mind.

While deployed differently at each site, the overall discursive strategy works to efface the history of slavery. The plantation museums continuously voice the unsaid and focus on creating a nostalgic colonial tableau that celebrates the former opulence of their noble family lineages. The splendour framed within recalls, as one of the leaflet states, 'l'or blanc' ['the white gold'] era, or the 'grande époque de croissance économique' ['great period of economic growth']. The visitor is invited to seize 'l'âme de [la] plantation qui, suspendue dans le temps, semble nous transmettre les grands moments de l'aventure sucrière de l'île' (Habitation Clément, 1994: 8–10).[18] The huts are those of the 'travailleurs' ['workers'] – a useful term that avoids speaking directly of slaves by stretching the euphemism to its fullest extent. Unlike the master's house, where all the furniture and other objects attesting to its former wealth are preserved, the slave hut must avoid referring to the past in any way. It is transformed instead into boutiques, toilets or air-conditioned bungalows for tourists.

Metamorphosed into a botanical or architectural Eden that validates the identity and continued presence of the former colonizers, the plantation museum becomes a mirror in which the self can be 'admired, desired, emulated' (Preziosi, 2004 [1996]: 79). These patrimonialized habitations thus develop a common rhetorical strategy that Eichstedt and Small excavate in their remarkable work on plantation museums in the US, or what they term 'white-centric' rhetoric (2002: 10–11). Centred on a white universe, or codified accordingly, this rhetoric is derived from a desire to both efface/

18 Translation: 'the soul of the plantation, which is suspended in time and seems to speak of the great moments of the island's sugar trade adventure'.

destroy slavery and emphatically valorize the world associated with the former plantocracy.

In the closed island space in which black and *béké* populations continue to confront each other – and despite the fact that the memory boom claims to recognize the ignominy of slavery – the composition of the patrimonial field demonstrates the persistent efficacy of the symbolic system in which a hierarchy of values endorses socio-racial groups. Rather than educating or informing visitors about the past, these witness sites, which transform the remains of slavery into authorized sites of self-congratulation, serve to reproduce these same hierarchical values. For all these reasons, we can transpose Eichstedt and Small's analysis to Martinique (an overseas department with such close ties to the Republic) in order to see its museal strategy as the development of a 'racialized regime of representation' – one that is identical to the plantation museums in the American South (2002: 9).

The Monumentality of the Memorial Strategy

This final strategy no doubt responds to the absence of ruins in the Antilles, and looks for other sites where the slave experience could have escaped from the imprisonment of slavery. What is required is to construct anew in order to speak of that which the architectural remains seem incapable of voicing. And the construction of memorial projects abounds. Some have already been erected, such as *Cap 110* in the commune of Diamant in Martinique, created by the artist Laurent Valère. Comprising fifteen busts in white stone that stand at over two metres high, and which have been placed in an evocative triangular formation, the sculpture's figures appear to rise out of the earth, their faces turned towards the sea in a posture that implies distress. They commemorate both the memory of slavery and the fate of the captives of a slave ship that was shipwrecked off the coast of the bay in 1830.[19] As Laurence Brown (2002) suggests, this is one of the rare Caribbean memorials that can be labelled as a 'counter-monument'. By rejecting more standardized artistic forms, this memorial sounds an unusually emotional note as it endeavours to represent the 'before' of abolitionism – the slaves' condition – and no longer the heroism of freedom celebrated by other statues. The monument has nonetheless been criticized, as Richard Price notes (2001: 60), for being modelled in white, despite the fact that this colour symbolizes grief. These criticisms recall the recurrent polemics in Jamaica over representations of slaves and national heroes in

[19] Although the slave trade had been abolished, this ship was illegally transporting three hundred slaves, of which eighty-six are thought to have survived (Brown, 2002: 111).

public spaces, which more often than not echo the content of contemporary socio-racial conflicts (Dacres, 2004).

The forthcoming project *Mémorial ACTe* in Guadeloupe produces yet another distinctive type of memorial language (or at least, this is what can be gathered by viewing the *Dailymotion* video presentation).[20] This imposing architectural site, which is composed of a metallic structure with footbridges that criss-cross over the sea and the routes below, is presented as a place of contemplation that aims to express a memory that is global in scale. The voiceover speaks at one and the same time of its conceptual inspiration drawn from the surrounding environment, of its solemnity, of its reflection upon the city, of museographical sites, of public spaces and of multimedia projections. The images display an impressive, hyper-modern monumentality, moving between open walkways suspended above the ground and interspersed with consumer outlets, to enclosed spaces, filled with state-of-the-art technologies, where its museographical approach can be located. The sense of airy tranquillity evoked by the background music, along with the dramatic and sinister tone of the voiceover, whose heterogeneous message provides a narration for a stream of multi-coloured images, constructs a kind of trailer for a blockbuster movie, piquing the spectator's interest through its suspense, before reaching a 'Happy Ending'. Meanwhile, the spectator has passed through spaces featuring the *Code Noir* and slave ships, before emerging into a carnivalesque celebration exploding with colour. The journey then continues on a kind of ghost train punctuated with horrifying objects, before finally exiting into the sunlit openness of the architectural space. Not dissimilar to a theme park, its construction is far more in tune with its own present era than with the past made into memory.

This patchwork of visual, textual and audible signs, offering a miscellany of signs and signposts, is in many ways typical of our postmodernity. It recalls the hyperspace as defined by Frederic Jameson (1984) in his seminal analysis of our contemporaneity. In other words, it is one of those simultaneous and synchronous spaces sprawling across massive architectural constructions. It is a space that is saturated with signs that strive towards totality, or a mini-town in which everything is contained under one roof, including leisure activities, consumerism and mass information. These permanently disconnected spaces make it impossible to locate oneself, or to connect the self to the external world, or to have a coherent experience linking the self to the

20 More on *Mémorial ACTe* can also be found online: 'Mémorial ACTe: Centre Caribéen d'expressions et de mémoire de la traite et de l'esclavage'. Available at http://www.cr-guadeloupe.fr/upload/documents/Macte12P.pdf (consulted on 19 November 2013).

past, present and future. In this case, the sort of devices that are supposed to allow memories of a lived past to emerge are stymied by the very fabric of the postmodern architecture. Markers of self-identification are drowned in a muddle of references that, even more than in the museum, offer only a simulacrum of the object being represented.

Museum, Patrimony and Slavery: An Impossible Balance?

In this way, the field of patrimonial practices relating to slavery in France is characterized by a double lacuna. First it remains faithful to a political context in which the desire to 'break the silence' is subordinated to a strategic need to save the republican model; and second it resorts to practices that are highly limited in nature since they remain dependent upon a nationalist and Euro-centric understanding of patrimony. If the process of 'breaking the silence' has been less than convincing, it is because it is swallowed up by an approach to memory in which all ethical intentions are submerged by a political strategy which, rather than constructing a legitimate and just memory, produces a 'moral economy of suspicion'. Patrimonial action is nothing more than an echo of this huge misunderstanding, since it seeks not to voice slavery, but rather to demonstrate that slavery has now entered the well-tested discursive space of national representations. The study of these four patrimonial strategies, which rely on the use of museographical codes, witness sites and memorials, raises questions as to the place of the experience of slavery within strategies that only seem to touch upon that experience through what they do not say (or through the unspoken). If we gather together all that is excluded, hidden, silenced or transfigured, perhaps we can arrive at a more truthful sense of the social realities that have been born out of slavery – notions such as the continuation of the dominant order, the perpetuation of racialized relationships and the pain of creolization. Since recognition has yet to occur, should it not logically be the case that an encounter, in its fullest sense as a dialogue, takes place before the construction of these museographical narratives that lay claim to recognition? Furthermore, we might ask if a museum, as an institution that is profoundly marked by the fantasy of modernity, and whose postmodern trimmings only double its capacity to create a fiction nourished by the West, is a suitable tool for voicing the complex cultural structure born out of slavery. As authors such as Paul Gilroy (1993) and Edouard Glissant (1990) have repeatedly asserted in relation to this structure, it remains inhabited by 'the especially acute consciousness of both life and freedom which is nurtured by the slave's "mortal terror of his sovereign master"' (Gilroy, 1993: 55). If identity ought to be constructed on the idea of what Glissant defines as 'Relation' (1990), can such a relation be claimed and blossom through the inertia of objects that are separated, classified, sequenced and far removed from everyday life? This critical analysis of the museum and of patrimonial practices thus leads us ineluctably to the illuminating comments of Achille Mbembe. And it is here that I will conclude by adding my voice to his in stating that the slave's experience is diametrically opposed to that of the museum, since slavery contains within it the 'scandalous' version of the very modernist project that the museum works to consecrate.

> De par son existence même, *la communauté des esclaves* ne cesse de fonctionner comme une critique radicale de la contradiction vivante que constituent les *démocraties esclavagistes* [...]. L'esclave rentrerait-il véritablement dans le musée tel qu'il existe de nos jours que le musée cesserait automatiquement d'être un musée [...]. L'entrée de l'esclave dans le musée consacrerait doublement l'esprit d'apartheid qui se trouve à la source de ce culte de la différence, de la hiérarchie et de l'inégalité [...]. Or justement, il faudrait garder à l'esclave sa puissance de scandale [...]. Ce à quoi nous invite l'histoire de l'esclavage atlantique, c'est donc à fonder la nouvelle institution que serait *l'anti-musée*. (2013: 38–40; emphasis in original)[21]

Works Cited

Amselle, Jean-Loup. 2008. *L'Occident décroché. Enquêtes sur les postcolonialismes*. Paris: Stock.

Anderson, Benedict. 1996 [1983]. *L'imaginaire national: Réflexions sur l'origine et l'essor du nationalisme*. Trans by Pierre-Emmanuel Dauzat. Paris: La Découverte.

Anonymous. 2009. 'Nouvel espace permanent du Musée d'Aquitaine. Regarder l'histoire en face et valoriser ses héritages'. *Bordeaux magazine* 364: 16–19.

Bristol City Council and Bristol Museums & Art Gallery. 'Slave Trade Trail around Central Bristol'. Available at http://www.audioguide2go.com/guide.php?guide=743 (consulted on 19 November 2013).

---

[21] Translation: 'By its very existence, *the community of slaves* never stops functioning as a radical critique of the real contradiction represented by *slaving democracies* [...]. Were the slave ever to truly enter the museum, as it exists today, it would automatically stop being a museum [...]. The slave's entrance into the museum would doubly consecrate the spirit of apartheid found at the root of this cult of difference, hierarchy and inequality [...]. It is therefore more fitting that the slave retains his or her power to scandalize [...]. What the history of the transatlantic slave trade thus invites us to do is to create a new institution, one that is an *anti-museum*.'

Brown, Laurence. 2002. 'Monuments to Freedom, Monuments to Nation: The Politics of Emancipation and Remembrance in the Eastern Caribbean'. *Slavery & Abolition* 23.3: 93–116.

Célius, Carlo. 1998. 'L'esclavage au musée. Récit d'un refoulement'. *L'homme* 145: 249–61.

Chivallon, Christine. 2001. 'Bristol and the Eruption of Memory: Making the Slave-Trading Past Visible'. *Social and Cultural Geography* 2.3: 347–63.

—. 2002. 'Construction d'une mémoire relative à l'esclavage et instrumentalisation politique: le cas des anciens ports négriers de Bordeaux et Bristol'. *Cahier des Anneaux de la Mémoire* 4: 176–203.

—. 2005. 'L'émergence récente de la mémoire de l'esclavage dans l'espace public: enjeux et significations'. *Revue d'histoire moderne et contemporaine* (RHMC) 52.4: 64–81.

—. 2006. 'Rendre visible l'esclavage. Muséographie et hiatus de la mémoire aux Antilles françaises'. *L'homme* 180: 7–42.

—. 2009. 'Museography and Places of Remembrance of Slavery in Martinique, or the Gaps in a Memory Difficult to Express'. In Horace Levy (ed.), *The African-Caribbean Worldview and the Making of Caribbean Society*. Kingston: University of the West Indies Press: 114–31.

—. 2012. *L'esclavage, du souvenir à la mémoire. Contribution à une anthropologie de la Caraïbe*. Paris. Karthala.

Comité pour la mémoire de l'esclavage. 2007. 'Mémoires de la traite négrière, de l'esclavage et de leurs abolitions'. *Rapport à Monsieur le Premier Ministre*. Available at http://www.comite-memoire-esclavage.fr/IMG/pdf/Rapport_CPME_2007.pdf (consulted on 19 November 2013).

Dacres, Petrina. 2004. 'Monument and Meaning'. *Small Axe* 16: 137–53.

De Lépine, Édouard. 1999. *Dix semaines qui ébranlèrent la Martinique*. Paris: Maisonneuve & Larose.

Eichstedt, Jennifer, and Stephen Small. 2002. *Representations of Slavery: Race and Ideology in Southern Plantation Museums*. Washington: Smithsonian Institution Press.

Exhibition catalogue. 1981–82. 'Bordeaux, le rhum et les Antilles'. Bordeaux: Musée d'Aquitaine.

Eyerman, Ron. 2008 [2001]. *Cultural Trauma: Slavery and the Formation of African American Identity*. Cambridge: Cambridge University Press.

Fassin, Didier. 2005. 'L'ordre moral du monde. Essai d'anthropologie de l'intolérable'. In Didier Fassin and Patrice Bourdelais (eds), *Les constructions de l'intolérable. Études d'anthropologie et d'histoire sur les frontières de l'espace moral*. Paris: La Découverte: 17–50.

—. 2006. 'Du déni à la dénégation. Psychologie politique de la représentation des discriminations'. In Didier Fassin and Éric Fassin (eds), *De la question sociale à la question raciale. Représenter la société française*. Paris: La Découverte: 133–57.

Findlen, Paula. 2004 [1989]. 'The Museum: Its Classical Etymology and Renaissance Genealogy'. In Bettina M. Carbonell (ed.), *Museum Studies: An Anthology of Contexts*. Oxford: Blackwell Publishing: 23–50.

Fondation du Mémorial de la Traite des Noirs. Available at http://www.fondationdumemorialdelatraitedesnoirs.com/ (consulted on 19 November 2013).

Gensse, Murielle. 2013. 'Le député-maire de Six-Fours: Jean-Sébastien Vialatte devant la justice pour un tweet'. *France 3 Côte d'Azur* 21 August. Available at http://cote-d-azur.france3.fr/2013/08/21/le-depute-maire-de-six-fours-jean-sebastien-vialatte-devant-la-justice-pour-un-tweet-305187.html (consulted on 19 November 2013).

Gilroy, Paul. 1993. *The Black Atlantic: Modernity and Double Consciousness*. London: Verso.

Giraud, Michel. 1999. 'La patrimonialisation des cultures antillaises. Conditions, enjeux et effets pervers'. *Ethnologie française* 29.3: 375–86.

Glissant, Édouard. 1981. *Le discours antillais*. Paris: Seuil.

—. 1990. *Poétique de la relation*. Paris: Gallimard.

—. (Interviews with Lise Gauvin.) 2010. *L'imaginaire des langues*. Paris: Gallimard.

Guillaume, Marc. 1990. 'Invention et stratégies du patrimoine'. In Henri-Pierre Jeudy (ed.), *Patrimoines en folie*. Paris: Éditions de la Maison des Sciences de l'Homme: 13–20.

Habitation Clément. 1994. *Éditions Grand Sud*.

Hargreaves, Alec. 2007. 'Chemins de traverse. Vers une reconnaissance de la postcolonialité en France'. *Mouvements* 51: 24–31.

Hourcade, Renaud. 2012. 'La mémoire de l'esclavage dans les anciens ports négriers européens. Une sociologie des politiques mémorielles à Nantes, Bordeaux et Liverpool'. Doctoral thesis. Rennes: Université de Rennes 1.

International Council of Museums (ICOM). 'ICOM Definition of a Museum'. Available at http://uk.icom.museum/about-us/icom-definition-of-a-museum/ (consulted on 20 March 2014).

Jameson, Frederic. 1984. 'Postmodernism, or, The Cultural Logic of Late Capitalism'. *New Left Review* 46: 53–93.

Le Goff, Jacques (ed.). 1998. *Patrimoine et passions identitaires*. Paris: Fayard.

Marie-Jeanne, Alfred. 1995. *Ecomusée de la Martinique. Histoire vivante d'une culture et d'une communauté*. Écomusée de Rivière-Pilote (catalogue).

Martin, Michael, and Marylin Yaquinto. 2004. 'Reparations for "America's Holocaust": Activism for Global Justice'. *Race and Class* 45.4: 1–25.

Mbembe, Achille. 2001. 'The Subject of the World'. In Gert Oostindie (ed.), *Facing Up to the Past: Perspectives on the Commemoration of Slavery from Africa, the Americas and Europe*. Kingston: Ian Randle: 21–28.

—. 2013. 'L'esclave, figure de l'anti-musée ?'. *Africultures* 91: 37–40.

'Mémorial ACTe: Centre Caribéen d'expressions et de mémoire de la traite et de l'esclavage'. Available at http://www.cr-guadeloupe.fr/upload/documents/Macte12P.pdf (consulted on 19 November 2013).

'Mémorial ACTe, musée de l'esclavage'. Available at http://www.dailymotion.com/video/x5iiht_memorial-acte-musee-de-l-esclavage_news (consulted on 19 November 2013).

Nora, Pierre. 2008. 'Malaise dans l'identité historique'. In Pierre Nora and Françoise Chandernagor (eds), *Liberté pour l'histoire*. Paris: CNRS-Éditions: 11–24.

Preziosi, Donald. 2004 [1996]. 'Brain of the Earth's Body: Museums and the Framing of Modernity'. In Bettina M. Carbonell (ed.), *Museum Studies: An Anthology of Contexts*. Oxford: Blackwell Publishing: 71–84.

Price, Richard. 2001. 'Monuments and Silent Screamings: A View from Martinique'. In Gert Oostindie (ed.), *Facing Up to the Past: Perspectives on the Commemoration of Slavery from Africa, the Americas and Europe*. Kingston: Ian Randle: 58–62.

Région Guadeloupe. 'Mémorial ACTe, musée de l'esclavage'. Available at http://www.dailymotion.com/video/x5iiht_memorial-acte-musee-de-l-esclavage_news (consulted on 19 November 2013).

Ricœur, Paul. 1998. 'Vulnérabilité de la mémoire'. In Jacques Le Goff (ed.), *Patrimoine et passions identitaires*. Paris: Fayard: 17–31.

—. 2000. *La mémoire, l'histoire, l'oubli*. Paris: Seuil.

—. 2004. Memory, History, Forgetting. Trans. by K. Blamey and D. Pellauer. Chicago: University of Chicago Press.

Rivière, Claude. 1995. *Les rites profanes*. Paris: Presses Universitaires de France.

Rousset, Julien. 2009. 'Prêts à tourner la page'. *Sud-Ouest* 11 June.

Trouillot, Michel-Rolph. 1995. *Silencing the Past: Power and the Production of History*. Boston: Beacon Press.

UNESCO. 'The Slave Route'. Available at http://www.unesco.org/new/en/culture/themes/dialogue/the-slave-route/ (consulted on 21 March 2013).

Valognes, Stéphane. 2013. 'Slave-Trade Memory Politics in Nantes and Bordeaux: Urban Fabric between Screen and Critical Landscape'. *Journal of African Diaspora Archaeology & Heritage* 2.2: 151–71.

Vanneste, Christian (interview). 2011. 'Des chiens de chasses sont en train d'égorger la liberté d'expression'. *Nouvelobs.com* 3 March. Available at http://tempsreel.nouvelobs.com/opinions/20110303.OBS9072/interview-christian-vanneste-des-chiens-de-chasses-sont-en-train-d-egorger-la-liberte-d-expression.html (consulted on 19 November 2013).

Walcott, Derek. 1962. 'The Royal Palms… An Absence of Ruins'. *London Magazine* 11: 12–13.

—. 1992. 'The Antilles: Fragments of Epic Memory'. Nobel Lecture. Available at http://nobelprize.org/nobel_prizes/literature/laureates/1992/walcott-lecture.html (consulted on 19 November 2013).

Telling Stories of Slavery: Cultural Re-appropriations of Slave Memory in the French Caribbean Today

Catherine Reinhardt

'What images does the word slavery bring to your mind?' was the starting point that initiated my interviews of Guadeloupians in the summer of 2013. 'Shame', 'suffering', 'misery', 'fear', 'chains', 'whips' and 'sugarcane fields with overseers' were the immediate, instinctive replies. From these premises, the interviewees delved further into their perceptions of how slavery has been remembered, commemorated and taught in Guadeloupe for the past twenty years. I was interested in their personal appreciation of erected memorials, statues and museums, and in their ability to identify with the yearly celebrations marking the anniversary of the abolition of slavery on 27 May 1848. I asked them to reflect further on the remnants of slavery in contemporary society, among their families and in their daily habits. Finally, I had them share their thoughts on education: is Guadeloupian society, in general, sufficiently knowledgeable about its slave heritage?

The idea of conducting these oral interviews originated in 2010 as a follow-up investigation to my book *Claims to Memory: Beyond Slavery and Emancipation in the French Caribbean* (2006). The last chapter focused on the sites of memory that I had photographed in Guadeloupe and Martinique – sites which either date back to the seventeenth and eighteenth centuries or were erected in recent years to commemorate the slaves' struggle for freedom and the abolitionary process (Figures 1–4).[1] The 200th anniversary of the

[1] Visit the author's website of photographs: http://www1.chapman.edu/~reinhard/.

first abolition of slavery in the French Caribbean in 1993, and even more so the 150th anniversary of the second abolition of slavery in 1998, marked turning points in the way that Guadeloupian and Martiniquais societies have expressed their slave heritage. Statues and monuments commemorating these islands' slave heroes have sprung up throughout the cities and countryside, breaking the silence that had prevailed since the abolition of slavery in 1848. Shortly thereafter – under the impulsion of the socialist minister Christiane Taubira – the French government voted into effect the law of 21 May 2001 qualifying slavery and the slave trade as crimes against humanity. Subsequently, the governmental decree of 5 January 2004 founded the Comité pour la mémoire de l'esclavage [Committee for the Memory of Slavery], originally headed by the Guadeloupian writer Maryse Condé. This committee would define places and dates of national commemoration and revisit the French curriculum with a view to integrating France's slave past into its history lessons. In 2006, it proposed 10 May as a national date for commemorating the abolition of slavery.[2]

Within ten years, the silence – or 'la politique d'oubli' ['the politics of forgetting'][3] – that had prevailed for generations in French Caribbean societies (Cottias, 1998) was replaced by proactive governmental and non-governmental initiatives to bring the past to the attention of the public, both in metropolitan France and in its overseas territories. Nonetheless, historians and anthropologists have been leery of these overt signs of memory that have failed to go beneath the surface to reveal the depths of slavery, or that 'festering wound at once shameful and dangerous' (Price, 2001: 61). These inadequacies have resulted in what Price describes as a 'silent screaming' that has not been appeased by 'bricks and mortar', which leads him to rally instead for teaching the slave past '*in all its complexities*' to 'every schoolchild in Europe, the Americas and Africa' (2001: 61; emphasis in original). The 'frénésie mémorielle' ['memorial frenzy'] resulting from the 'fétichisme de la stèle' ['fetishization of the statue'] artificially represents the realities of the slave past, but without shedding any further light on it, like a 'mémoire mécanique' ['mechanical memory'] without any transformative impact (Chivallon, 2012: 441, 452, 55). In this regard, Price cited the example of a travelling commemorative exhibition in Martinique: '150 years of Abolition –

[2] In Guadeloupe, slavery was abolished on 27 May. Since slavery was abolished on different days in various colonies, a common national date had to be chosen. Tenth May became the date of choice since it corresponded to the Senate's adoption of the Taubira law in 2001.

[3] This translation and all subsequent translations are the author's own, unless otherwise stated.

1848–1998'. There was no mention of slavery in Martinique and Guadeloupe anywhere in the exhibition, as though this '"crime against humanity" [...] happened "somewhere else"' (2001: 59–60). Paul Ricœur describes compulsive repetitions, which substitute action for true memory and reconciliation with the past as 'trop de mémoire' ['surplus memory'] (2000: 96). The forty-four-day-long strike headed by the Lyannaj Kont Pwofitasyon (or LKP),[4] which completely paralyzed the island of Guadeloupe in January and February 2009, had the additional effect of exposing the Guadeloupians' uneasy relationship to their slave heritage. While the strike was primarily focused on the social injustices arising from excessively expensive food prices and insufficient pay, links to the slave past were quickly made to explain the continuing economic structures marked by the domination of white Creoles, descendants of the *békés* or white colonial planters.[5] Slavery was instrumentalized in this highly politicized context, and yet it did not provide catharsis. Interestingly, the sociologist Michel Giraud's critique of such references to slavery for political ends (cited in Chivallon, 2012: 83) was also echoed by my interviewees. As far as the future museum about slavery, Mémorial ACTe, is concerned, Monsieur R., for instance, believes that politically motivated commemoration leads nowhere: '*Mémorial ACTe* est un grand délire de politiciens qui construisent le musée pour qu'on se souvienne d'eux'.[6] Madame C. similarly deplores the politicians' exclusive focus on their own interests and their superficial engagement with societal concerns.

The growing interest in the slave past during recent years – visible in the proliferation of memorials, the increasingly elaborate celebrations of

---

4 '*Lyannaj Kont Pwofitasyon* can be loosely translated as the 'Alliance against Profiteering' (Bonilla, 2010: 129).

5 See Bonilla (2010) for an excellent in-depth study of the strike, the social relations between the general population and the economic elites, and definitions of the terms *béké* and 'white Creole': 'The economy in Guadeloupe has long been controlled by a small white minority, commonly referred to as the *békés*, that dominates the majority of the import-export industry and most major wholesale and retail operations. These elites are seen as the direct descendants, in both biological and economic terms, of the area's previous generations of plantation owners and slaveholders' (Bonilla, 2010: 130).

6 Translation: '*Mémorial ACTe* is an extravagance of politicians who want to construct it for themselves in order to be remembered by posterity'. See the brochure about the museum *Mémorial ACTe, Centre caribéen d'expression et de mémoire de la traite et de l'esclavage* at the following web address: http://www.cr-guadeloupe.fr/upload/documents/Macte12P.pdf. The project was first conceived in June 2007 and is currently still under construction. The museum is built on the site of the dilapidated sugar factory Darboussier in Pointe-à-Pitre.

abolition day and the amplified references to slavery in political debates – has inspired the questions underpinning this chapter: how does the Guadeloupian population in general apprehend this overt memory of slavery? To what extent do people from various educational, economic and social backgrounds feel concerned and personally touched by the sudden abundance of visible signs of the past? And are the politicians' and intellectuals' increasing concerns with the island's heritage shared by their fellow citizens?

Altogether I interviewed twenty-three Guadeloupians from all walks of life. I interviewed the first four in June 2010 and the remaining nineteen in June and July 2013. There were ten women and thirteen men between the ages of 35 and 75. Since I wanted to sample the widest array of viewpoints possible, I chose individuals from varying educational and socio-economic backgrounds. Among my interviewees were self-employed craftsmen, an artist, business owners, shop keepers, state employees in local government offices, a retired school teacher, an English teacher, a university professor, retirees who had been previously unemployed, a retired professional cook and a physician. Each time I asked the interviewees a series of seven questions pertaining to the memory of slavery and recorded their answers on a digital recording device.[7] I then transcribed the recordings and searched for patterns or themes that came up repeatedly in the different interviews.

My analysis articulates the interviewees' reiterated concerns with suffering, humiliation, race, politics, history and national identity, all of which represent the archipelago of themes that arise from the silences of the past. 'La mémoire est un archipel' ['Memory is an archipelago'], states Edouard Glissant, emphasizing the interconnectedness of peoples and cultures, 'nous y sommes alors des îles que les vents inspirés mènent à dérader' (2006: 163).[8] While forgetting is offensive, shared memory abolishes

[7] These are the seven questions I asked each interviewee: 1. When the word slavery is evoked, which images or words come to mind? 2. Are the *lieux de mémoire* of slavery such as the statues of Mulâtresse Solitude, Ignace or Delgrès, the vestiges of plantations such as the Grivelière, or the slave cemetery on the beach of Sainte-Marguerite meaningful for you? 3. Are the abolition day celebrations successful in rendering the memory of the past alive? Do you feel personally touched by these celebrations? 4. Do you believe contemporary Guadeloupian society to still be marked by slavery? Can you give any examples? 5. Do you think contemporary Guadeloupian society is sufficiently conscious and educated about the slave past? 6. What do you think of the construction of the museum Mémorial ACTe at Darboussier? 7. Does the memory of slavery have an impact on your daily life?

[8] Translation: 'and we are thus the unanchored islands that have been scattered by the creativity of the winds.'

this offence. We need each other's memory to create new clarity through our relationship with others (Glissant, 2006: 161). Likewise, the manner in which my interviewees assess the physical and virtual memorialization of slavery is not oppositional, but rather relational and interconnected. Sites of memory are not considered to take away the prevailing silence of the past; local celebrations of abolition day are not directly opposed to commemorative initiatives originating in France; nation-centred debates on slavery do not stand face to face with local political agendas. What is striking, instead, is the wide variety of socio-cultural subjects the interviewees touched upon as they thought through the problem of slavery. The six above-mentioned themes are interwoven in most interviews, making for a non-linear approach to slavery. The initial positive reaction to sites of memory among some respondents is immediately nuanced by concerns with hidden political agendas. Some find the statues important; others do not feel that those sites speak to them in any way. While most agree that Guadeloupe has come a long way in terms of openly discussing slavery, this positive impression is dampened by the realization that the people still have a long way to go to come to terms with the heritage of the past, and to be transformed by a collective memory that incorporates its slave past.

The French sociologist Maurice Halbwachs (1992) pioneered the concept of memory as a collective faculty. A group within a given society can reconstruct its past at any given moment by relying on the social memory of the group at large. Once people or historical facts have permeated the memory of the group, they gain meaning as a teaching point, notion or symbol, and become part of society's system of ideas (Halbwachs, 1992: 182–83, 188). The French historian Pierre Nora (1996) calls such moments, places, people or objects that symbolize a community's memorial heritage 'lieux de mémoire' ['realms of memory']. These symbolic spaces become 'lieux de mémoire' when they are characterized by an overwhelming presence of the past (Nora, 1996: xvii, 3). When considering how these notions might work in the geo-cultural sphere of the Caribbean, it quickly becomes evident that it is difficult, if not impossible to aspire to a 'system of ideas' or a unified 'memorial heritage'. In both cases, a singular system of thought does not account for the multitude of voices and perspectives so characteristic of this geo-cultural region of the world (Chivallon, 2012: 133). The gradual transformation of moments, places, people and objects into 'lieux de mémoire' in Guadeloupe means that one can certainly speak of a reconstruction of the past; yet, the result is an explosion of memory into multiple narratives about the past. There is no 'encompassing narrative' at the end of the road of memory (Chivallon, 2008: 886).

The French philosopher and historian Michel Foucault's notion of 'counter-memory' articulates memory positioned against the 'continuity' expressed by 'official' history; it articulates 'marginal' stories that have typically been silenced (Reinhardt, 2006: 5–6; Chivallon, 2008: 115). As far as my Guadeloupian interviewees are concerned, however, the rebellion against a coercive French history is pushed to the background in favour of dynamic debates around contemporary societal issues. Glissant summons a memory that is alive, continually changing and changed by other memories, rather than a historical memory that is static in its approach to the past (quoted in Chivallon, 2012: 149). Paul Gilroy calls this a 'non traditional tradition' (1993: 198), and Stuart Hall an experience of 'hybridity' (2003: 244). Chivallon also points to the importance of the 'interstices of memory': what happens between the said and the 'not-said' (2008: 884–86).

In the end, the commentaries of my sampling of the population transcend the rhetoric of self-celebration expressed through the proliferation of museums and monuments (Chivallon, 2012: 432). My interviewees do not position themselves against a nation-centred view of history originating in France, but instead ponder Guadeloupe's historical, cultural and political expressions, wondering if they represent their own daily experiences. Glissant's approach to memory best articulates my interviewees' branching out into a wide array of subjects. In *Quand les murs tombent: L'identité hors-la-loi?* (2007), Glissant and Patrick Chamoiseau elaborate the notion of globality within which our identities are no longer nationally, linguistically and geographically bound; instead we continually enter into relation with other nations, languages and places. This unbounded identity

> ne se trouve [...] que dans les imaginaires: la façon de se penser, de penser le monde, de se penser dans le monde, d'organiser ses principes d'existence et de choisir son sol natal. La même peau peut habiller des imaginaires différents. Des imaginaires semblables peuvent s'accommoder de peaux, de langues et de dieux différents. (2007: 15–16)[9]

I would argue that the Guadeloupians I interviewed do not define themselves as victims of their heritage and of centuries of silence, but instead reflect on the multifaceted relationships between different social groups. These relationships are the legacy of the past and define the way Guadeloupians experience the present and envision the future. Glissant's 'pensée archipellique, qui invente à chaque moment les effets de la Relation, disperse et éclabousse

[9] Translation: 'can only be found in the imagination: how one imagines oneself, how one imagines the world, how one imagines oneself in the world, how one organizes one's principles of existence and chooses one's native soil. The same skin can clothe different ways of imagining. Similar ways of imagining can adapt to different skins, languages and gods.'

les identités en rapport, les renforce chacune cependant et les garantit de l'autisme identitaire' creatively expresses the way Guadeloupians exist in their insular environment (2007: 166).[10] Though small, my sample of the population can hardly be reduced to any kind of homogenous thinking. On the contrary, I was surprised that my interviewees reacted so differently to my questions. Their reflections crisscrossed along very different paths. And yet, in the end, I found a commonality in the recurrence of key themes. As in Glissant's 'archipelic thought', these issues overlap, while branching out in different directions. They do not directly break the silence, but instead engage with it, transforming it into novel perspectives on ever-changing identities within the Caribbean archipelago.

Suffering and humiliation characterize the images and words immediately brought to mind by my initial questioning about slavery: 'il y avait beaucoup de misère' ['there was a lot of misery'], 'beaucoup de souffrance' ['a lot of suffering'], 'de l'abus' ['abuse'], 'les esclaves étaient au dernier rang' ['slaves were always at the bottom'], 'le travail c'était la souffrance' ['work was suffering'], where the whip regimented work without rules; today people feel shame in speaking about slavery. For the most part, the interviewees drew on their emotions, rather than on any intellectualized reflection on injustice or 'crime against humanity'. They did not, however, dwell on these issues and immediately moved onto other themes. When asked whether they thought slavery had left any traces in contemporary Guadeloupian society, almost all the interviewees elaborated at length on the question of race, before leading into a web of further reflections on history, work, identity and humiliation.

Mademoiselle D. vehemently emphasized the existence of 'un grand, grand, grand fossé entre blancs et noirs'.[11] Even in her small village, she finds that racist attitudes prevail: 'quelqu'un de plus claire "porte la lumière"'.[12] Light-skinned people are automatically favoured at school and in society in general, whereas blacks with kinky hair are at a great disadvantage and are looked down upon: 'La couleur ça joue beaucoup. Si t'es noir il faut être très intelligent et instruit pour t'en sortir.'[13] Monsieur DL. similarly recollects racial contempt during his childhood: 'on préférait les chabines aux jolies

---

10 Translation: 'archipelagic thought, which continually invents the effects of Relation, dispersing and spattering across identities-in-relationship, while reinforcing each of them and protecting them from identity autism'.

11 Translation: 'a large, large, large gulf between whites and blacks'.

12 Translation: 'Somebody with lighter skin "carries the light"'.

13 Translation: 'Your skin colour makes a huge difference; if you are black you have to be very intelligent and educated to make it.'

filles noires.'[14] When he listens to his boys, he realizes that such attitudes continue to prevail today. Racial concerns were directly linked to slavery in Monsieur B.'s interview. He explained his compatriots' negative reactions to his sustained efforts since 1993 to bring the memory of slavery to the attention of the public through statues and commemorative celebrations. He was reproached for trying to foment hatred between blacks and whites by continually bringing up this topic: 'Les gens pensent que les blancs et noirs sont bien comme ça et qu'il ne faut pas chercher à déranger cette entente avec la mémoire de l'esclavage.'[15] Racial balance is precarious and easily unsettled by societal events. Monsieur D., for instance, deplored the fact that political interest behind the forty-four-day-long strike led by the LKP in 2009 opposed blacks to whites by using slavery to deepen these racial divisions.[16]

Racial concerns are intertwined with the general theme of work in many interviews. Several interviewees drew on their personal experiences to underline that link. Madame C., for instance, pointed out that she was the only black woman working in a managerial position at the head of her state administration when she began more than thirty years ago. Only whites are typically hired for such positions, while the local population is relegated to subaltern occupations. Furthermore, stated Madame C., Guadeloupians do not feel that work can personally advance them or offer them the opportunity to blossom; they only see work in terms of the racial divide between whites and blacks. Monsieur V. added that slavery was equated with an experience of work as suffering. Work was not valorizing for slaves and continues to be associated with pain even today.

Madame F.'s discourse elaborated on the same disparities. Based on her personal experience as an accountant in a bank, she recounted her tribulations

---

14 Translation: 'People preferred light-skinned girls, or *chabines* to pretty black girls.'

15 Translation: 'They think the relationship between blacks and whites is fine as it is and that this mutual understanding mustn't be disturbed by the memory of slavery.'

16 I transcribe my interviewees' racial terminology directly as they express themselves during the interviews, even though this terminology is not always sociologically and historically appropriate. My interviewees typically referred to Guadeloupians of African descent as black, and Guadeloupians of European descent as white. These descendants of colonial planters are also called *blancs créoles* (white Creoles). Recent arrivals from France, who are not descendants of seventeenth- to nineteenth-century colonial planters, are also referred to as white, and I clarify that each time in the text. For an in-depth study of these complex racial relations and the terminology used to describe different racial and ethnic groups, see Sainton (2009).

working under incompetent white supervisors. She deplored the unjust hiring practices she had witnessed in Guadeloupe: 'On ne donne pas le travail aux Antillais mais aux blancs incompétents.'[17] White supervisors are supposedly more effective in controlling the workers. While she admitted that there were lazy 'Antillais', she found it unfair to make that assumption about all West Indians: 'Il ne faut pas penser en noir et blanc; il faut juger la personne à sa juste valeur, pour ce qu'elle est, pour sa capacité.'[18]

From a wider perspective, Monsieur Z., a retired French and history teacher, considers the power relations inherent to the tensions between blacks and whites, in particular descendants of colonial planters. Looking at the relationship between blacks and whites from the perspective of a historian, he notes that white Creoles still hold most of the power since they own the majority of the land. Even though people have started to question these power relations, they are still submissive to white Creoles and continue to see them as the masters. Workers unions now oppose the owners and bosses – who are often white – making demands on behalf of the black workers. Racial politics dominate the relationship between different social groups in Guadeloupian society. An important inheritance of the slave past, they continue to govern contemporary societal structures, infusing interpersonal relationships with a mistrust that is difficult to shake.

The memory of slavery is as politically charged as the question of race. Several interviewees are concerned that there is a political agenda behind commemorative celebrations and museums that obstructs the potentially transformative impact of remembering the past. Monsieur DL., for instance, feels that the new museum about slavery, Mémorial ACTe, will not embody 'l'âme guadeloupéenne' ['the Guadeloupian soul'] if the government takes charge of its elaboration. Monsieur R. questions the content of government-led commemorations. According to him, the Guadeloupian heroes of the 1802 rebellion against the restoration of slavery by Napoleon's troops – Ignace, Delgrès and Mulâtresse Solitude – concretize 'une commémoration politique' ['a political commemoration'] that does not interest or touch Guadeloupians (Figures 1 and 2). His belief is borne out by the reactions of other interviewees: both Madame C. and Mademoiselle D. shared their complete indifference to commemorative practices taking place yearly on 27 May. Madame C. finds it pointless to commemorate just for the sake of commemoration. She would like to see the commemoration of the past inscribed into a larger

17 Translation: 'The job is not given to the West Indians, but to incompetent whites.' In this case, she is referring to recent arrivals from France.

18 Translation: 'One must not think in black and white; one must judge the person for their merits, for who they are, for their competencies.'

Figure 1: Statue of Ignace, one of the heroes of the 1802 revolution in Guadeloupe, on the Boulevard des Héros in Pointe-à-Pitre. The statue was erected on 27 May 1998. Photo taken by the author in February 2009.

framework that takes humanity in general as a reference point. Although personally touched by the statues of Ignace, Delgrès and Mulâtresse Solitude, Monsieur D. is nonetheless suspicious of the potential political motivations behind their erection. He hopes that those who create these statues have honest and sincere motivations and are not driven by a political agenda.

The mistrust that laces interracial work relations similarly feeds into memories of slavery. Hence, the positive impact of commemoration is questionable. While commemoration is unanimously applauded to the extent that it takes away the prevailing silence, its relationships to race and politics turn it into a contentious subject. Interestingly, these debates focus not, for the most part, on the relationship between France and Guadeloupe, but rather on local governing bodies and race relations. Monsieur S. is the only one who stepped out of the insular context to evoke France's political interest in dampening the militant backdrop of memorials raised around the island. While the symbolic power behind those concrete sites may be problematic, France cannot directly get involved in their elaboration. Monsieur S. uses the Prefects' inaugural discourses throughout the years to exemplify the way

Figure 2: Statue of Louis Delgrès, the most important leader of the 1802 revolution. The statue was erected on 27 April 1998 in the Fort Delgrès, a large fort in the capital Basse Terre. Photo taken by the author in July 2009.

in which France flatters the Guadeloupian population. During the 1970s, Guadeloupe was represented as an island of enchantment, then during the 1980s and 90s as an island of champions, and today as an island with a strong identity rooted in a well-founded memory. This is not true, contends Monsieur S. On the contrary, Guadeloupian culture has no defined borders and is in constant flux, permeable to outside influences. The population is no longer attached to, or identified with, its territory. Throughout the Caribbean in general, strong national identities can only be found in Cuba, Haïti and Jamaica. Again, memory is used for political ends and the population is led to believe in a fictitious strength it does not have. Built up in this way, the population may take the exterior signs of memory at face value without questioning the underlying significance of turning to the past.

My interviewees unanimously deplore the inadequacy of teaching methods with regard to the history of slavery. This history is either not taught at all, comment the older generations of interviewees, or poorly taught, comment the younger ones. Because of the lack of instruction, Mademoiselle Z. and Mademoiselle D. both claim to have only an extremely vague idea of the

Figure 3: Vestiges of the past: the restored house of the master on the Habitation La Grivelière. Photo taken by the author in June 2000.

slave past. Monsieur B. regrets the absence of historical markers regarding the Caribbean in the public school curriculum. Regardless of the lack in systematic teaching at the school level, visible signs recalling the past abound throughout the island. To what extent then do these vestiges and erected sites 'speak' to the general population? Apparently, my interviewees are considerably more taken by vestiges than by constructions. Madame P., for instance, thinks that the Mémorial ACTe museum is better than nothing, but that the vestiges of the seventeenth-century coffee and indigo plantation La Grivelière, nestled in the mountainside, convey the past much more meaningfully (Figure 3). Monsieur DL. acknowledges the 'aliveness' of old plantations. In his town of Trois-Rivières, there are slave dungeons people walk by unknowingly. He laments the population's unawareness of these historical sites and rallies for a proactive dissemination of this rich history.

Nonetheless, these visible signs of memory only gain their full significance when the population can fit them into a meaningful historical context taught at school. Anthropologist Mademoiselle A. emphasizes that history in and of itself does not necessarily make people conscious. Dates, events and heroes are not sufficient to explain the ways in which key historical events impact society. Haitians have a historical consciousness that is connected by a main thread, which Guadeloupians in turn lack. The statues of their heroes do not bring Guadeloupians closer to their history on a more personal level – these fragments of history are not connected by a main thread and do not create a well-founded historical consciousness. The population may wonder what the meaning is behind the statues that they see around them without having a deeper understanding of their significance and their interconnectedness to the historical backdrop. The yearly celebrations on 27 May do not have a practical, personal impact on the population. Mademoiselle A. largely holds education responsible for the people's inability to relate to their history: 'on leur [students] apprend pas à réfléchir sur l'histoire'.[19] Educators must first reflect on the significance to be given to the curriculum in order to make the historical material coherent. Madame DL. similarly distinguishes between a style of memorialization that gives more media coverage, in particular during the celebrations and commemorative events of 10 May and 27 May, and a deeper, less visible transformation of people's consciousness that will take considerably longer. Having been taught exclusively French history in school, she had to learn the history of Guadeloupe on her own while she was a university student in France. However, she finds that her knowledge of local history is still not thorough enough to be able to share it effectively with her students.

The process of rendering the population conscious of its slave past through the vehicle of education will be a painstakingly slow one, predicts historian Monsieur S. The problem lies in the way that memory is perceived by the people: cultural memory, linked to behaviours, language, cultural expressions and first-hand experiences, is very personal and real for people, while also being deeply buried in their lives. The explicit, visible memory that searches for exterior signs of slavery makes people uncomfortable. Monsieur S. calls this a 'fausse mémoire' ['false memory']: it is militant, puts forward claims and has not yet been integrated into any kind of curriculum. For Madame C., these exterior signs, or 'memory markers' ['marqueurs de mémoire'], are sought by intellectuals, but do not move her in the slightest. This history has been suppressed and makes people ill at ease because they have not been exposed to it during their schooling. Madame DL., who is similarly untouched by slavery on a personal level, believes that the memory of slavery is brought forth in a militant context only. Specifically, the forty-four-day strike of the LKP in 2009 awakened this consciousness in the general population through the repeated claims of the strike leaders.

Monsieur R. reiterates the same ideas in his interview: the statues of Delgrès, Ignace and Mulâtresse Solitude do not 'speak' to the general population because they do not represent their own personal history. They

19 Translation: 'students are not taught to think about history'.

Figure 4: Slave cemetery on the beach of Sainte-Marguerite near Le Moule. Visible here are the billboard and the seven coconut trees and flagpoles. Photo taken by the author in July 2013.

symbolize the revolution of 1802 against the restoration of slavery, but are at a remove from people's sensibilities. Similarly, the Mémorial ACTe museum is a 'coque vide' ['empty shell'], as the objects to be exposed will first have to be bought throughout the Caribbean. In a sense, the museum has to be almost pieced together artificially rather than taking shape organically with local materials.

In contrast, Monsieur R. believes that the filiation with ancestors is a meaningful approach to history that arises from within individuals rather than being imposed from the outside. Discovered in 1994 after the devastating effects of several hurricanes, the slave cemetery on the beach of Sainte-Marguerite, Le Moule, localizes the commemorative work of the association Lanmou Ba Yo. Three hundred graves were exhumed by a team of French archaeologists between 1997 and 2002. Some of them are still being studied in France, but most have been stored at the Musée Edgar Clerc in Le Moule.[20]

---

[20] Sainte-Marguerite is the best-documented slave cemetery in the Caribbean. It was used from the second half of the eighteenth century until 1848. The study of the grave sites has allowed archeologists to determine the African origin of

Figure 5: Billboard with the charter of the association Lanmou Ba Yo. Photo taken by the author in July 2013.

Under the impulsion of Lanmou Ba Yo, founded in 2005 and headed by Monsieur R., the site of Sainte-Marguerite provides the grounds upon which people can come to commune with their slave ancestors. Although there are no physical structures resembling a cemetery, a museum or a monument, a large billboard describes the motto of Lanmou Ba Yo in the form of a poem and seven flagpoles and coconut trees are aligned in a half-circle on the grounds of the excavated cemetery facing the ocean (Figures 4 and 5).[21] The

the deceased and the conditions of sanitation, as well as the stress factors and diseases to which they were subjected.

[21] Lanmou Ba Yo means 'Love for them' in Creole. The seven coconut trees and flagpoles make reference to the seven rhythms of the traditional *gwoka* drum and to the fact that, in the early eighteenth century, it was thought to take seven days to make a slave. The essence of the motto of Lanmou Ba Yo described in the concluding stanza on the billboard translates as follows: 'From now on, We, the great grandsons and daughters of slaves have decided: To rehabilitate the memory of our slave parents, to list them as our relatives, to assert their full dignity, to render a sacred homage: Strength to us!'

yearly celebrations during the month of May in honour of the slave ancestors bring to life the lineage between the population and the ancestors buried there. A website allows people to find their ancestor, making the history real on a personal level.[22] Monsieur R. cited various examples of individuals who were deeply moved once they found the name and identity of their slave ancestor. Artist Mademoiselle F. said she witnessed hair-raising reactions by people who found the name of their ancestor at an exhibit organized by Lanmou Ba Yo during the May celebration in 2013. For her, the identification of the slave ancestor makes all the difference, as people are able to find a link to the past – a past that is personally relevant for them. While she senses that people have mostly been disconnected from their own history, the work on the ancestors provides the missing link that allows people to reconnect. On the other hand, she finds the erected monuments and statues in Guadeloupe utterly 'silent'.

How does the first-hand experience of slave ancestry facilitated by Lanmou Ba Yo, for instance, factor into Guadeloupians' perceptions of their identity as a nation? The 'porous' identity, analysed by Monsieur S., makes it difficult for Guadeloupians to find a stronghold. West Indian cultures in general tend to be more fluid and changing in contrast to 'older' Asian, European and African cultures: 'Nous ne nous sommes pas réapproprié notre espace mental, notre vécu. On subi encore; "je fais l'esclave révolté", "je joue à l'esclave". [...] Nous devons dépasser ces blocages et nous réapproprier l'histoire.'[23] According to Monsieur R., this troubled identity arises directly from the lack of identification with slave ancestors: 'les Guadeloupéens doivent comprendre qu'ils descendent des esclaves mais ne sont plus esclaves eux-mêmes [...] ils ont besoin de devenir conscients de qui ils sont et continuer à vivre en paix.'[24] The path of memory is materialized through the act of lighting a candle for the ancestors, for instance, thereby giving homage during the May celebrations revolving around the slave cemetery.

Monsieur DL. approaches the question of national identity from an entirely different angle, focusing instead on the interrelations between different racial and ethnic groups in Guadeloupe: 'L'enseignement de l'histoire ça devrait faire émerger une véritable conscience Guadeloupéenne [...] Il faut que les

---

22 The website can be found at http://www.anchoukaj.org/.

23 Translation: 'We have not appropriated our mental space, our lived experience; we still endure and act as "the slave" or the "revolted slave". [...] We must go beyond these blockages and re-appropriate history.'

24 Translation: 'Guadeloupians must realize that they descend from slaves, but are no longer slaves themselves [...] they need to become conscious of who they are and go on to live in peace.'

Guadeloupéens aient un esprit commun, une nation, une identité à part, que les gens se sentent reliés, se sentent "uns", se sentent fiers.'[25] Monsieur DL. insists that people should have these feelings regardless of their racial or ethnic belonging – in particular blacks, white Creoles and Indians. He regrets that only the black community is mobilized around the abolition day on 27 May; neither the descendants of the colonizers or white Creoles nor the Indian community get involved in the commemorative celebrations. Mademoiselle A. similarly laments the absence of the white Creoles, the Indians and the Lebanese at the commemorative celebrations.[26] There is no coherent project uniting the people. For Monsieur DL., the memory of slavery symbolized by a specific day should rally interethnic and interracial support, bringing these communities together so they talk to one another. History lived in this way ceases to be a handicap and instead is transformed into an asset. Monsieur DL. emphasizes the richness of the different cultures present in Guadeloupe. Unfortunately, the people are unaware of their cultural wealth, as the cultures are juxtaposed and do not mix enough, despite the fact that black and white Guadeloupians like the same food and the same music. There is a common ground that needs to be exploited to make possible 'l'avènement de la nation guadelouéenne' ['the advent of the Guadeloupian nation'].

The potential of a Guadeloupian identity is pragmatically rooted in the people's relationships to one another and to their slave ancestors. According to several of my interviewees, these relationships form the foundation of the Guadeloupians' attitudes to race relations, education, work, politics and history. My interviewees dynamically engage 'living relationships between memories, vertiginous intermingling' – to reiterate Glissant's words from the beginning of this chapter. My sampling of the Guadeloupian population is clearly more concerned with contemporary societal issues than with traditional historical memories expressed through explicit memorial constructions and celebrations. While many do find the statues, museums and vestiges important as reminders of the past, they do not dwell on the inefficacy of the 'lieux de mémoire' in expressing the silenced past. Instead, they voice their personal experience of societal phenomena that continue

25 Translation: 'The teaching of history should allow a true Guadeloupian conscience to emerge [...] Guadeloupians should have a common spirit and feeling of national belonging, a unique identity [...] people should feel connected, united, proud.'

26 Indians were brought to Guadeloupe after the abolition of slavery in 1848 to work on the sugar plantations. The Lebanese and Syrians immigrated to Guadeloupe at the end of the nineteenth century.

to be deeply marked by the slave heritage. This 'undigested' heritage – if one may call it so – pervades all aspects of society and is part and parcel of Guadeloupians' everyday life. Based on my interviewees' commentaries, I would argue that they do not for the most part consider their story to be 'marginal' to the 'official' French discourse. Instead of delving into this binary relationship, they mostly direct their criticism internally, at the way their society (mis-)functions because of, and despite, an inheritance that continues to be raw even today. These considerations draw the interviewees into a web of thoughts spreading far and wide, yet continually overlapping like 'rhizomes' and interconnecting like an 'archipelago'. The Martiniquais authors Chamoiseau and Glissant capture precisely this movement: 'la repentance [...] ne peut pas se demander ni se réclamer: pour les esclavages, pour les génocides ou les holocaustes, pour les colonisations, il s'agit à chaque fois de mettre l'histoire à plat et de conjoindre les mémoires, et non pas pour qui que ce soit de battre sa coulpe, mais qu'elle peut se recevoir et s'entendre' (2007: 24–25).[27] Inspired by his immediate geographical environment, Glissant poetically incites his compatriots to recompose 'la trame archipélique et continentale de nos mémoires et la rhizomer sur toute l'expansion de nos histoires et [...] de nos géographies' (2006: 162).[28] All is possible within this creative perspective that starts afresh by facilitating new and unforeseen connections – drawing upon the past, while engaging the present and envisioning the future.

Works Cited

Bonilla, Yarimar. 2010. 'Guadeloupe Is Ours: The Prefigurative Politics of the Mass Strike in the French Antilles'. *Interventions: International Journal of Postcolonial Studies* 12.1: 125–37.

Chivallon, Christine. 2008. 'On the Registers of Caribbean Memory of Slavery'. Trans. by Karen E. Fields and Michael Stambolis-Ruhstorfer. *Cultural Studies* 22.6: 870–91.

—. 2012. *L'esclavage, du souvenir à la mémoire: Contribution à une anthropologie de la Caraïbe*. Paris: Karthala.

[27] Translation: 'repentance [...] can neither be requested nor demanded [...]: as far as slaveries, genocides, holocausts or colonizations are concerned, history must be levelled and memories joined together, not so as to make anybody feel guilty, but rather so that history can be received and heard.'

[28] Translation: 'recompose the archipelic and continental texture of our memories and rhizome it over the whole expansion of our histories and [...] geographies'.

Cottias, Myriam. 1998. 'La politique de l'oubli'. *France-Antilles: Supplément-Edition (Guadeloupe)* 25 May.

Gilroy, Paul. 1993. *The Black Atlantic: Modernity and Double Consciousness.* Cambridge: Harvard University Press.

Glissant, Edouard. 2006. *Une nouvelle région du monde: Esthétique I.* Paris: Gallimard.

—. 2007. *Mémoire des esclavages: la fondation d'un centre national pour la mémoire des esclavages et de leurs abolitions.* Paris: Gallimard.

Glissant, Edouard, and Patrick Chamoiseau. 2007. *Quand les murs tombent: l'identité nationale hors-la-loi?* Paris: Galaade Institut du Tout-Monde.

Halbwachs, Maurice. 1992. *On Collective Memory.* Chicago: University of Chicago Press.

Hall, Stuart. 2003. 'Cultural Identity and Diaspora'. In Jana Evans Braziel and Anita Mannur (eds), *Theorizing Diaspora: A Reader.* Oxford: Blackwell Publishing.

Nora, Pierre. 1996. *Realms of Memory. Vol. 1, Conflicts and Divisions.* Trans. by Arthur Goldhammer. New York: Columbia University Press.

Price, Richard. 2001. 'Monuments and Silent Screamings: A View from Martinique'. In Gert Oostindie (ed.), *Facing Up to the Past: Perspectives on the Commemoration of Slavery from Africa, the Americas and Europe.* Kingston: Ian Randle Publishers: 58–62.

Reinhardt, Catherine A. 2006. *Claims to Memory: Beyond Slavery and Emancipation in the French Caribbean.* New York: Berghahn Books.

Ricœur, Paul. 2000. *La mémoire, l'histoire, l'oubli.* Paris: Seuil.

Sainton, Jean-Pierre. 2009. *Couleur et société en contexte post-esclavagiste: La Guadeloupe à la fin du XIXe siècle.* Pointe-à-Pitre: Jasor.

The Art of Reconciliation: The Memorial to the Abolition of Slavery in Nantes

Nicola Frith

On 1 May 1998, a statue created by an art student, Lisa Marcault-Dérouard, in honour of the abolition of slavery in 1848 was found desecrated on the quayside in the city of Nantes.[1] It had been inaugurated six days earlier as part of the nation-wide celebrations of the 150th anniversary of the 1848 Abolition Act. Commissioned without the authorization of the municipal council by a group of citizen-led associations, the statue's illicit unveiling in the midst of a state-led ceremony was intended to alert Nantes's politicians to the need for a permanent memorial site (Chérel, 2012: 58). The violence subsequently committed against the statue represented a clear refusal on the part of an undisclosed sector of public opinion to engage with the memory of slavery, the statue having been knocked down from its standing position and its ankles re-shackled.[2] Its creation and destruction forced the elected representatives, notably the then mayor and socialist minister Jean-Marc Ayrault, to recognize the necessity of creating a permanent memorial site to assist

[1] The primary materials (as yet not archived) referred to here were consulted and have been cited in this publication with the kind permission of the Direction du Patrimoine et de l'Archéologie in Nantes. This work was supported by the Arts and Humanities Research Council (grant number: AH/L003937/1).

[2] Importantly, the statue has been reclaimed by the city of Nantes and now stands in the regional Musée des ducs de Bretagne as an explicit reminder of the city's troubled past.

the city of Nantes in confronting the history of its slave past (Chérel, 2012: 58). After twelve years of negotiation between the municipality, citizen-led associations and the artists Krzysztof Wodiczko (a world-renowned artist now based in New York, but originally from Poland) and Julian Bonder (an architect originally from Argentina), the Memorial to the Abolition of Slavery was inaugurated on 25 March 2012.

The realization of this memorial raises a number of important questions concerning the flexibility of republican discourse when confronted with histories that do not serve to glorify the French nation. Traditionally, the function of state memorialization has been to celebrate itself and its values (Barcellini, 2010: 210). In recent years, however, demands to commemorate historical traumas in which the French state has been directly implicated have meant that the 'victim', not the state, has emerged as the 'moteur de la vie mémorielle française' ['driving force behind French memorialization'] (Barcellini, 2010: 216).[3] The political response to this shift has been either to reposition the Republic as the symbolic champion of the victim's rights and/or to place itself at a careful temporal remove from a past which now exists in 'a world apart' and defines 'what we are in the light of what we are no longer' (Nora, 1989: 17–18). Where memories of slavery are concerned, the result has been an excessive emphasis on the role of the state in abolitionism, notably during the 1998 sesquicentenary of the Abolition Act, which erases the complex history of slavery, while forgetting the existence of slave-led revolts and other forms of resistance against the system (Vergès, 2006: 30). Driven by a desire to promote republican values, the state's excavation of a 'shared' and celebratory national narrative thus distorts the potential for a far more complex reading of the colonial past (Frith, 2013).

The problem remains that a more open and intellectual engagement with France's long history of colonialism would force the state to absorb into its national narrative memories that threaten to undermine the very foundations of its republican discourses. As Bancel, Blanchard and Vergès have noted, France's *République coloniale* is an impossible linguistic construction since the creation of 'un empire colonial où s'épanouiraient les idéaux de la République' is paradoxically the opposite of France's much-celebrated discourse of *liberté, égalité, fraternité* (2003: 11).[4] The difficulties of confronting France's long history of slavery without damaging local pride or undermining the Republic would continuously shape the debates over the memorial's conceptualization in its attempt to position itself between the assertion of a strong, republican

[3] Unless otherwise stated, all translations are the author's own.

[4] Translation: 'a colonial empire throughout which republican ideals would spread'.

memory of human rights on the one hand, while recognizing France's history of human rights abuse on the other.

Importantly, the municipality selected the internationally acclaimed artist Krzysztof Wodiczko to create the Nantes memorial.[5] If abolitionist iconography had functioned on behalf of the state's monolithic memorial apparatus, Wodiczko, as an 'outsider', had the advantage of offering an external vision with the potential to disentangle Nantes from the discursive knots of France's state-centred narrative by forcing it to move beyond its abolitionist focus.[6] This 'republican' project therefore presents an opportunity to explore the suppleness and limitations of the discursive field in which memories of slavery are being constructed in contemporary France, while also evaluating the potential for public art to negotiate the socio-political tensions between the state's celebratory discourse and citizens' demands for more genuine forms of recognition. In this way, the memorial can be seen as a cultural artefact of the difficult process of creating a memory that belongs to both state and citizen, and as a microcosm of the broader tensions relating to the visibility of minority identity within French society today.

Commemoration or Action?

The first steering committee meeting was held on 5 July 2000 to discuss the creation of a permanent memorial in Nantes. It brought together representatives of the state, members of Nantes's artistic and architectural community and representatives of Nantes's citizen associations grouped under a 'Collective for the 150th Anniversary of the Abolition of Slavery'. The collective included groups such as 'Mémoire de l'Outre-Mer', who had

---

[5] Wodiczko was one of eight names selected from twenty-one possible artists who had been put forward by different members of the steering committee that oversaw the memorial's development and production. Of the final eight, three were from the international community, four were from Paris and one was from Nantes.

[6] Indeed, during the selection process, one of the committee members, the director of Nantes's Ecole régionale des Beaux-Arts, commented on the potential usefulness of choosing an artist who was '"extérieure" aux événements' ['"external" to the events'] by citing the example of the Judenplatz Holocaust Memorial in Vienna. This had been designed and executed by the British-born artist Rachel Whiteread in honour of the Austrian victims of the Holocaust. Such external interpretations are advocated by Bancel and Blanchard, not simply for the Holocaust – following the example of Robert Paxton, whose seminal work on *La France de Vichy* (1973) transformed French historiography of the Occupation – but additionally for the whole history of France's colonial past (2006: 142).

commissioned the original statue by Lisa Marcault-Dérouard. The public tender that emerged from the committee's discussions set out the guidelines within which the selected artist would have to operate. The memorial was to carry a dual, but complementary, message. It would sit within a national discourse on republican universalism, celebrating France's national motto through the abolition of slavery in 1848, and a transnational discourse on human rights, of which Nantes was to become the shining example. Its initial conceptualization was therefore less about confronting the past than rebuilding Nantes's image as contradistinct to its past.

This tactical approach to memories of slavery is certainly not specific to France. As Marcus Wood notes, Britain's bicentennial of the abolition of the slave trade in 2007 mass-marketed a fiction whereby 'Slavery dies, or is slain, suddenly by the forces of good, inevitably manifested as abolition enlightenment' (2012: 367). The stage-management of the bicentennial in the UK was constructed from a few key motifs or figures that acted as a 'visual shorthand' (2012: 263), including the Abolition Seal ('Am I not a man and a brother') and the plan of the Brookes Ship, and narrated a story of 'black passivity developed by the white imagination' (Wood, 2012: 61). The constant recycling of these images not only reveals the limits of the (white) abolitionist imagination, which Wood argues has become locked into its 'freedom fetish' (2012: 318), but also suggests that it has reached a point of cultural exhaustion where abolitionist iconography is concerned. A shift in emphasis is required so that 'the policing mechanisms of white abolition art' are replaced by the need 'to think about how slaves expressed freedom within slavery' (2012: 356), specifically by moving from a top-down, state-led construction to a bottom-up, slave-centred narrative.

Nantes's decision to select Wodiczko meant engaging with an artist whose vision was (and remains) informed by a desire to speak out against the kinds of hegemonic discourses that have shaped France's commemorative processes. At the very centre of Wodiczko's art is the Foucauldian concept of '*parrhesia* – a special class of speech in the ancient world through which a speaker, the *parrhesiastes*, risks his civic status (perhaps also his life) to publicly speak a truth' (Kwinter, 2011: 6).[7] The *agora* is the public space in which Wodiczko's art overtly stages its bold statements and speaks a political 'truth' whose nature is 'critical, harsh, necessary… and dangerous' (Kwinter, 2011: 6). From the outset, then, Nantes's municipality was dealing with an

[7] For more information on Foucault's concept of *parrhesia*, listen to the six lectures that he delivered at Berkeley University in 1983, which are available as audio files at the following website: http://www.lib.berkeley.edu/MRC/foucault/parrhesia.html.

artist whose approach to the city, or *polis*, would be antagonistic, being rooted in the need to speak unspeakable truths through the medium of art as *parrhesia*. Necessarily, his work would offer a critical engagement with the state's 'myth' of abolitionism by viewing the 1848 Abolition Act as an ephemeral moment of democracy that must be re-imagined in the present and 'fought into the future' (Wodiczko, 2001: 4).

Wodiczko's approach was clearly outlined in his preliminary proposal (2001). Rather than honouring the nation-state, he began by stating that 'no single event of liberation, no matter how glorious, ensures that slavery will not reappear' (Wodiczko, 2001: 1).[8] He envisaged three components, each of which would move the memorial away from state commemoration and towards citizen action. First, a tax would be imposed on the sale of all coffee and sugar in Nantes (an impossible request due to the centralization of French tax laws). Second, the funds raised through taxes (revised to 'voluntary contributions'; Wodiczko, 2002: 2) would finance citizen projects run by associations 'specifically linked to contemporary forms of enslavement and their impact' and housed in the nearby Maison de la mer (Wodiczko, 2001: 2). Third, a passage would link the Maison de la mer to an 'underground archival chamber' running alongside the Loire River and embedded into the quayside (Wodiczko, 2001: 3). The importance of this chamber lay precisely in its proximity to the Loire River, which remains as a site of memory for 'the returning and departing ships [that] would have moored and been in contact with the town and its residents' (Wodiczko, 2001: 3). By positioning the archive belowground, Wodiczko intended to achieve a bottom-up perspective by evoking 'what the slaves themselves must have seen on their arrival at their ports of call' (Wodiczko, 2001: 3).[9] The connection between the archives as a site for 'mourning, thinking and "working through"' (Wodiczko, 2001: 4) and the Maison de la mer would ensure that the visitor's compassion did not fall into the trap of melancholia, but was instead translated into collective action. Rather than honouring the state, this passage would venerate the memory of the slaves by listing the 400,000 names of those who had been

---

[8] The reintroduction of slavery under Napoleon Bonaparte in 1802 after its first abolition in 1794 suggests just such a lack of guarantee.

[9] When Edouard Glissant was commissioned by the French government to write a proposal for a Centre national pour la mémoire des esclavages et de leurs abolitions (which was supposed to be constructed in Paris, but has yet to see the light of day), he similarly envisaged an archival core at the site's centre. Specifically, this archival and study centre would act as a site in which to connect all other centres, museums, institutions and commemorative sites (Glissant, 2007: 152).

transported as a result of Nantes's trading activities.[10] The retrieval of their names would serve to individualize and re-humanize the abstract figure of the slave in opposition to the faceless monochrome forms that neatly line the plan of the Brookes Ship.

The memorial would therefore be an integral part of 'la lutte constante qui se joue pour la libération des esclaves aujourd'hui' (Wodiczko, 2003: 3; emphasis in original).[11] It would serve as a reminder that the law is not enough to bring about absolute change, and that the anti-slavery struggle must continually be fought in(to) the present. This problematizes the state's abolitionist narrative construction by challenging the complacency brought about by celebratory commemoration. Action is shown to function in direct opposition to the state's discourse, through which a legal decree substitutes the need for more to be done in the present.

Monumentality or Horizontality?

The schisms that quickly appeared among members of the steering committee resided in different conceptions of the memorial's form and function. Initially, debates centred on whether the project should be 'une œuvre que l'on verra ou que l'on ira voir?' (Comité de Pilotage, 10 May 2001: 2).[12] For those with architectural and artistic backgrounds, the horizontality of Wodiczko's project was compelling because visitors would necessarily have to come and see it ('aller voir') – whereas representatives of Nantes's citizen associations considered Wodiczko's proposal as far removed from their own preference for 'une œuvre monumentale' ['a monumental work'] in keeping with Marcault-Dérouard's statue (CP, 10 May 2001: 2).[13] That the heart of the memorial would be an 'underground archival chamber' (Wodiczko, 2001: 3) was seen as problematic since it suggested, however unintentionally, a continuation of the municipality's former refusal to confront Nantes's involvement in slavery and the slave trade (Guyvarc'h,

---

10 The memorial website – available at http://memorial.nantes.fr/esclavage-et-lutte-pour-la-liberte/nantes-la-traite-negriere-et-l'esclavage/ – states that the figure was nearer to 550,000.

11 Translation: 'the ongoing fight for the liberation of slaves today'.

12 Translation: 'something that you can see or something that you go to see?' 'Comité de Pilotage' is hereafter rendered 'CP'.

13 Glissant's recommendations for a Centre national pour la mémoire des esclavages et de leurs abolitions would be similarly attuned to the need to 'see' the centre. His defining chapter opened with the statement that 'Le Centre national sera visible' ['The National Centre will be visible'] (Glissant, 2007: 145).

1999: 128–29).[14] It appeared to be a figurative reburial of the past, which contravened the important steps taken to disinter and sensitize the public to Nantes's slave-trading history, notably through the important exhibition at the Château des ducs de Bretagne entitled 'Les Anneaux de la Mémoire' (1992–94), and risked rendering the past invisible once more.[15]

Although the collective's calls for something more traditionally monumental seemed antiquated to those members of the committee with artistic and architectural backgrounds, they can also be seen as signalling two priorities for the associations: first, for visibility and recognition within the republican framework; and, second, for a shift away from 'traditional' abolitionist iconography. The emphasis on visibility can be linked to a socio-political context in which Antillean and black identities remain paradoxically 'invisible' and 'visible' within republican society.[16] As Pap Ndiaye notes, France's Antillean and black communities are trapped in a double bind. Blackness is determinedly not a 'sujet politique' ['political subject'] (2008: 390), which means that 'les Noirs de France sont individuellement visibles', while remaining 'invisibles en tant que groupe social [et politique]' (2008: 21).[17] Unlike British multicultural models, which are potentially more open to privileging the visibility of ethnic minorities (Chivallon, 2002), the republican model of neutrality before group identity (most notably captured by its policy

[14] This refusal was notably the case under the former right-wing mayor Michel Chauty (Rassemblement pour la République, 1983–89), who was replaced by the socialist minister and former prime minister Jean-Marc Ayrault (Parti Socialiste, 1989–2012). Like the memorial's 'underground' space, whose suitability for remembering slavery was questioned, Liverpool's former 'Transatlantic Slavery Gallery' was placed in the Maritime Museum's basement. As Marcus Wood notes, 'Slavery is consequently excised from the overall narrative of Liverpool's development and sent down to the basement. [...] Slavery is physically separated, as if it exists in contradistinction to, and down below, indeed out of sight of, the normal growth of the port' (2000: 297).

[15] A virtual exhibition can be found online (http://www.anneauxdelamemoire.org/fr/ressources/outils-pedagogiques/expositions-virtuelles/item/208-exposition-les-anneaux-de-la-m%C3%A9moire/208-exposition-les-anneaux-de-la-m%C3%A9moire.html). The exhibition was visited by 400,000 people (http://fr.wikipedia.org/wiki/Anneaux_de_la_M%C3%A9moire).

[16] It is worth noting that not all of the associations on the steering committee were representing the interests of Antillean and/or black minorities. For example, the primary aim of the association Nantes Histoire was to ensure that Nantes's white abolitionists were also remembered (CP, 5 November 2001: 2).

[17] Translation: 'Black people in France are visible as individuals', while remaining 'invisible as a social [and political] group'.

of *laïcité*, or secularism) insists that French associations actively avoid any accusations of 'communitarianism', especially around concepts of ethnicity. As such, the associative network offers a means by which many black French citizens are able to make their presence more manifest within public spaces. Memorialization has become, as Ndiaye suggests, 'un des volets importants de l'expression identitaire de la minorité noire' (2008: 398).[18] Within the construction of this identity, verticality is a symbol that departs from abolitionist iconography, which traditionally depicts the slave kneeling or supine (Wood, 2012) and in contrast to which Marcault-Dérouard's statue had been built upright, holding its chains aloft in an act of *self*-liberation. A vertical memorial was therefore implicitly connected to the desire for a visible identity within the Republic, while moving symbolically beyond the hackneyed images of black passivity.

In three further revisions of his proposal, Wodiczko sought to incorporate this vertical element, settling on the abstract idea of 'un phare' ['a beacon'] (2003: 3) that would shine out from the Maison de la mer, drawing attention figuratively to 'les combats menés actuellement contre les formes de l'esclavage moderne' (2004: 3).[19] The 'beacon' satisfied all members of the committee. Spatially, it would mark the memorial's location within the cityscape and perform an important act of recognition of the city's past. It would always be 'seen', while inviting people to 'come and see'. Temporally, it would link the past to the present, marking a transition from the former invisibility of Nantes's slaving history to its current visibility as part of the city's narrative: 'L'histoire existe dans le sol (le "passage") et émerge avec le phare' (CP, 12 January 2004: 2).[20] Symbolically, it would signify the need for constant vigilance against discrimination in the present and action against modern-day forms of slavery, not through simplistic equations between past and present, but by actively seeking to share responsibility and encourage public engagement. As Wodiczko commented, 'S'il n'y a pas de lien entre la traite et l'esclavage moderne, il sera difficile de comprendre le passé', just as 'Si on ne parle pas de l'antisémitisme aujourd'hui, il est impossible de parler de l'holocauste' (Minutes, 3 July 2001: 3).[21]

---

[18] Translation: 'an important component for expressing the identity of black minorities'.

[19] Translation: 'the ongoing fight against all forms of modern-day slavery'.

[20] Translation: 'History lives in the ground (the "passage") and emerges with the beacon'.

[21] Translation: 'If no connection is made between the slave trade and modern-day slavery, it will be difficult to understand the past', just as 'it is impossible to speak about the Holocaust without speaking about anti-Semitism today'.

What does it mean then that the final memorial ended up with no vertical element to complement its horizontality and no physical space in which to house citizen action? A major stumbling block was the financial constraint placed upon the project, which led to the difficulty of relocating the maritime associations that were then, as now, residing in the Maison de la mer (CP, 29 September 2004: 2). The municipality's decision to cut this aspect of the project was vehemently contested by the associations, who noted that the removal of the Maison de la mer would leave 'une "dent creuse"' ['a "hollow tooth"'] (CP, 29 September 2004: 2), while commenting that a project connected to the idea of symbolic reparations should not be subject to these kinds of financial restrictions (CP, 29 June 2005: 3).

Although financial support was sought from the central government via the Ministry of Culture ('Projet de lettre au président de la République', [2006]), no funds ever materialized. As Chérel notes, the refusal of the state, then under Chirac, to participate financially in this project was undoubtedly linked to party politics, it being likely that 'le gouvernement UMP ne souhaite pas soutenir un projet d'une ville socialiste' (2012: 164).[22] The much-lauded political unanimity with which France had voted in the (socialist) Taubira law (2001), which retrospectively recognizes slavery and the slave trade as 'crimes against humanity', thus crumbles under the weight of real political opposition and thwarts the potential to fully realize France's symbolic or moral reparation.[23] For the collective, the cuts consequently made were 'un recul politique' ['a political backstep'], leaving only 'un passage sous le quai sans un élément fort extérieur' [a passage under the quay without a strong external component'], which was not 'souhaitable' ['desirable'] (CP, 29 September 2004: 3). Yet this was ultimately what would remain of the original proposal.

Ownership and Identity

With these financial cuts imposed, the steering committee shifted their attention away from the memorial's form and towards its content, namely how to define its meaning and identity. Their discussions act as a microcosm

---

22 Translation: 'the UMP government did not want to support a project within a socialist city'.

23 Note, however, that the actual word 'reparation' was deliberately removed from the final wording of the Taubira law due to its controversial nature, while the law itself was viewed as a form of 'moral reparation' that has been instrumentalized politically to exempt the government from any real financial commitment.

of the many difficulties that abstract republicanism faces in coping with the demands of French multiculturalism and group identity. In this way, they reflect broader national concerns over the future of French identity and ownership of the past, notably within the context of what Schor (2001) has previously described as a crisis over the meaning of French universalism.

The memorial, stated Wodiczko, should transcend ownership – 'Just as a human may not become the property of another, the archive, too, must be the property of no one' (2001: 3) – but this did not mean that its identity would be 'neutral' in the republican sense. On the contrary, the underground passage was overtly concerned with the retrieval and valorization of the slaves' identity, and is linked to recent moves, notably by Antillean associations residing in France, to retrieve and honour their slave ancestries. The emphasis, Wodiczko repeatedly stressed, 'should be on the experience of the slaves themselves and those in contact with them, through their own testimonies, rather than on nameless masses of victims past and present' (Wodiczko, 2001: 3). The memorial was therefore designed to 'evoke the hold of a ship', with image and sound to be used to create a highly emotive space and 'a powerful account of the experiences of slavery and liberation' (Wodiczko, 2002: 1). In Foucauldian terms (1984), Wodiczko envisaged a heterotopia, or an 'extra'-ordinary space that would contrast with the everyday world existing aboveground. Indeed, the hold represents a kind of 'hétérotopie par excellence': a place of deviation that breaks with the linear flow of time aboveground into which the visitor enters aware that they are retreating into an unimaginable and almost sacred past. More specifically, it represents a 'hétérotopie de crise' ['heterotopia of crisis'] by recreating (without actually being) that indescribable site of trauma and pain (Foucault, 1984).

Unless treated with extreme care, such an encounter with the reimagined past risks producing a vulgar simulacrum, or a three-dimensional replica of the Brookes Ship, its supine bodies replaced by ghostly images and sounds. Instead, Wodiczko wanted to create a place of filiation (2001: 3), the 'archive' housing technologies to allow visitors to search for 'sailors, captains and officers, *armateurs, négociants,* resistants and abolitionits [sic]' (2002: 1).[24] While this would avowedly be 'délicat à traiter car on touche à la vie privée des descendants' (CP, 31 January 2002: 2), it would nonetheless reaffirm the multifaceted and non-possessive nature of the site, while speaking to other sites of memorialized trauma – such as the Memorial to the Murdered Jews of Europe, in Berlin, and the Mémorial de la Shoah, in Paris – where visitors

[24] In 2013, UCL launched a British equivalent of this project, entitled 'Legacies of British Slave Ownership', a database where visitors can search for ancestral links to persons connected with the slave trade (http://www.ucl.ac.uk/lbs/).

can search for their family histories.[25] Balancing carefully the associations' desire for a memorial 'dédié à la mémoire du peuple noir meurtri par la traite' (Minutes, 3 July 2001: 3)[26] and the state's desire for a republican and universal object, the memorial's principal function would be 'la commémoration de la **résistance** décisive **des esclaves noirs** eux-mêmes [...] non seulement au nom de la libération mais également au nom des droits fondamentaux de l'homme' (Wodiczko, 2003: 2; emphasis in original).[27] This dual strategy combining the language of human rights with a bottom-up methodology that privileged the slaves' perspective thus enabled Wodiczko to negotiate the demands of state discourse and the associations' claims for recognition.

The prominence given to slave histories within this memorial construction and the links made to the revalorization of particular group identities would prove highly problematic in the eyes of the municipal council. Directly contradicting the associations' (and the artist's) calls for a memorial to commemorate the transatlantic slave trade (Minutes, 3 July 2001: 3), the municipality specified that the memorial 'doit traiter l'histoire de l'abolitionnisme, non de la traite qui sera bien sûr abordée mais sans être l'objet principal des réflexions' (CP, 29 September 2004: 4).[28] This message was made incontrovertibly clear in a letter written by the committee's president to the then deputy mayor of Nantes, Jean-Marc Ayrault: 'Les débats récents ont montré qu'il fallait absolument accentuer le plus qu'on pourra le thème de l'abolition en regard de l'autre thème, c'est-à-dire le souvenir de la traite. En clair, il faut accentuer l'aspect informatif sur les luttes en faveur de l'abolition' (Guin, 2006; emphasis in original).[29] This unequivocal

---

25 Translation: 'Filiation [...] is a delicate subject to treat because it means reaching into the private lives of descendants'. In 2008, a French-based association, Comité marche du 23 mai 1998 (CM98), would undertake precisely this project on behalf of those descended from slavery by retrieving and displaying the family names arbitrarily assigned to the former slaves during the 1848 abolition (http://www.cm98.fr/).

26 Translation: 'dedicated to the memory of black people who suffered under the slave trade'.

27 Translation: 'the commemoration of black slaves and their active forms of resistance [...] not only in the name of liberation, but also and equally in the name of basic human rights'.

28 Translation: 'must deal with the history of abolitionism, not the slave trade, which will be addressed but without being the primary subject of reflection'.

29 Translation: 'Recent debates have demonstrated that it is absolutely necessary to emphasize as much as we possibly can the topic of abolition over and above that other topic, the memory of the slave trade. To be quite clear, we must stress the informative aspects of the fight for abolition' (emphasis in original).

statement suggests the longevity of nation-centred desires to bury the history of slavery beneath that of abolitionism, and to do so even in the wake of the Taubira law, which was intended to perpetuate a national memory of slavery. It attests to the persistent presence of what Ricœur terms 'une mémoire empêchée' ['a forbidden memory'] that serves to block any realization of, or awakening concerning, a traumatic event (2000: 575–79), in this case in the name of republican unity. There are unfortunate echoes here with the provisional governor of Martinique, Claude Rostoland, who coupled the declaration of abolition in 1848 with a general amnesty, which cleared the names of those involved in the uprisings against the plantation owners, while exhorting a state of forgetfulness towards the slave past (Garraway, 2008: 373–74). Then, just as now, the suggestion remains that the memory of slavery 'has the potential to sabotage a tenuous peace between social groups' (Garraway, 2008: 374). The state's desire to forget through abolitionism tacitly acknowledges therefore 'feelings of unrepaired victimization on the part of slaves' (Garraway, 2008: 374), while suggesting a kind of discursive stasis that traverses colonial and postcolonial histories.

It can be surmised that the letter's vague reference to 'recent debates' is an allusion to the 'tenuous peace' that had recently been disrupted as a result of heated national discussions over the legacies of France's colonial past. At a national level, these debates reached their peak with the controversial 23 February law (2005) stipulating the need to remember 'les aspects positifs de la colonisation' ['the positive aspects of colonialism']. But at a regional level too there had been strong disagreements over the first annual commemoration of the slave trade, slavery and their abolitions in 2006, when a new Nantes-based association, Passerelle Noire, had broken away from the official ceremonies by performing a controversial piece of street theatre that re-enacted the slave past (Chérel, 2012: 213–20; see also Hourcade's chapter in this volume). Cognisant of these national and regional fractures, the letter to the deputy mayor warned against the taking of 'positions communautaristes, voire même sectaires' ['communitarian, even sectarian, positions'] (Guin, 2006), stating that

> il nous faut absolument mettre une distance entre les associations locales et la Municipalité (républicaine). Nous allons fortement affirmer que c'est la Municipalité qui gérera le lieu, et que celui-ci sera entièrement tourné vers l'abolition de l'esclavage, ancien ou contemporain, de telle sorte que nous évitions que les associations s'imposent quasiment comme propriétaires du lieu et en ayant la disposition. (Guin, 2006; emphasis in original)[30]

---

30 Translation: 'it is absolutely essential for us to distance the (republican)

In addition to understanding this statement within the context of the contemporaneous debates mentioned above, it must also be positioned more broadly within the French republican model of abstract universalism. If the French state is traditionally committed to 'public neutrality' contrary to 'the privatization of culture', the so-called memory laws (including the Taubira law and the 23 February law) can be viewed as a diversion away from the state's desire to recognize 'individuals, not communities, as bearers of rights' (Laborde, 2001: 720). But, equally, if universalism 'makes of the citizen of the republic a neutered subject devoid of all particularities', its failing lies, as Schor suggests, in the fact that 'the neutering operation is not complete, for the neuter is a man' (2001: 62). We might add to this by stating that the neuter is a *white* man.

For the municipality, as representatives of the state, the only possible language that could transfer the memorial away from its focus on collective (black and/or Antillean) identity and towards a more abstract and 'neutered' form of universal identity was therefore the discourse of abolitionism. The history of slavery was to be rejected as its memory was seen as racially divisive. Yet the danger of ejecting the history of slavery from France's national narrative – which allows the state to eschew its legacies of racial discrimination and avoid confronting the socio-economic disparities between the metropole and its outre-mer – is, as Cottias notes, that national history will produce nothing more than 'des discours ineptes et idéologiques de tout bord, soit un rejet total du projet national, soit encore le développement d'identités fragmentées construites à partir de leur propre lieu et utilisant l'esclavage comme ressort politique' (2005: 61–62).[31] This then represents 'l'inverse du parcours de la reconnaissance' ['the opposite of achieving recognition'] (Cottias, 2005: 62) – or rather the opposite of what the Taubira law set out to achieve by fully recognizing France's slave past. This leads us to suspect then that abstract universalism, which acts in the interests of republican nationalism, can never offer an adequate framework for understanding the colonial and slave pasts.

Municipality from the local associations. We must strongly assert that it is the Municipality that will manage the site and that the site will be entirely focused on the abolition of slavery, past or present. This must be done to prevent the associations from imposing themselves as the quasi-owners of a site that they see as being at their disposal.'

[31] Translation: 'broadly ineffectual and ideological discourses, a total rejection of the national discourse, or even the proliferation of fragmented identities constructed from their own bases and using slavery as a political resource'.

Teleology or Transition?

If demands by citizen groups to recognize the roots of their collective identity in the colonial and slave pasts reveal the paradoxical limitations of republican universalism, the process of assimilating the memorial's message into state discourse also suggests the possibilities of negotiating these difficulties through more pluralist approaches. Initially, however, the state insisted on having ultimate control over the content and ordering of the texts that would line the back wall of the underground passage, seeing this as a way of ensuring the 'neutrality' and 'universality' of the memorial. As noted earlier, Wodiczko's intention was that the 'archive' or 'hold' would honour the 400,000 names of those who had been transported on Nantes's ships. The apparent lack of archival data meant a change in content, but not perspective, so that the names would be substituted with carefully chosen textual 'fragments' relating to 'les différentes facettes de la vie d'esclave' ['different facets of a slave's life'] (Wodiczko, 2003: 2).[32]

Problems quickly arose over who would be responsible for the content of those 'fragments'. In 2005, the local state announced that 'les artistes ne peuvent pas avoir une place privilégiée dans le processus du choix des textes' (CP, 29 June 2005: 5).[33] Their contracts were adjusted accordingly to ensure that the committee remained 'souverain dans le choix final des textes, de l'iconographie et des éléments audiovisuels', even if the artists were permitted to participate in this process (CP, 29 June 2005: 7).[34] This would help to ensure that the memorial remained focused on abolition, not slavery – or rather on its universal message as opposed to the collective identity of slave descendants.

The state's first decision was a directive from Jean-Marc Ayrault to place the Taubira law in prime position at the bottom of the main steps into the memorial, thereby framing it within a contemporary political setting with specific links to the Socialist Party. Ayrault would rubberstamp the textual excerpts himself (CP, 25 June 2006: 3). Prior to seeking this official approval, a subcommittee was set up under the guidance of a local historian of medicine, Yannick Le Marec. The report he produced one year later

---

[32] It is worth noting that despite these obstacles, the association CM98 has succeeded in retrieving the names given to former slaves during the process of abolition through the purchase of private archives.

[33] Translation: 'the artists cannot take a lead role in the process of choosing the texts'.

[34] Translation: 'sovereign in the final choice of the texts, the iconography and the audio-visual elements'.

(30 May 2007) highlighted a fundamental split operating at material and symbolic levels between the artists and the municipality of Nantes. Quoting from Reinhardt Koselleck, Le Marec noted that difficulties had arisen because 'les monuments ont un "potential excédentaire"' ['monuments have a "potential for excess"'] (2007: 1); in other words, since all memorials are constructed within particular socio-political contexts, they will inevitably lose their initial meaning and give themselves over to new interpretations: 'Le symbolique s'en va. L'architecture demeure. Les monuments se mettent à "tenir un langage qui n'avait pas été prévu par leurs fondateurs"' (Le Marec, 2007: 1).[35]

In the case of the Nantes memorial, this resulted in two diametrically opposed approaches to architecture (form) and text (content). For the artists, visitors would be able to move freely through the memorial, passing west to east or east to west, dropping down from the everyday flow of the world aboveground into the interruption of the past below, or 'd'un monde à l'autre, d'une perception à une autre' (Le Marec, 2007: 1).[36] The architecture offered a transitional, emotive and reflective space in which to recall the transatlantic crossings, while the contents of the texts would 'venir nourrir cette méditation mais laisser cette dernière aboutir' (Le Marec, 2007: 1) and therefore allow multiple and unexpected meanings to occur naturally and meditatively.[37] The message would be neither didactic nor prescriptive, but would rather foster interpretative meanings so that the architectural space was prioritized over textual content: 'C'est le monument et sa symbolique qui doivent d'abord "parler"' (Le Marec, 2007: 1).[38]

In contrast, the state wished to control the text and 'fixer le sens' ['fix the meaning'], thus ensuring that the message of the memorial was clearly presented (Le Marec, 2007: 1). Instead of allowing room for (mis)interpretation, the visitor's transition through the passage would be guided by 'un discours historique cohérent, des repères précis, une vision chronologique des abolitions' (Le Marec, 2007: 1).[39] Propelled from west to east, visitors would follow a carefully constructed teleology narrating the history of abolitionism

---

35 Translation: 'The symbolism leaves, but the architecture remains. Monuments begin to "acquire a language that their creators had not anticipated"'.

36 Translation: 'from one world to another, from one perception to another'.

37 Translation: 'stimulate this meditative process, while allowing thought to emerge'.

38 Translation: 'It is the symbolism of the monument that must "speak" first and foremost'.

39 Translation: 'a coherent historical discourse, precise markers and a chronological presentation of abolition'.

– or rather a macro-history, beginning with the Enlightenment, the French Revolution and the struggle for human rights fought during the nineteenth century, before emerging into the present-day – 'Un temps fort' ['A high point'] – where the battle has been won by the Republic and slavery safely consigned to the past. In an almost complete negation of the original aims of the artist and his intention to foreground contemporary slavery, ahistorical emotivity is replaced by historical teleology that prescribes meaning for the visitor, so that the content is 'fortement symbolique des valeurs que nous portons aujourd'hui, auxquelles nous attribuons une portée universelle' (Le Marec, 2007: 1).[40]

Broadly supportive of this macro-historical approach, the report assured the committee that there would still be room to 'faire la juste part aux paroles des esclaves' ['make sufficient space for the slaves' voices'], so that 'les actions des esclaves ont été aussi importantes que les idées des philosophes et des hommes politiques' (Le Marec, 2007: 1).[41] There is no understanding that history serves to valorize a Franco-French perspective and is unable a priori to make adequate room ('sufficient space') for the micro-historical perspectives of individual slave voices and memories. Moreover, the spurious celebration of the nineteenth century as a period of emerging human rights entirely overwrites the important connections between the abolition of slavery and France's drive for colonial expansion under the Second Empire and Third Republic (Delaye, 2003; Frith, 2014). Instead, the memorial is assimilated into a state-centred discourse that celebrates the Republic through what Schor defines as a 'monoversalist' form of universalism (2001: 61), which is only slightly decentred by gestures towards both the 'other' and the international community.

The initial selection presented to the committee was viewed as a 'compromise' between the two positions outlined above, but it was immediately obvious that the voice of the white French abolitionist and/or Enlightenment *philosophe* would dominate. Of the thirty-two texts, nearly two-thirds (62.5%, or 20 out of 32) related to French thinkers and laws, of which only five were from France's overseas colonies. In contrast, only three texts (9%, or 3 out of 32) represented the voices of slaves, none of whom were enslaved in the French colonies. This distortion of the original concept was, as Chérel notes (2012: 197), of deep concern for the artists.

In 2009, a new subcommittee under Françoise Vergès (appointed President

[40] Translation: 'strongly symbolic of the values to which we hold today and which are universal in scope'.

[41] Translation: 'the actions of the slaves were as significant as the ideas of the philosophers and the politicians'.

of the Committee for the Memory and History of Slavery from 2009 to 2012) and compiled of experts in slavery and the slave trade ensured that the textual content moved away from this monoversalist vision and towards something more 'pluriversalist' in its outlook. Consequently, the dominance of the French abolitionists and *philosophes* was tempered by increasing the presence of black voices from international and overseas communities. The result is that now over half of the memorial's texts are from non-French sources (51%, or 19 out of 37) and a small majority are from the black and/or Creole communities (54%, or 20 out of 37). Significantly, only three white French abolitionist voices remain, with more space being given instead to French legal documents relating to abolition and contemporary slavery, which reintroduces Wodiczko's desire to connect the past to the present. Importantly, a further two panels were added to include the voice of the enslaver with quotations from slave ship logbooks. Also in keeping with the artist's vision, the a-chronological structure of the texts allows the visitor to construct a dialogue between the different texts, creating 'complex connections and divergences across and between polyphonic voices' (Frith, 2013: 36–37).[42]

Yet the memorial remains undeniably gendered – only three women appeared in the first selection (9.4%, or 3 out of 32), and only four made the final cut (10.8%, or 4 out of 37) – while the voice of the former slave (male or female) remains markedly marginalized (13%, or 5 out of 37). This is no doubt due to the paucity of published slave narratives from French history, their voices having primarily been gleaned from legal archives. If the memorial has succeeded in moving away from its macro-history and towards plurality, the texts nonetheless remain far removed from Wodiczko's initial proposal. Indeed, the absence of slave voices within the important site of the hold testifies to the difficulty of retrieving the memories of those who suffered the most.

Iconography or Heterotopia?

The Memorial to the Abolition of Slavery in Nantes is now part of Nantes's patrimony and identity. As it embeds itself into the local landscape and its significance for Nantes and France is constructed, so its message and symbolism will continue to evolve. The question remains as to whether it succeeds in answering the demands to adhere to the municipality's drive for neutrality and universalism, as well as to the associations' desire for visibility

[42] The planned exhibition space eventually became a historical timeline room that complements the a-chronicity of the memorial's interior.

and recognition, while still retaining an artistic vision rooted in the concept of *parrhesia*. If its negotiation is successful, then in what ways might it offer a way forward for French society as it continues to struggle to confront its colonial and slave pasts?

Questioning whether or not the memorial is 'successful' is, of course, a highly subjective process, but in terms of this chapter, 'success' might be measured in three interconnected ways. First, does the memorial transcend the kinds of abolitionist iconography that have dogged the West's ability to confront the slave past? In other words, is the end result simply another recycled version of the Brookes Ship diptych in three-dimensional form, the texts propped up against its back wall replacing the silent monochrome bodies of the slaves from the original print? Second, does it offer a sufficiently complex space in which multiple memories and voices can be heard and within which the tensions between these memories are not simply smoothed out under a thinly shared abolitionist narrative? Third, does it meet the artist's original objective of forming a bridge between the past and present by moving towards citizen action?

The answers to these questions are both negative and positive. There is no doubt, as noted above, that the voices of slaves are in the minority, their 'space' having been replaced or even usurped by other voices, both past and present – the law, the abolitionist, the politician, the singer, the poet, the intellectual and even the slaver. That these multiple voices lie hidden from view is a reminder that those who were enslaved are often unheard and their histories forgotten, and that greater efforts are needed to retrieve them in the present. It also cannot be denied that, as Chérel notes, 'l'État reste le grand absent' ['the State remains the missing link'] (2012: 199). Its failure to provide funding meant removing key elements, such as the complementary vertical structure, the Maison de la mer and the exhibition spaces. These were desired not only to make the memorial visible, but also to connect it to communal action in the present. As such, the 'incompletion' of the memorial also points to an incomplete process of working through, one that stops short of action as a direct result of the state's unwillingness (in terms of funding) to move beyond action that is symbolic and moralistic.

What remains is the traumatic site of the hold, in which the French state, despite its financial absence, is clearly presented and perhaps even privileged through the textual display of five French laws condemning slavery. Importantly, however, the dominance of France's national narrative has been tempered by positioning it within a broader international context that moves the site beyond regional and national spaces. In the end, it is neither the slave nor the abolitionist who is allowed to dominate, but rather the importance of global, political action and resistance at all levels to fight against slavery in its multiple forms, as connoted by the multiplicity of legal, literary, autobiographical, political and historical texts.

Arguably, its greatest success might be located in its architectural form, which allows the memorial to escape the clutches of state discourse. Although positioned at the periphery of the city centre (but near the Loire), it remains an 'other' space that interrupts the everyday. The voices lining the 'hold' rise up from this reimagined site of historical trauma, the tops of the glass panels appearing aboveground and inviting the passer-by below. The visitor is forced to immerse themselves by sinking below the level of the water and passing through at their own pace and in their own direction, before finally re-emerging into the flow of humanity aboveground. It is a site that forces the visitor to stop and think by entering a void that has been filled with the (written) voices of those deemed to be most prominent in the fight for human rights. It is a memorial whose very architectural form means that the visitor cannot help but meditate upon the crimes of slavery and the slave trade. It is this physical structure that acts as a metaphor for the memory of trauma by connecting the experiences of the slaves to the coterminous emergence of slave resistance against the system. As such, and despite attempts to the contrary, it manages to transcend white abolitionist art by providing the necessary contrapuntal tension between slavery and abolitionism.

This analysis of the memorial's conceptualization thus sketches out the discursive field in which memories of slavery are currently operating, as well as the kind of political barriers that remain. The memorial object itself will always attest to a shared will to create something of significance to Nantes's and, by proxy, France's historical involvement in slavery and the slave trade. It is a site that, through its textual polyphony, demonstrates the absolute value of dialogue between multiple subject positions, as well as the usefulness of rearticulating 'national' debates within an international forum. By engaging with external perspectives (in this case, that of the artists), the limitations of republican universalism are called into question and its borders expanded. This engagement leads to a rethinking of French identity not in order to replace one model (universalism) with another (multiculturalism), but rather to create an 'other' space that allows pluralized identities to co-exist.

Works Cited

Primary Sources

In chronological order (with thanks to the municipal offices of the Direction du Patrimoine et de l'Archéologie in Nantes):

Comités de Pilotage. Held on 5 July 2000, 10 May 2001, 5 November 2001, 31 January 2002, 12 January 2004, 29 September 2004, 29 June 2005, 25 June 2006.

Wodiczko, Krzysztof. March 2001. 'A Memorial of Slavery in Nantes: A Preliminary Proposal'.

Minutes of the 'Recontre avec l'association Mémoire d'Outre-Mer et Krzysztof Wodiczko'. 3 July 2001.

Wodiczko, Krzysztof. January 2002. 'A Memorial Commemorating the Abolition of Slavery in Nantes: An Evolving Proposal'.

Wodiczko, Krzysztof. May 2003. 'Monument pour la commémoration de l'abolition de l'esclavage'.

Wodiczko, Krzysztof, January 2004. 'Mémorial à l'Abolition de L'Esclavage'.

'Projet de lettre au président de la République'. [2006].

Guin, Yannick. 6 June 2006. 'Note confidentielle à Jean-Marc Ayrault'.

Le Marec, Yannick. 30 May 2007. 'Choix de textes abolitionnistes: Passage du Mémorial à l'Abolition de l'esclavage'.

Secondary Sources

'Anneaux de la mémoire'. Available at http://fr.wikipedia.org/wiki/Anneaux_de_la_m%C3%A9moire (consulted on 5 March 2014).

—. Available at http://www.anneauxdelamemoire.org/ (consulted on 5 March 2014).

Bancel, Nicolas, and Pascal Blanchard. 2006. 'Les origines républicaines de la fracture coloniale'. In Pascal Blanchard, Nicolas Bancel and Sandrine Lemaire (eds), *La Fracture coloniale: La société française au prisme de l'héritage colonial*. Paris: La Découverte: 35–46.

Bancel, Nicolas, Pascal Blanchard and Françoise Vergès. 2003. *La République coloniale*. Paris: Albin Michel.

Barcellini, Serge. 2010. 'L'État républicain, acteur de mémoire: des morts *pour* la France aux morts *à cause* de la France'. In Pascal Blanchard and Isabelle Veyrat-Masson (eds), *Les guerres de mémoires: La France et son histoire. Enjeux politiques, controversies historiques, strategies médiatiques*. Paris: La Découverte: 209–19.

Chérel, Emmanuelle. 2012. *Le Mémorial de l'abolition de l'esclavage de Nantes: enjeux et controverses, 1998–2012*. Rennes: Presses Universitaires de Rennes.

Chivallon, Christine. 2002. 'L'émergence récente de la mémoire de l'esclavage dans l'espace public: enjeux et significations'. *Cahiers d'histoire. Revue d'histoire critique* 89: 2–15.

Comité Marche du 23 mai 1998. Available at http://www.cm98.fr/ (consulted on 5 March 2014).

Cottias, Myriam. 2005. 'Et si l'esclavage colonial faisait histoire nationale?' *Revue d'histoire moderne et contemporaine* 52: 59–63.

Delaye, Karine. 2003. 'Slavery and Colonial Representations in Indochina from the Second Half of the Nineteenth to the Early Twentieth Century'. *Slavery & Abolition: A Journal of Slave and Post-Slave Studies* 24: 129–42.

Foucault, Michel. 1983. 'Discourse and Truth: Parrhesia'. Berkeley College. Available at http://www.lib.berkeley.edu/MRC/foucault/parrhesia.html (consulted on 1 August 2014).

—. 1984. 'Des espaces autres'. In *Dits et écrits* (1954–1988), vol. IV (1980–1988). Paris: Gallimard: 752–62. Available at http://foucault.info/documents/heterotopia/foucault.heterotopia.en.html (consulted on 5 March 2014).

Frith, Nicola. 2013. '"Working Through" Slavery: The Limits of Shared Memories in Contemporary France'. *Irish Journal of French Studies* 13: 17–39.

—. 2014. *The French Colonial Imagination: Writing the Indian Uprisings, 1857–58, from Second Empire to Third Republic*. Lanham, MD: Lexington Books.

Garraway, Doris L. 2008. 'Memory as Reparation? The Politics of Remembering Slavery in France from Abolition to the Taubira Law (2001)'. *International Journal of Francophone Studies* 11: 365–86.

Glissant, Edouard. 2007. *Mémoires des esclavages. La fondation d'un centre national pour la mémoire des esclavages et de leurs abolitions*. Paris: Gallimard.

Guyvarc'h, Didier. 1999. 'Les troubles de la mémoire nantaise de la traite de noirs au 20ème siècle'. *Cahiers des Anneaux de la Mémoire* 1: 127–39.

Kwinter, Sanford. 2011. 'Introduction'. In Duncan McCorquodale (ed.), *Krzysztof Wodiczko*. London: Black Dog Publishing: 6–8.

Laborde, Cécile. 2001. 'The Culture(s) of the Republic: Nationalism and Multiculturalism in French Political Thought'. *Political Theory* 29: 716–35.

Loi no. 2001-434 du 21 mai 2001 tendant à la reconnaissance de la traite et de l'esclavage en tant que crime contre l'humanité. Available at www.legifrance.gouv.fr (consulted on 1 May 2011).

Loi no. 2005-158 du 23 février 2005 portant reconnaissance de la Nation et contribution nationale en faveur des Français rapatriés. Available at http://www.legifrance.gouv.fr (consulted on 27 June 2013).

'Mémorial de l'Abolition de l'Esclavage: Nantes'. Available at http://memorial.nantes.fr/esclavage-et-lutte-pour-la-liberte/nantes-la-traite-negriere-et-l'esclavage/ (consulted on 5 March 2014).

'Mémorial de la Shoah'. Available at http://www.memorialdelashoah.org/index.php/en/ (consulted on 5 March 2014).

'Memorial to the Murdered Jews of Europe'. Available at http://www.stiftung-denkmal.de/en/home.html (consulted on 5 March 2014).

Ndiaye, Pap. 2008. *La Condition noire: Essai sur une minorité française*. Paris: Gallimard.

Nora, Pierre. 1989. 'Between Memory and History: Les Lieux de Mémoire'. *Representations* 26: 7–24.

Ricœur, Paul. 2000. *Le Mémoire, l'histoire et l'oubli*. Paris: Éditions du Seuil.

Schor, Naomi. 2001. 'The Crisis of French Universalism'. *Yale French Studies* 100: 43–64.

UCL. 'Legacies of British Slave-Ownership'. Available at http://www.ucl.ac.uk/lbs/ (consulted on 5 March 2014).

Vergès, Françoise. 2006. *La Mémoire enchaîné: Questions sur l'esclavage*. Paris: Hachette.

Wood, Marcus. 2000. *Blind Memory: Visual Representations of Slavery in England and America*. Manchester: Manchester University Press.

Wood, Marcus. 2012. *The Horrible Gift of Freedom: Atlantic Slavery and the Representation of Emancipation*. Athens: University of Georgia Press.

Shaping Representations of the Past in a Former Slave-Trade Port: Slavery Remembrance Day (10 May) in Nantes

Renaud Hourcade

In 2005, the French government chose 10 May as the annual date for its national day for remembering the slave trade, slavery and their abolitions. The creation of this official day of remembrance fulfilled one of the criteria set out in the so-called Taubira law (2001), which sought to inscribe the slave trade, slavery and their abolitions into national memory. Since the 1983 decree under François Mitterrand, each of France's overseas departments and former slave colonies has had its own official commemorative date to celebrate abolition. But until 2005, France as a nation had neither a specific date nor any other *lieu de mémoire* to officially recall and commemorate this past, as if slavery was only a matter for the outre-mer. The stipulations made by the Taubira law dramatically changed this situation. Since 2006, prefects and city mayors have been asked to make sure that an official ceremony marks this date every year and everywhere in the country. Aside from national institutions, however, the event of 10 May – which tends to involve exhibitions, ceremonies, conferences and/or concerts – are organized in a minority of places around France. They mainly draw attention in cities where there is a large and active black community, such as Paris and its suburbs, where there is a higher concentration of African or Caribbean migrants, and where concerned civil society actors often help compose the commemorative programme and fill the audience. In addition to areas with high levels of ethnic diversity, slavery-related events are also commonly seen in those French port cities with a direct link to the transatlantic slave trade.

However, even if cities, like Bordeaux or Nantes, have a relatively large black community, the slave past has not been a subject for collective remembrance until relatively recently.

Indeed, in these former slave-trade ports, the fear of collective stigmatization typically resulted in unanswered local memorialization claims until the turn of the century (Hourcade, 2014). By taking Nantes – once France's main slave-trade port – as a case in point, this chapter aims to analyse the ways in which the new legislative instruction to commemorate slavery has been answered in cities burdened with a particular responsibility. This chapter focuses in particular on the symbolic codes of commemoration and the explicit discourses used by local authorities to frame collective understandings of the slave-trade past and its consequences for the present. Collective rituals, such as those that take place on 10 May, have a significant political dimension. According to the classical Durkheimian approach (1960), groups use rituals to reaffirm their existence as a community, enhancing shared identity, values and a sense of solidarity. However, other analyses suggest that when commemorations refer to a past that is not fully accepted or that remains controversial, they may crystallize social oppositions and feed political contention rather than uniting a community and forging a collective identity. When this happens, these acts are likely to take the shape of what Vinitzky-Seroussi calls a 'fragmented commemoration' (2002), whereby different groups compete through separated ceremonies in order to create specific interpretations of the past or particular identities, or even to make certain values prevail.

Home to the descendants of slave-traders, active black communities and politicians concerned with their city's public image, the former slave-trade ports might be expected to be the place for precisely these kinds of antagonistic commemorations. By focusing on Nantes, the different meanings and uses of memory put forward by local memory activists and public authorities will be explored. Particular attention will be paid to analysing the ways in which these meanings and uses converge on and/or confront each other, as well as the frames that have come to dominate through the official commemorative ritual. The first half of this chapter describes the approach of Nantes's authorities to commemoration and demonstrates how the official 10 May ritual at a local level politically legitimates republican discourses on identity. The second half examines the ways in which opposing actors have managed to penetrate the scene with views that challenge the 'official' memory frames, particularly where concepts of race and racism are concerned. Both parts look closely at how these contrasting perspectives on memory are embodied in competing symbolic languages of commemoration.

Inventing a Ritual: Controlling Slavery's Uses

With more than 1700 voyages, Nantes's share in the slave trade amounts to 45 per cent of all French expeditions, a figure that makes the Loire city by far the nation's leading slave-trade port (Pétré-Grenouilleau, 2007: 4). In spite of its particularly weighty involvement, for many years Nantes chose silence and discretion where its past was concerned, much like all the other French ports once involved in the so-called 'ebony trade' (notably Bordeaux, Saint-Malo and La Rochelle). The city only started to officially acknowledge its role in the slave trade in the 1990s, when an exhibition on this theme was organized with strong municipal support (Les Anneaux de la Mémoire, 1992–94). However belated, this successful operation helped the city appear avant-gardist at a time when other slave-trade ports, and the nation as a whole, remained reluctant to make slavery a part of public memory. This exhibition was made possible in the wake of a significant political shift in Nantes: Jean-Marc Ayrault, a socialist, won the 1989 local election over his conservative opposition. During the campaign, he had promised to 'réveiller la belle endormie' ['awaken Sleeping Beauty'], a programme that intended to enliven the city's image, breaking up its 'bourgeois' reputation and setting up innovative cultural policies. This ambition led his team towards a new strategy regarding the history of slavery, which opposed that of the previous municipality. In 1983, fearing bad publicity for Nantes, the former mayor had refused to support a local commemoration on the occasion of the tercentenary of the Code Noir (the code regulating slavery issued in 1685 by Louis XIV). In contrast, the new political majority led by Jean-Marc Ayrault took a different approach, choosing to confront the past, instead of denying it, and thereby embodying Nantes's modern values and attitude. Consequently, political communication and place marketing derived the maximum possible benefit from the 1992 exhibition, allowing the city to 'reverse the stigma' of its past by transforming shame into civic pride through its courageous engagement. In 1998, the city's authorities also began discussing the construction of an ambitious memorial, a decision that was meant to confirm Nantes's pioneering attitude regarding acknowledgement of its past.[43]

Race, Place and Memory Activism

Against this political backdrop, the Taubira law's measures did not represent any kind of real challenge for Nantes's elected representatives. Dialogue and good cooperation with local civil society actors were already in place,

[43] See, in particular, Nicola Frith's chapter in this volume.

thus reducing the risk of making commemoration a weapon in the hands of opposing groups. Although a small group of radical African activists had protested against Les Anneaux de la Mémoire, calling the exhibition a 'sanitized' version of history and claiming that it had marginalized African voices, their critical views did not succeed in attracting significant attention after the exhibition. Other memory stakeholders, whether they came from the region's historians or its black minority, praised the exhibition and later engaged in durable cooperation with local authorities on public memorialization issues. Memory activists from the Antilles region proved particularly committed at a local level, represented in the main by the association Mémoire de l'outre-mer, whose views on the topic are broadly aligned with the vision promoted by the city's authorities. Gathering members from France's overseas departments, notably Martinique, Guadeloupe, French Guyana and Réunion, this association also includes white 'friends' of the Antilles. By highlighting their cultural and biographical particularity as 'descendants of slaves', the members of Mémoire de l'outre-mer claim the necessity for Nantes to acknowledge its slave-trading past and are thus generally supportive of the city's efforts in this direction. As a result of this good working relationship, the municipality has regularly consulted this group on memory matters. Moreover, Octave Cestor, the founder and at the time leader of Mémoire de l'outre-mer, a member of the socialist party, was an elected member of the city council. In stark contrast with Bordeaux, for instance, where memory entrepreneurs in the same period were fiercely fighting the city council's reluctance to acknowledge its past, the context for the emergence of Nantes's memory of slavery appeared to be relatively peaceful and indeed consensual.

When Mémoire de l'outre-mer was created in the late 1980s, it was highly unusual for people from the overseas departments to consider their slave genealogy as something valuable (Jolivet, 1987; Bonniol, 2007). Especially in metropolitan France, where the desire of migrants to integrate lent itself to discretion, the 'slave-descendant' identity was largely unrecognized among the overseas community, and even more rarely voiced in public. But the leaders of Mémoire de l'outre-mer held other views. They were sensitive to the new cultural paradigm that had emerged in the 1970s and 1980s, claiming slavery and the racial mixing to which it had given rise as the distinctive feature of Caribbean identity. Following Edouard Glissant's conceptualization of the 'rhizomic', or multiple, nature of Caribbean roots (Glissant, 1981), and seduced by the *Créolité* movement, which places the history of slavery and resistance at the centre of Caribbean cultures and identities (Bernabé, Chamoiseau and Confiant, 1989), the members of Mémoire de l'outre-mer were at pains to emphasize both their distinctive ethnic legacy, as slave descendants, and their full belonging to Nantes (and, by proxy, the nation). The former aspect led them to take action inside their own community in order to 'faire sauter les chaines qui restent fortement liées dans [leurs] têtes',[44] by reclaiming slavery as a heritage: 'Cela nécessite une démarche consciente d'acceptation de notre héritage historique: oui, le peuple d'Outre-mer a comme héritage son origine, nous sommes enfants d'esclaves et de négriers' (Anonymous, 1993: 1).[45] It was notably this latter aspect that made them push Nantes's official memory to be more inclusive and respectful of its black minority, and to request full recognition of the slave past.

When the group was first created in 1986, the achievement of such an objective was still remote. The cancellation of the Code Noir commemoration, following Mayor Michel Chauty's opposition, had only happened a few years before, and the reluctance of the city's political leaders seemed particularly strong at that time. In response to this situation, Mémoire de l'outre-mer's members decided to create their own commemorative ceremony. Each year, at the end of May, they would gather on the banks of the Loire River in the city centre and hold a ceremony to commemorate the abolition of slavery. Octave Cestor would give a speech, and there would be some Caribbean dances and drums, followed by a moment of greater solemnity when some members of the association, often accompanied by a guest, would throw flowers into the river, representing the symbolic 'tombeau de milliers d'Africains' ['grave of thousands of Africans'].[46] According to Cestor, this ritual was the best way to raise awareness among Nantes's population (Anonymous, 2000: 9). Often, local politicians, friends from other associations, local sport champions or school children would be invited to participate as a way of demonstrating that these kinds of ceremonies belong not just to one specific community, but to all the people of Nantes.

The 'Quai de la Fosse' where the activists invariably met for this ceremony was once the place where transatlantic ships were moored on the Loire River, just a short distance away from the Atlantic Ocean. Among them were many slave vessels, whose owners would often live in the graceful

---

44 Translation: 'break the chains that remain linked in the minds of the Caribbean people'. This and all subsequent quotations from this source and others were translated by the author of this article, unless otherwise stated.

45 Translation: 'This requires a conscious process of accepting our historic heritage. Indeed, for people from the outre-mer, their origin is their heritage; we are the children of slaves and slave-traders.'

46 As Cestor often explains, 'Cette eau qui relie les continents [...] fut le tombeau de milliers d'Africains'. Translation: 'This water that links the continents [...] is the grave of thousands of Africans' (Hazera, 2006: 183).

hôtels particuliers that had been built right on the quayside. Still standing today, these eighteenth-century buildings are among the few remaining physical testimonies to the city's past. With its equivocal nature – death and sufferance on one side, and commercial entrepreneurship and wealth on the other – the quay perfectly illustrates the contrasted legacies of the slave trade. It therefore also presented Nantes's municipal authorities with a problem, namely the difficulty of constructing a local memory out of a divisive history that still preserves social cohesion and the sense of shared belonging. By setting aside an official day of remembrance, the Taubira law has provided cities with a valuable political tool. While it offers the local community an opportunity to demonstrate the level of respect they wish to pay to the past, it also supplies dominant actors with an instrument to put forward their own visions, values and interests. The type of commemorative activity, the discourses within which commemoration is staged and the cultural or historic references that it highlights collectively create a specific memory frame. In Nantes, three dominant perspectives structure this frame: it centres on the city's pioneering acceptance of the past; it eludes the question of culpability and debt; and it remains silent regarding the racial legacies of slavery.

Memory Governance and the Political Production of Memory Frames

When Nantes's authorities were required to organize the first 10 May commemoration in 2006, they kept things simple by adopting Mémoire de l'outre-mer's ceremony as their own official ritual and closely involving civic activists in designing the programme of events. The already established relationship between the main memory entrepreneurs and the city council facilitated this process. As Sarah Gensburger (2010) has suggested in her study of the national commemoration of the 'Righteous among the Nations', this kind of governance has become a norm for contemporary policies of memory. Memory governance allows memory entrepreneurs and public authorities to share the benefit of a 'cross-legitimization' process (Gensburger 2010: 93): the associations receive official recognition and their visions gain better access to the public sphere, while public authorities benefit from the assurance of strong civil society support that endorses their actions in the field of memory.

As a result of this process in Nantes, it is now the mayor who ceremoniously throws flowers into the river, while Caribbean activists stand close by, but to one side. With the mayor in this central position, the ritual acquires new meanings. It is no longer a specific community that pays tribute to the victims of the slave trade or that celebrates abolition, but rather the whole city, irrespective of race or ethnicity. The fact that this commemoration follows the classic symbolic pattern of all republican ceremonies, such as 11 November and every other official tribute, is noteworthy: a wreath is laid at the foot of a monument (although the wreath is thrown into the river, the meaning remains the same), which is followed by a minute's silence and then finally a speech pronounced by the highest authority present. Insofar as it echoes the ritual patterns of other commemorations, the memory of the slave trade can be said to receive equal recognition to these other events, and thus becomes yet another strata of local (and national) identity. In other words, it is *patrimonialized* – slavery and the slave trade deserve to be preserved, not because of their significance for a particular political party, but rather for all of Nantes's citizens, who are represented by their mayor. Thus, by integrating the victims of slavery into the local collective memory, Nantes recognizes slave descendants as full members of the community. Jean-Marc Ayrault's discourse at the 2011 ceremony gives a sense of this symbolic act of recognition: 'Cette histoire est celle d'un crime qui concerne notre histoire, et qui n'est l'apanage d'aucune communauté. [...] L'enjeu est que chacun, quelles que soient ses origines, se sente partie intégrante de l'histoire nationale et citoyen à part entière'.[47] When interviewed a few days later, the vice mayor in charge of culture presented a similar viewpoint:

> Nous nous sommes beaucoup fixés sur la position d'Aimé Césaire, lorsqu'il dit en particulier que ce qui compte c'est le récit national. [...] Césaire s'est toujours opposé à des réparations, mais Césaire a toujours exigé que la République assume, dans son enseignement scolaire, dans son rituel républicain, qu'elle assume cette portion de l'histoire qui est une portion de nos concitoyens français. Ils ne seront français qu'à partir du moment où la République dit 'oui, ça fait partie de notre histoire, vous faites partie de notre histoire, au même titre que les paysans français'. (Guin, 2011)[48]

---

[47] Translation: 'This is the history of a crime that concerns our history and it is not owned exclusively by any one community. [...] This is about making everyone, irrespective of their origins, feel a part of national history and like a full citizen.'

[48] Translation: 'We have been greatly inspired by Aimé Césaire's position, particularly when he says that what counts most is the national narrative [...]. Césaire always opposed reparations, but Césaire also always asked the Republic to acknowledge, in its school teachings and in its republican ritual, this part of its history, which is a part of all of our French fellow citizens. They will only become French when the Republic says "yes, that's a part of our history, you are a part of our history, just as much as the French peasants".'

As Johann Michel (2010) suggests, such processes of patrimonialization are also processes of de-politicization. He observes that France as a nation commemorates opposing moments of history, the Revolution and royalty, Napoleon's empire and the Republic. These multiple layers are part of our common identity. While the state integrates these complex and potentially divisive events into the shared national narrative, it ensures that contentious representations of the past are eluded and the political divisions of past events put to one side.

In a sense, then, patrimonialization involves sterilization. The language of commemoration makes the ceremony a space where cohesion is displayed and heated debates are put to one side. The abstemious, ritualistic form of the ceremony translates such focalization on unity. The flowers and the minute's silence both have a religious dimension. Even in modern societies, flowers have preserved their ancient signification as an offering made to the dead (Goody, 1993), whereas the minute's silence can be interpreted as a secular form of prayer. Both symbolic gestures thus construct the symbolic presence of the victims and, as such, the ritual calls for respect, dignity and discretion, rather than voicing claims.

Public discourses appear consistent with these symbolic codes. Nantes's mayor is at pains to emphasize that the public memorialization of the slave trade is neither a matter of looking for responsibilities nor a question of accepting collective guilt. Memory is a subject of neither debt nor reparation, the underlying purpose being to show union, not division. Hence, there is a strong insistence on the fact that memory must not be interpreted as 'repentance'. There should be no victims on the one side and perpetrators on the other, but only present-day citizens, reunited under the same banner, one that attests to Nantes's acceptance of its past and endorses its common values in the present. As Jean-Marc Ayrault frequently states, 'Il serait réducteur de penser que nous concédons, les uns et les autres, à la culpabilité: comment pourrions-nous être comptables de ce qui fût en dehors de nous-mêmes? Nous sommes cependant redevables de ce qui ne doit plus jamais être'.[49] In terms of identity construction, these political discourses typically emphasize collective belonging to the city and shared humanitarian values, and only rarely mention other perspectives of slavery's cultural or racial legacies. Citizens are invited

---

[49] Translation: 'It would be simplistic to think that we recognize all of our own culpability. How could we be held responsible for what happened in our absence? However, we do have a responsibility for what must never happen again.' This statement is frequently made by Jean-Marc Ayrault, for instance during the 1998 commemoration (Anonymous, 1998: 7) and again at the Abolition Memorial unveiling ceremony on 25 March 2012.

to feel proud of a city that dared to confront its past at a time when Nantes stood alone in this position. It is therefore local identity, more than anything else, which is at the core of these memorialization discourses.

One additional aspect of the dominant memory frames worth stressing is the absence of a 'black' or racial perspective. Comparative studies show that in many contexts, whether in the US, the UK or Brazil, the memory of slavery is inevitably bound up with the issue of the durable racial prejudice derived from the system of slavery and its ideology (Araujo, 2012). Commemorative gatherings or monuments around the world are generally structured by – or at least make reference to – the struggle of black people against domination, and often underline links between the past and today's racial discrimination and social inequalities. In 2007, the bicentenary of the abolition of the slave trade celebrated in the UK was an opportunity for public authorities to demonstrate their concern regarding the disadvantages still suffered by the nation's black community (Waterton et al., 2010). In Nantes, however, the memory of slavery is only rarely associated with such issues. As mentioned by Nicola Frith in her chapter in the present volume, the fact that local politicians were at pains to make sure the city's Memorial to the Abolition emphasised universalism, as opposed to recognising the 'black dimension' of slavery memory, is revealing. While this feature coincides with the traditional racial blindness of the French Republic (Ndiaye, 2007), one may note that it is particularly pronounced in Nantes when compared, for instance, with Bordeaux.

This can be explained in terms of the different nature of the memory entrepreneurs in these two former slave-trade ports (Hourcade, 2014). In Bordeaux, memory entrepreneurs are predominantly of African origin and have mainly conceived of memory in terms of racial diversity and ethnic minority integration; whereas in Nantes, it is Mémoire de l'outre-mer and a few other memory groups with identity rooted in the Caribbean who have led the mobilization of memory. As was already clear during the slavery exhibition organized by the city in 1992, perspectives that are more concerned with a 'black' or Afro-centric identity tend to be marginalized. Moreover, local Caribbean memory militants often radically reject racial identifications. In their opinion, recent mobilizations based on black identity, such as the creation of the Conseil Régional des Associations Noires, or CRAN (2005), can only result in *communautarisme* (communitarianism) and division. Such initiatives are deemed to betray the republican pact of colour-blindness to which these activists strongly adhere. The close relationship between the city of Nantes and these dominant memory entrepreneurs allowed this perspective to become instilled into the frame of the official commemorations. Hence, for instance, the multiple references made to

Edouard Glissant's conceptions of the 'tout-monde' and the frequent mention, more generally, of Caribbean authors. Guests are also often culturally linked to the Antilles: Edouard Glissant in 2009, Yannick Lahens in 2010 and Christiane Taubira in 2011. By contrast, Afro-centric or black perspectives on the slave trade and slavery are much less frequent. It is also worth noting that this outre-mer-centred feature of Nantes's commemoration matches the general memory frame promoted at a national level by the Taubira law and the Comité pour la Mémoire de l'Esclavage [Committee for the Memory of Slavery] (CPME), the consultative body that was set up following the 2001 law. In their recommendations regarding the 10 May commemoration, the committee asked that it serve as an opportunity to 'mettre en lumière les contributions des Guadeloupéens, Martiniquais, Réunionnais, Guyanais à la culture, à la pensée, à la création artistique et à la démocratie' (CPME, 2005: 29).[50] In contrast, race and blackness are marginalized in this document.

Getting Politics Back: The 'Marche des Esclaves' as an Alternative Ritual

From 2006, the institutionalization of an annual remembrance day for slavery appeared to be an opportunity for a variety of local civil society groups. The new actors that emerged, as well as those that already existed, decided to engage with memory issues, bringing with them new visions of the significance of slavery for the present. Participation in the 10 May celebrations gave them access to modest public funding, to the 'Village de la mémoire' ['Memory Village'], and, perhaps more importantly, to a share of public attention. The 'Village de la mémoire' is a plastic tent area installed in a public square near the Quai de la Fosse during the day of commemoration and is the location where the associations involved can display exhibits, communicate their activities and meet visitors. There is also a stage for concerts and shows. From 2007, the city council began asking participants to gather under an umbrella group, the 'Collectif du 10 mai' ['Tenth May Collective'], which would be recognized as the unique direct partner and would help coordinate the multiple initiatives attracted by this new tribune. The Collectif's expansion from sixteen groups in 2007 to twenty-five in 2009 brought with it disputes over who would have ultimate control over this structure. By 2009, the 'old' central associations (Mémoire de l'outre-mer, Métisse à Nantes and Les Anneaux de la Mémoire) were in the minority and had lost control, which

[50] Translation: 'highlight the contributions of people from Guadeloupe, Martinique, Réunion and Guyane to culture, thinking, artistic creation and democracy'.

meant they had also lost control over the messages of the commemoration. Instead, other views inspired by a more race-orientated perspective prevailed. In 2010, the Collectif decided that the topic of that year's commemoration would be 'les résistances noires à l'esclavage' ['the resistance of black people to slavery'] (Prochasson, 2010). Their plan was to draw a connection between the Resistance to the Nazis during the Second World War and the slaves' resistance to oppression through revolts and *marronnage*. This did not please the 'historical' associations, who put forward 'métissage' as their preferred topic for 2010, this being a theme that was more in line with customary local memory frames. A heated controversy broke out, during which the members of Mémoire de l'outre-mer defended their legitimacy against the newcomers, who were accused of opportunism and radicalism (Mvé, 2010). No more at ease with the framework of 'black resistance', the authorities finally withdrew the Collectif's prerogatives and imposed 'Haïti' as the official theme for 2010 (the former slave colony having been stricken by a devastating earthquake some months earlier).

The 'Marche' and Black Memory

This episode was a clear indication of the rising competition between contrasting concepts of memory in Nantes. Deeply involved in this competition was a small group of memory entrepreneurs called Passerelle Noire. Led by Peter Lema, an actor born in the Democratic Republic of Congo, this association mainly gathers activists of African origin, but also some from the French Antilles. Many of its members had long been active in Nantes's African milieu before taking action in the field of memory in the context of 10 May commemorative events. Others, like the Martinique-born musician André-Joseph Gélie, were involved in the local Rasta musical scene. Taking advantage of their professional abilities, they decided in 2006 to create their own programme to mark Nantes's slavery commemorations. Political visions were also at stake. Passerelle Noire's activists aimed to make alternative voices heard and to stress other aspects of slavery and its legacies. The programme they created in 2007, called 'La marche des esclaves' ['The march of the slaves'], sought not to evoke the past symbolically, as the official ritual does, but rather to recreate the past through theatre and playacting.

The march travels along the commercial streets of Nantes's city centre either on 10 May or the day before. A pair of soldiers mounted on horseback walks ahead of a file of black slaves. The slaves are dressed in rags, some bending over, other wearing chains, as they are forced to walk before white guards who shout at them and whip them. They are men, women and children who proceed falteringly, stumbling as they go, moaning or singing melancholic songs together. At various moments during the procession, short sketches are played out. They evoke episodes from the plantation system, such as a slave auction featuring slave merchants from Nantes, or an attempted escape that ends up with the death of the unfortunate runaway. The march finally arrives at the stage of the 'Village de la Mémoire', where the play terminates. According to its creators, the 'Marche des esclaves' brings more content to the representations of slavery by helping people to figure out 'what it was like'. In a 'world of images', they consider that this recreation of slavery is more 'pedagogical' (Patrice, 2008).

These aesthetic choices contrast strikingly with the language of the official commemoration. In Passerelle Noire's re-creation, violence, suffering, fear and scandal are prioritized over restraint and contemplation as a means of making the past come alive in people's consciousness. While throwing flowers in the Loire can trigger emotion, if only through interpretation, the march offers a far more tangible 'experience'. It is a performance that is meant to create a more direct 'memory' constructed from images that are immediately accessible. It is also, therefore, a memory that is more political. The performance does not try to devitalize the past and damper passions, as the official ceremony does, but rather seeks to liberate them.

Seen through this lens, the march is evocative of the social functions of carnivals in popular culture, and notably in post-slavery societies (Cohen, 1993). Carnivals can be understood only in relation to the social order, its dominant actors and prevailing values, which the carnival seeks to challenge through performance. This similarity is not circumstantial. As one of the leaders of Passerelle Noire explained (Jonathan, 2011), the idea of the march dawned on him while watching, but not participating in, a Caribbean carnival in Nantes:

> J'ai fait le carnaval mais aujourd'hui je n'ai plus envie de faire ça, parce que je sens que nous passons encore pour des gens qui dansent, qui jouent, qui n'ont pas de souci. Je me suis dit, pour que je refasse le carnaval, il faudrait quelque chose qui soit un peu au niveau de la mémoire, à Nantes. Et je voyais effectivement qu'on pouvait aussi marcher dans les rues, avec des chaînes, en esclaves. C'est ça l'origine.[51]

---

[51] Translation: 'I used to go to carnivals, but I've no desire to do that any more because I feel we are depicted again as people who just dance and play, and have no worries. But I thought that in order to return to the carnival I would need to do something that was more related to memory in Nantes. And I also realised that we could walk the streets dressed in chains as slaves, so that was where it started.'

If challenging the establishment was a goal, the 'Marche des esclaves' appears to have hit its target, as made clear by the many commentaries in the media. Indeed, speaking to the press, dominant memory entrepreneurs deemed the procession 'sinistre' ['sinister'], because, as Octave Cestor stated, 'on n'a pas le droit de singer une telle souffrance' (Anonymous, 2011).[52] He added in the same interview: 'C'est comme si on demandait aux Juifs de théâtraliser leur marche vers les fours crématoires'.[53] The vice mayor in charge of culture shared a similar position: 'Il y a, aujourd'hui, une *"Marche des esclaves"*. Alors nous, on est complètement contre ça. Pour nous, c'est calamiteux. Des images comme ça sont calamiteuses!' (Guin, 2011).[54] Thus, from the outset, the city's authorities did not take kindly to this initiative and were very reluctant to provide public funding to support it. In response, the members of Passerelle Noire developed an increasingly critical stance, blaming the city for its 'frilosité' ['feebleness'] and 'manque de sincérité' ['lack of sincerity'] (Patrice, 2008). Meetings with city councillors often gave way to confrontations. As a Nantes civil servant explained, 'La ville n'a aucune obligation de soutenir tous les projets, surtout quand elle ne s'y reconnaît pas au point de vue politique. [...] Franchement on n'a aucun objectif commun! On n'est pas sur les mêmes planètes!' (Dominique, 2011).[55]

Initiators of the March of the Slaves also challenge dominant visions through the cultural references that they bring to the commemoration. The black American struggle for civil rights is one of these references. In 2008, Passerelle Noire introduced Amelia Boynston Robinson, 'a friend of Martin Luther King and Rosa Parks', according to the flyer they distributed, as the sponsor of the march. In 2011, they invited Malaak Shabazz, one of Malcolm X's daughters, to take part in the procession, along with Dowoti Desir, the former director of the Malcolm X and Dr. Betty Shabazz Memorial, Educational and Cultural Center in New York. 'Nous voulons faire entendre d'autres voix [...] Les Noirs anglophones ont moins une complexe d'infériorité' (Patrice, 2008).[56] This 2011 march also displayed the support of a group of

52 Translation: 'We have no right to ape such suffering.'

53 Translation: 'It's like asking Jews to playact their march to the crematorium furnaces.'

54 Translation: 'Now there is this march of the slaves. We are totally against it. For us, it is calamitous. Images like these are calamitous!'

55 Translation: 'The city has no obligation to support every project, particularly when we don't identify with them from a political point of view. Frankly, we don't have any common objective. We don't even live on the same planet!'

56 Translation: 'We want to make other voices heard [...] Anglo-American blacks don't suffer as much from an inferiority complex.'

activists, the Brigade Anti-Négrophobie. This recently created group gathers young black men and women from the Paris region. They militate for strong public action in the field of racial equality and have been involved in various operations to denounce racism and discrimination. The participation of dozens of Brigade Anti-Négrophobie members in the 2011 march spectacularly accentuated its apparent radicalism. Fully dressed in black, the Brigade members paraded at the back of the procession of slaves. A handful of strong, tall men, with shaved heads, wearing sunglasses and earpieces, also flanked the two American guests throughout the performance. Looking like bodyguards, their appearance was an inevitable reminder of images of radical black American activism. Partly because of this striking image, the slave march that year met with particular political disapproval.

But suspicion towards this kind of activism was not limited to Nantes. The day after this demonstration, the Brigade Anti-Négrophobie tried to join the official national ceremony on 10 May in the Jardin du Luxembourg in Paris, in the presence of the then President of the Republic Nicolas Sarkozy. At the park's entrance, however, Brigade members were pushed back by security guards, which resulted in a confrontation and a number of arrests. Notwithstanding their striking dress code and actions, the ideology of these militants is nonetheless quite different from that of radical black nationalists. They do not conceive of blackness as a substantive identity and even call themselves 'Republicans' (Thompson, 2012). What they seek is mainly to make the nation aware of the level of racial disadvantage suffered by a part of its citizens, and to do so through more outspoken and direct means than are commonly seen in France. The level of attention raised by the commemoration of slavery thus offers a good opportunity to voice their concerns within an overtly spectacular setting.

Race or Reunion? The Limited Polysemy of Slavery Commemorations

Prior to the Taubira law, very few commemorations of slavery existed in France, but the institutionalization of a day of remembrance led to a mushrooming of actors and initiatives. As the example of Nantes clearly shows, there is a wide range of messages, values and interests that can utilize 10 May as their political vehicle. So the question remains: is a shared commemoration still possible within this context and, if so, what can its goal be? The main objective of the Taubira law was to make slavery and the slave trade part of France's national identity, thus providing slave descendants with a moral form of recognition from the nation-state (Cottias, 2007). The commemoration in itself ought to 'rappeler à la France qu'elle participa à la traite et à l'esclavage,

[...] inviter l'ensemble des citoyens de la République française à se pencher chaque année solennellement sur cette page douloureuse de son histoire, en favorisant à cette occasion la plus large diffusion d'un récit partagé' (CPME, 2005: 29).[57] While political authorities may pursue specific objectives through their policies of memory, once the instrument of memory is created, social dynamics step in to strengthen, amend, contest or supplement the initial message. While official memories have all too often been studied uniquely from a top-down perspective that focuses on the uses of public memory by political powers, it seems much more preferable to understand them as an interactive process, where appropriation or contestation plays a key role in shaping collective representations. Commemorations are malleable and often polysemic. This may particularly be the case when the past being remembered is painful or ambiguous, and when unanimity and solidarity are therefore more difficult to obtain. In their study of Washington's National Memorial to the Vietnam War, as a particularly uncomfortable episode of the history of the US, Robin Wagner-Pacifici and Barry Schwartz (1991) come to the conclusion that social interactions constantly challenge the symbolic message of the state, in this case by reintroducing heroism and pride into an anti-heroic monument.[58] But even if symbolic forms, whether ritual or material, are capable of conveying a variety of meanings, disagreements over these meanings do not prevent a memorial from playing its role. In line with Durkheimian thinking, this diversity of appropriations should not have significant consequences for the commemoration's function, insofar as the multiple meanings that can be derived from rituals count less than their actual existence. As David Kertzer writes, 'rituals can promote social solidarity without implying that people share the same values, or even the same interpretation of the ritual' (1988: 69).

As far as modern societies are concerned, however, it may be considered that, when a certain level of dissensus has been reached, a single commemorative form stops being capable of incorporating the diversity of all the visions of the past. Such a situation may indeed lead to the emergence of alternative forms of memorialization, more apt to demonstrate and promote opposite feelings or values. Vered Vinitzky-Seroussi (2002) calls this model

57 Translation: 'recall that France participated in slavery and the slave trade [...], invite all French republican citizens to look solemnly into this painful part of its history on an annual basis, while contributing, on this occasion, to diffuse a shared narrative as widely as possible.'

58 For example, visitors tend to bring national flags and/or other personal items that introduce alternative visions of the past into what was fundamentally designed as a humble symbolic landmark for an inglorious past.

'fragmented' commemoration. This form of public memorialization does not serve to enhance unity, but rather 'sharpens social conflicts by offering contentious collectives what they scarcely could have laid claim to before the monuments were erected and the memorial days were set: a place to meet, a time to share and a discourse to cherish' (Vinitzky-Seroussi, 2002: 48). The tenth of May in Nantes is just such an example of a commemoration that has become 'fragmented'. Notwithstanding the state's intention to foster solidarity, it reminds us that public memory remains a place for political struggles in its own right (Bertrand, 2005). This may be particularly true regarding memories of slavery and colonialism, which have been a much-disputed political arena in the last years (Bancel et al., 2010).

Conclusion

Both the 1998 national commemoration of the abolition of slavery and the passing of the Taubira law that followed in 2001 are commonly seen as key steps for the integration of slavery into France's national memory. From then on, slavery – and not simply its abolition – has indeed gained institutional recognition. While this is still an ongoing process, this new understanding of the collective past is not dissociable from a changing approach to the national politics of identity, insofar as memory has been used as an instrument for the recognition of some of the Republic's 'minorities'. However, this study of Nantes's 10 May commemoration indicates that the extent of such recognition and the limitations of the ethnic 'minority' remain contested questions. What the Taubira law recognized, not in direct terms but rather 'incidentally', as Myriam Cottias writes, was 'l'identité distincte d'une minorité culturelle défavorisée issue de l'esclavage transatlantique et de l'océan Indien' (Cottias, 2007: 84).[59] Since the 1980s, activists from the Antilles, Guyana and Réunion have termed themselves 'descendants d'esclaves' and have convinced authorities to recognize them as such. This leads the nation, at least once a year, to recall the past, to stress its cultural legacy and to value the contribution of the outre-mer territories and its people to the nation. The 10 May commemorations communicate messages relating to the morally grounded 'devoir de mémoire' ['duty of memory'], to the need to ensure that the past does not repeat itself and/or to political self-satisfaction for having the courage to face up to such a painful past, as was the case in Nantes. But official memory policies also prove dominantly unsupportive of militants who present themselves as 'blacks' and try to

[59] Translation: 'the distinct identity of a disadvantaged cultural minority born from transatlantic and Indian Ocean slavery'.

make the legacy of slavery a race-orientated issue. Particularly in Nantes, where such social movements are in effect, this has created the conditions for a contested 10 May ceremony, in terms of both genre and the message that it conveys. In the French context, where racial struggle remains suspect and where demands for the implementation of policy instruments directly relating to racial discrimination (such as ethnic monitoring and positive discrimination) tend to yield limited results, focusing on memory politics may have appeared a reasonable choice to these activists. The tenth of May has created the opportunity for them to translate their political outlook into symbolic politics, through a counter-commemoration that attracts public attention. With their March of the Slaves, Passerelle Noire's activists support a less consensual approach to the legacies of slavery – one that puts racial identities and contemporary inequalities in the foreground. Thus, with the 10 May commemoration, Passerelle Noire has found an arena through which activists can define group boundaries along different lines, challenge dominant conceptions of identities and make their voices heard.

Works Cited

Anonymous. 1993. 'Où est l'intérêt général ?' *Dom Tom Com* 6: 1.

—. 1998. 'Extrait du discours de Jean-Marc Ayrault, Député-maire de Nantes, 25 avril 1998'. *Dom Tom Com* 25: 6–7.

—. 2000. 'Intervention d'Octave Cestor au congrès des jeunes avocats de France'. *Dom Tom Com* 35: 9.

—. 2011. 'La fille de Malcom X à la *Marche des esclaves* de Nantes'. *Ouest-France* 5 May. Available at http://www.ouest-france.fr/la-fille-de-malcom-x-la-marche-des-esclaves-de-nantes-367273 (consulted on 10 March 2014).

Araujo, Ana Lucia (ed.). 2012. *Politics of Memory: Making Slavery Visible in the Public Sphere.* New York and London: Routledge.

Ayrault, Jean-Marc. 2011. Public speech transcribed by the author. 10 May.

Bancel, Nicolas, Florence Bernault, Pascal Blanchard, Françoise Vergès and Achille Mbembe (eds). 2010. *Ruptures postcoloniales: Les nouveaux visages de la société française.* Paris: La Découverte.

Bernabé, Jean, Patrick Chamoiseau and Raphaël Confiant. 1989. *Eloge de la créolité.* Paris: Gallimard.

Bertrand, Romain. 2005. *Mémoires d'Empire: La controverse autour du fait colonial.* Bellecombe-en-Bauges: Le Croquant.

Bonniol, Jean-Luc. 2007. 'Les usages publics de la mémoire de l'esclavage colonial'. *Matériaux pour l'histoire de notre temps* 85: 14–21.

Cohen, Abner. 1993. *Masquerade Politics: Exploration in the Structure of Urban Cultural Movements.* London: Berg.

Comité pour la mémoire de l'esclavage. 2005. 'Mémoires de la traite négrière, de l'esclavage et de leurs abolitions'. Paris: La Découverte.

Cottias, Myriam. 2007. *La question noire: Histoire d'une construction coloniale.* Paris: Bayard.

Dominique (civil servant from the municipal department of culture). 2011. Interview with author. Nantes. 28 May.

Durkheim, Emile. 1960 [1912]. *Les formes élémentaires de la vie religieuse.* Paris: PUF.

Gensburger, Sarah. 2010. *Les Justes de France: Politiques publiques de la mémoire.* Paris: Presses de Sciences Po.

Glissant, Edouard. 1981. *Le discours antillais.* Paris: Le Seuil.

Goody, Jack. 1993. *The Culture of Flowers.* Cambridge: Cambridge University Press.

Guin, Yannick (vice mayor in charge of culture). 2011. Interview with author. 25 May.

Hazera, Jean-Claude. 2006. 'Esclavage: Les ports français se souviennent'. *Les Échos* 5 May.

Hourcade, Renaud. 2014. *Les ports négriers face à leur histoire: Politiques de la mémoire à Nantes, Bordeaux et Liverpool.* Paris: Dalloz.

Jolivet, Marie-José. 1987. 'La construction d'une mémoire historique à la Martinique: du schoelchérisme au marronisme'. *Cahiers d'études africaines* 27: 287–309.

Jonathan (Passerelle Noire). 2011. Interview with author. 22 May.

Kertzer, David. 1988. *Ritual, Politics and Power.* New Haven: Yale University Press.

Michel, Johann. 2010. *Gouverner les mémoires: Les politiques mémorielles en France.* Paris: PUF.

Mvé, Etienne. 2010. 'Mémoire noire toujours à vif'. *Presse Océan* 20 July.

Ndiaye, Pap. 2007. *La condition noire: Essai sur une minorité française.* Paris: Calmann-Lévy.

Patrice (Passerelle Noire). 2008. Interview with author. 6 December.

Pétré-Grenouilleau, Olivier. 2007. *Nantes et la traite négrière.* Nantes: RMN – Château des Ducs de Bretagne.

Prochasson, David. 2010. 'Le collectif du 10 mai devra revoir sa copie'. *Vingt Minutes – Nantes* 4 March. Available at http://www.20minutes.fr/nantes/388544-collectif-10-mai-devra-revoir-copie (consulted on 10 March 2014).

Thompson, Vanessa. 2012. '"We Are Not What We Seem": Radical Black Activism in Contemporary France'. Unpublished communication. Madrid: 22nd Congress of the International Political Science Association.

Vinitzky-Seroussi, Vered. 2002. 'Commemorating a Difficult Past: Yitzhak Rabin's Memorials'. *American Sociological Review* 62: 30–51.

Wagner-Pacifici, Robin, and Barry Schwartz. 1991. 'The Vietnam Veterans Memorial: Commemorating a Difficult Past'. *American Journal of Sociology* 97: 376–420.

Waterton, Emma, Laurajane Smith, Ross Wilson and K. Fouseki. 2010. 'Forgetting to Heal: Remembering the Abolition Act of 1807'. *European Journal of English Studies* 14: 23–36.

Haiti and the Memorial Discourses of Slavery after 1804

Kate Hodgson

> Esclavage! que ce mot par lui-même est dur et repoussant! Combien il retrace de souvenirs amers! Que de turpitudes, d'attentats il renferme, à lui seul, contre l'espèce humaine! Que de tourmens il a causés à ses déplorables victimes, et que de fléaux il apprête encore à ses abominables auteurs!
>
> (Chanlatte, 1810: 10)[1]

Of all of the countries of the Americas, the people of Haiti have to go the furthest back in time to access collectively the 'souvenirs amers' ['bitter memories'] of colonial slavery. The beginning of the end of plantation slavery in the Americas occurred there, in August 1791, when a mass revolt broke out across the northern plain of what was then the French colony of Saint Domingue. Hundreds of sugar and coffee plantations were razed to the ground, and the de facto end of slavery began, as the former slaves-turned-revolutionaries deserted the ruins, forming rebel camps in the hills. By October 1793, the end of slavery had been officially proclaimed throughout

[1] Translation: 'Slavery! How hard and repulsive even the word is! How many bitter memories it brings back! How many depravities and attacks on human nature it alone contains! How many torments it has caused to its pitiful victims, and what a curse it brings upon its abominable authors!' This and all subsequent unattributed quotations were translated by the author of this article.

Saint Domingue by the French commissioners Léger Félicité Sonthonax and Etienne Polverel, who were desperately trying to maintain French control over what had, prior to the outbreak of revolution, been the most valuable sugar plantation colony in the world. The proclamations constituted the first legal abolition of slavery by representatives of a European colonial power. The colonial universe of sugar plantations, overseers, Creoles and African slaves, which persisted elsewhere in the Americas for nearly a century, thus largely ceased to exist in Saint Domingue from the early 1790s. After a further ten years of revolutionary politics, civil war and conflict with the British, Spanish and French armies, the independence of the renamed Republic of Haiti was proclaimed on 1 January 1804 by former slaves Jean-Jacques Dessalines, Henri Christophe and their leading generals. With this gesture, a population of predominantly African-born former slaves 'stood up for the first time and said it believed in its humanity' (Césaire, 1995: 24).

Whether because of or despite the lasting impact of this transformational revolutionary history, the memorial traces of colonial slavery among the Haitian people have been largely obscured. Gérard Barthélemy terms the retrieval of this legacy a 'difficult feat of memory' for the descendants of the enslaved in contemporary Haiti, due to the significant time lapse – over 220 years having passed since the first abolition of slavery in 1793 – and the dominant memorial impact of the events of Haiti's own subsequent revolutionary and independent national history (2004: 128). Perhaps, he suggests, awareness of the colonial slave past has faded from popular collective consciousness precisely because the French colonists were so roundly defeated and slavery constitutionally outlawed by the Haitian people after independence – 'we can allow ourselves to forget (because it [slavery] was defeated?)' (Barthélemy, 2004: 130).

Can the memorial narrative of slavery in Haiti be understood as a gradual process of forgetting; one that has occurred as the nation as a whole has moved over time from the 'bitter memories' of former slaves in the early nineteenth century to the distant surviving recollections among their descendants two centuries later? What competing Haitian narratives emerged out of colonial slavery and its overthrow? Was the memory of the colonial slave past conserved within certain social groups, more so than others, and what purposes has this collective memory served? As we shall see, faint traces of the unconscious presence of the slave past in collective memory have been detected by scholars in popular Haitian festivities, such as carnival and Rara, in folk songs and stories, and in the practice of Vodou. On a national level, competing memories of the colonial past and national resistance to slavery have had an ongoing political usefulness, and Haiti's revolutionary history is omnipresent in official commemorative contexts. Since the foundation of Haitian independence in the early nineteenth century, the Haitian state has commemorated various forms of resistance in national celebrations, monuments and museums, in the national press and in educational curricula.

Thus the traces of slavery live on in both official state and collective popular consciousness in often difficult and complex ways. To consider all of the memorial legacies and traces of slavery in Haiti in depth is beyond the scope of this chapter, which seeks to focus instead on a number of case studies that foreground this shared memory. In this way, the extent to which memorial discourses and practices surrounding the idea of slavery are shared across Haitian society, or conversely how far these discourses and practices diverge from one another across social, geographical and generational lines, can be considered.

Memories of Slavery: Memories of Africa?

The history of slavery on the island that Laurent Dubois has called the 'ground zero of European colonialism in the Americas' dates back to the late fifteenth century, with the indigenous Caribbean peoples enslaved and forced by Spanish conquistadors to work in mines and agriculture in the new colony of Hispaniola, and the first boatloads of enslaved Africans arriving to the island a few decades later (Dubois, 2004: 13). Yet, while these early attempts at colonization using enslaved and forced labour are recorded in histories of the island, the surviving memorial traces of slavery in present-day Haiti speak more clearly to an unprecedented expansion of the sugar plantation system in eighteenth-century Saint Domingue. The transatlantic slave trade at its peak brought over 1700 slave ships in just fifty years to France's most important colony, carrying on board hundreds of thousands of African captives from regions as diverse as Senegambia, the Bight of Benin, the Congo and Mozambique.

The question of what was lost and what was preserved in the Middle Passage has been repeatedly debated by cultural historians of the African diaspora in the Americas. It has often been surmised that the trauma of capture, transportation and enslavement, as well as deliberate policies among plantation owners and managers to disperse and separate slaves with shared origins or a common language, meant that African cultural heritages in the Americas have been fragmented and transformed over the centuries, rendering them almost unrecognisable in their original forms. Scholarship produced in recent years by academics such as Gwendolyn Hall (2005), Paul Lovejoy (2000) and John Thornton (1998) has challenged this assumption by emphasizing the profoundly interconnected nature of the Atlantic world and the relevance of an 'African-centred' narrative of the transatlantic slave trade, allowing for the preservation and communication of African identities across the Middle Passage and into the plantation worlds of the Americas. Such African cultural markers include shared linguistic groupings, corporeal modifications such as scarification, and cultural markers such as music, dance and religious practices. These historic indicators of Africanness in the Americas must often be pieced together by historians from an assortment of sources, including the accounts of travellers and settlers, court records, plantation lists of slaves and runaway slave advertisements, which detail distinguishing features, African origins and sometimes languages spoken. Less tangible, and more difficult to reconstruct, are the worldviews and lived historical experiences carried into slavery by those who survived the Middle Passage. These could include a familiarity with political conflict and techniques of warfare, as well as agricultural skills, knowledge of plants and their medicinal properties, and religious leadership. In the specific context of colonial Saint Domingue, John Thornton has made a ground-breaking contribution to our understanding of the perceptions of newly arrived African slaves in the colony, especially those from the war-torn Congo of the late eighteenth century. In his 1993 article '"I am the subject of the King of Congo": African Political Ideology and the Haitian Revolution', Thornton showed the impact of African political ideologies on the revolutionaries, many of whom had been born in West Central Africa, had fought in civil wars there and had been sold into slavery as prisoners of war. The article highlights how their understanding and participation in the revolution in Saint Domingue was shaped by their experiences prior to undergoing the Middle Passage.

On the plantations of the Americas, the 'nation' to which African-born inhabitants of the colony belonged was considered highly significant, both within the white planter community and to the enslaved themselves. For the planters, the nation was seen as indicative of a collective character or national temperament, which rendered slaves more or less susceptible to rebellion, hard work, suicide or other tendencies affecting their value as a financial investment. In Gabriel Debien's *Plantations et esclaves à Saint-Domingue* (1962), he used plantation records and letters from the late eighteenth century to show how certain ethnic groups were favoured over others by owners and managers. Perceived as most useful and sought-after were the 'Creole' slaves who had been born in the colony. But as Debien notes, the economic realities of running a Caribbean plantation usually meant that cargoes of slaves had to be purchased as and when they became available (1962: 44–51). Surviving plantation registers and lists of runaways published in the colonial press also provide clues as to the African origins of the enslaved. Some examples from the Saint Domingue colonial newspaper *Affiches américaines* in the 1780s and 90s include 'Congo', 'Nago', 'Mondongue', 'Arada' and 'Thiamba'. By far the most common identifying nation in the French colonial press's runaway slave advertisements, however, is 'Congo', with 3490 mentions in the *Marronage in Saint-Domingue* database, as opposed to the three or four hundred references to the other nations, supporting the idea widely held by planters at the time that West Central African slaves were most likely to maroon.

Scholars of slavery and its legacies have stressed the centrality of Vodou to formulating an African-centred understanding of how slavery, *marronnage* and revolt played out in late eighteenth-century Saint Domingue. The seminal text by Haitian ethnographer Jean Price-Mars *Ainsi parla l'oncle* (1928) made a series of connections linking Haitian rural culture, folklore and the practice of Vodou directly to Africa, via the slave ship, the plantation and the outbreak of revolution in Haiti. For Haitian *Vodouisants* (practitioners of Vodou), an alternative term signifying the nation, or *nanchon* in Creole, is *fanmi* ['family'] (Métraux, 1958: 75–76). The African 'nation' was clearly significant during the era of slavery in Saint Domingue not only as a predicator of value to the slave holders, but also as a source of solidarity and brotherhood to the enslaved, who formed secret mutual aid, social and religious societies with elected kings and queens of their respective nations (Thornton, 1993: 200). Carolyn Fick has argued that Vodou and other cultural practices served among the Africans in Saint Domingue to 'bind more closely the loose psychological ties arising out of the common experience of organized plantation labor and the material conditions of life under slavery, raising these to a form of collective consciousness' (1990: 42). As such, they can be understood as a 'source of psychological liberation', enabling slaves to retain a sense of human dignity, solidarity and *fanmi*, in order to survive immense oppression and brutal exploitation (Fick, 1990: 42).

As Price-Mars suggested, African cultural and religious assemblies continued to hold vital socio-political significance in Saint Domingue once revolution broke out. The Congo revolutionary leader Makaya was criticized by Toussaint Louverture for spending his days at the 'dances and assemblies of Africans of his nation' (Thornton, 1993: 204). The collective consciousness developed through Vodou has been channelled in Haiti through two broad groupings of spirits, or *Lwa*. These are *Rada* spirits (from the name of the kingdom of Arada, in Dahomey, West Africa) and *Petro/Lemba*, who are West Central African or Congo spirits. Even now, the latter are considered to be 'hotter' or more rebellious and difficult to control in nature, and are particularly strongly connected to slave resistance and the outbreak of the Haitian revolution (Averill, 2009: 142).

In the late eighteenth century, between thirty and forty per cent of the African-born slaves or *Bossales* of Saint Domingue, many of whom fought in the Haitian revolution, originated from West Central Africa, or the

Congo (Geggus, 2008: 39). It is this population that has been credited with introducing many of the most prominent African-derived elements of Haiti's peasant culture, including the revolutionary *Petro* rites in Vodou. Particularly relevant, insofar as it concerns the popular memory of slavery in contemporary Haiti, is the figure of the zombie (or *Zonbi* in Creole, derived from the Kikongo word *Nzambi,* meaning 'God' or 'spirit'). The zombie is considered by scholars of Haiti to be a creolized manifestation of a West Central African belief transported in the holds of slave ships to the Americas:

> The poignant plight of the *zonbi* as it is expressed in myth and ritual is a graphic memory of the experience of capture, transport and enslavement of the Africans in Saint-Domingue who lived and died far from home. As long as the myth of the *zonbi* exists in Haitian culture, this terrifying history is remembered. (McAlister, 2002: 107)

In contemporary Haiti, the *zonbi* is a deceased former member of society, forced to make the long journey back from the dead, robbed of his or her soul, and compelled to perform some kind of spiritual or physical work. The Haitian zombie, like its cinematic namesake, is characterized by its vacant stare and low moan, moves slowly, has no free will and cannot be reasoned with. McAlister describes in her book *Rara!* (2002) the folk bands that roam the Haitian countryside in the weeks leading up to Easter, and notes how zombies are recruited to serve in these ensembles. By seeking to enslave the deceased, McAlister argues, Rara band leaders are affirming their power in negotiating between worlds, from local political networks to the dead themselves. Thus, the descendants of the enslaved become the enslavers, in a reversal of power with clear symbolic overtones. Dayan's analysis of the re-enactment of the dynamics of slavery in Vodou and popular culture in Haiti highlights 'what historians often forget: the compulsion to serve, the potency and virtue of atrocity' (1995: 29). The phenomenon of possession in Vodou is thus shaped by the collective memory of enslavement, which is 'given substance through time by a spirit that originated in an experience of domination' (Dayan, 1995: 56).

The zombie in its New World manifestations has been variously considered by cultural commentators and critics as a folk memory of enslavement. This term should be understood in its widest sense as incorporating not only colonial or chattel slavery prior to the outbreak of revolution in 1791, but also domestic slavery and extreme forms of labour exploitation (McAlister, 2002: 103). The zombie is generally symbolic of the oppressed, the exploited or the slave. Yet, the balance of power between master and zombie is complex: the zombie retains his or her own power, often derived from a position held while alive (for example, a powerful *Vodouisant* who has been made a zombie in death), and has the power to enslave others. In a recent article, McAlister describes her puzzlement faced with the paradoxical situation of a formerly enslaved people symbolically enslaving the dead, who in turn create other zombies. She explains this process as '*tak[ing] charge*' of a troubling history of enslavement through spiritual practice or, citing Michael Taussig, 'history as sorcery' (McAlister, 2012: 464; emphasis in original). According to both McAlister and Dayan, contemporary manifestations of spiritual enslavement continue to create cultural meaning and affect social relationships between present-day Haitians. Instead of a defeated and buried history of colonial slavery, which ceased to have any meaning after the triumphant declaration of Haitian independence in 1804, Dayan and McAlister paint a very different picture 'from below', in which the myriad legacies of enslavement and forced labour are still being processed symbolically and spiritually through zombification and possession in Vodou. This research, which contributes towards the identification of 'African-centred' memories of slavery located in popular culture, offers an important departure point for scholars seeking to identify popular memories of slavery in post-revolutionary Haiti.

Commemorating Slavery through the Haitian Revolution and Its Legacies

While the significance of the popular memory of slavery in contemporary Haiti is only starting to be understood by scholars, the shared memory of the Haitian revolution is exceptionally prominent and visible in all areas of Haitian national life. The founding narrative of the nation is based on the history of the revolution: its key dates and events are commemorated every year in Haiti with national holidays, and its leaders are remembered in monuments, street names, the national education system, museums and especially the commemorative Place des Héros de l'Indépendance [Independence Heroes' Square]. Situated in central Port-au-Prince on the Champ de Mars, this public park is dotted with statues commemorating the key founding figures of the nation: Toussaint Louverture, Jean-Jacques Dessalines, Henri Christophe and Alexandre Pétion. The revolution, its leaders and the subsequent history of national independence are at the heart of the narrative told both to generations of Haitian schoolchildren and to visitors to the Museum of the National Pantheon (MUPANAH), where the history of Haiti from 1492 to the present day is recounted. Built in 1973–74 on the Champ de Mars, this memorial site incorporates a shrine to the memory of the founding fathers.

While the established national narrative of the Haitian revolutionary past has traditionally focused on the idea of these heroic fathers of the nation, prominent state-led commemorative practices have, in recent decades, increasingly invested in representations of the anonymous African-born masses who fought for freedom as maroons and as soldiers in the Haitian revolution, leading the way towards a systematic redefinition of Haitian national identity (Béchacq, 2006: 203). As one of the prime sites of institutionalized national memory, MUPANAH has made efforts to redress the balance of memory by honouring not just the pantheonized leaders of the revolution, but also the largely forgotten rank and file who fought alongside them, or as a wall plaque states, 'men and women who are renowned by their example of courage, wisdom, talent and virtuous citizenship'. The few names from this largely anonymous group that have survived in the historiography of the revolution are inscribed around the outer walls of the pantheon: 'Malouba, Jambon, Larose, Guerrier, Boisblanc, Batichon, Trois Balles, Coco, Grand Boucan, Toby, Sans Souci, Sylla, Jean Zombi, Bossou, Poisson, Dubosc, Titus, Fourmi, Lys, Doyon, Sanglaou, Cacapoule, Henriette St Marc, Kina [...]' This litany of names, along with the recognition of the roles played by the revolutionary masses, offers a powerful state-led narrative of the widespread and fundamental rejection of slavery that is central to Haiti's history and national identity.

In addition to the names inscribed around the walls of the Pantheon, the MUPANAH museum houses a gallery dedicated to the history of slavery in Saint Domingue, illustrated with large-scale reproduced images of slave ships, plantations and runaway slaves. The principal physical objects exhibited in this gallery are chains, an eighteenth-century sugar mould and a statue of an African woman wearing a white headscarf and robes. While the exhibits encourage the visitor to contemplate slavery as an integral part of Haiti's history, the focus on the colonial period is minimal when considered within the overall space of the museum. The majority of the exhibits displayed in the museum are official portraits and ephemera linked to the revolution and the subsequent independence (for instance Pétion's watch, Soulouque's crown, Boyer's knife and fork). The colonial era of plantation slavery is thus largely overshadowed in MUPANAH by the dominant national narrative of resistance culminating in the revolution of 1791–1804 and the ensuing history of Haiti. While the revolutionaries are commemorated within this space, the enslaved masses of Saint Domingue are only symbolized by the statue of the anonymous African woman at the heart of the slavery gallery.

Another important and highly politicized instance of state investment in the commemoration of those who fought for their freedom against colonial domination is the statue of 'Le Marron Inconnu' ['The Unknown Maroon']. This was unveiled in 1968 on the Champ de Mars by the then-president François Duvalier (1957–71), and was designed to promote a centralized national memory of the maroons, described in the inauguration ceremony

Figure 6: Monument to the Unknown Maroon, *Neg Mawon* by Albert Mangonès (1968).

as the 'pioneers' of Haitian liberty and independence (Duvalier, 1969: 24). The statue depicts a crouched maroon, or runaway slave, poised in the act of blowing into a conch shell (a historic means of communication between the Afro-descendent peoples of the Caribbean). In his other hand is a machete, a double-edged symbol of slavery (symbolizing sugar cane cutting on the plantation) and freedom, in its use as both a weapon and a tool of liberation. The 'Unknown Maroon' is a prominent example of state investment in and political appropriation of popular memories of resistance, especially given the context of its commission and unveiling during the Duvalier dictatorship. Despite his concern to maintain control over state institutions through state-led terror and repressive measures for ensuring his own power and his succession, Duvalier was keen to portray himself as a latter-day outlaw and popular hero, describing himself in a speech to the youth of the nation in 1967 as the 'dernier marron président à vie de la Republique'.[2] The statue illustrates how the national narrative of resistance against slavery has been, and continues to be, a useful discourse repeatedly drawn upon by the Haitian political elite.

[2] Translation: 'the last maroon, president for life of the Republic'. For more on the subject of this wholesale state appropriation of popular politics and revolt, see Hurbon, 1979.

In the context of contemporary Haitian politics, state-led discourses commemorating slavery and resistance have interacted with, and diverged from, popular memories of this shared history in a number of interesting ways. The memorial divide between state and nation observed by Michel-Rolph Trouillot can also be seen in the popular response to the statue of the revolutionary leader, and later king, Henri Christophe, on the Champ de Mars (Trouillot, 1990). The official monument, which depicts Christophe on horseback atop a tall column, is plated around the base with a series of bronze plaques depicting scenes from his life. In the early years of Haitian independence, the main concern of the ruling generals was to lead and coordinate a large-scale mobilization against the pressing threat of re-invasion by France. They induced a depleted and demoralized workforce to build a remarkable series of fortresses across the mountain ranges of Haiti, enabling the Haitians to operate a scorched earth policy and retreat into their mountain fortresses if French troops should return. Christophe's surviving correspondence from 1805 to 1806 conveys a desperate need for agricultural and military manpower, as the Haitian generals rushed to consolidate the gains of the revolution. The survivors of the war of independence were deployed into militarized labour forces to recover building materials from ruined sugar plantations and use them to build fortifications. 'Vous m'envoyerez [...] toutes les femmes, celles qui savent faire des briques', Christophe wrote to one of his generals on 14 February 1806.[3] During this period, colonial Saint Domingue was rebuilt, brick by brick, as former sites of slavery were stripped and transformed into revolutionary strongholds by former slaves-turned-labourers for the Haitian state.

But this workforce came at a price, as Fick's work on the Haitian people viewed 'from below' during the revolution and in the early days of independence has shown. Her research provides valuable insight into the surviving rebel factions, consisting largely of first-generation Africans, whose principal concern after 1804 was not the defence of the newly established Haitian state, but rather the preservation of their own freedom (Fick, 1990: 236). They pursued this goal by retreating into the hills and borderlands, and setting up subsistence communities. Rival groups, led by figures such as Lamour Dérance and Petit Noël Prière, continued to self-identify as African, taking the names of 'Congos, Aradas, Ibos, Nabos, Mandingoes, Hausas' (Madiou, III, 1848: 33). A kind of *marronnage* that sought to evade and/or oppose state control thus continued into the post-independence era, as Dessalines, Christophe and the other generals fought to bring the entire territory and its inhabitants under their control. Faced with a refractory

3 Translation: 'Send me all the women who know how to make bricks.'

Figure 7: Side panel of the Christophe monument on the Champ de Mars in Port au Prince, depicting his support for education (left) and state-imposed labour on fortifications (right).

workforce refusing to labour for the state, Christophe employed military force. In November 1805, for example, he sent a battalion to Manzanillo, on the northern border with the Dominican Republic, to re-establish Haitian state control over one such group of rebels: 'J'ai fait incendié les ajoupas qu'ils y avaient construits pour s'y loger, plusieurs ont été arrêtés, les cultivateurs renvoyés au commandeur militaire, et les soldats dans leurs derniers brigades respectives' (Christophe to Dessalines, 13 November 1805).[4]

Given that the state under Christophe imposed labour and military discipline throughout the Haitian territory in the early years of independence, it is perhaps not surprising that his legacy within the national collective memory remains somewhat problematic.[5] Surrounded by enemies and facing dissent from within, Henri Christophe shot himself in October 1820, and was succeeded by the president of the rival republic formed in the south of

[4] Translation: 'I have had the huts that they built for shelter burnt down, several have been arrested, the cultivators have been returned to the military commander and the soldiers to their most recent brigades.'

[5] See Bongie (2008: 25–35) on the 'scribal politics' of post-revolutionary Haiti and the problematic legacy of King Henri Christophe for his republican successors, who, in their written accounts of Christophe's kingdom, chose to mask similarities by asserting difference.

Figure 8: Side panel depicting the Haitian people, with graffito 'Esclave' in top-right corner.

Haiti, Jean-Pierre Boyer. The memorial frieze depicting the life of Christophe around the base of his statue on the Champ de Mars reflects the uneasy balance struck by the inheritors of the Republic of Haiti: while the majority of the panels depict his impressive military record and support for public education, the state-imposed labour and tyranny over the Haitian people who built this network of fortifications is also remembered in a panel which depicts workers transporting building materials in a human chain, overseen by Christophe himself. A graffito, photographed in February 2012, reinforces the impression of state-led tyranny at this time with an unexpected addition to the narrative surrounding Christophe's legacy in Haiti. Above one of the panels a single word in French, 'Esclave' ['slave'], is inscribed, raising questions as to the significance of the word in independent Haiti and the broader conclusions that can be drawn regarding popular memory and the legacies of slavery. Whose enslavement is evoked by this image – that of Christophe himself, believed to have been born into slavery in Grenada and sold to a Saint Domingue planter in the 1770s, or that of the Haitian labourers painstakingly building his legacy, brick by brick?

A Living Memory of Colonial Slavery in Early Haitian Writing

The multiple forms that popular memories of slavery in post-independence Haiti have taken continue to pose historical and methodological questions. Yet historians do have access to numerous written testimonies by members of the nineteenth-century Haitian literary elite that provide us with a contemporary perspective on French colonial slavery and its legacies. These are not 'slave narratives', like those written in the Anglophone abolitionist context, but they do offer an insight into how the final days of French colonial slavery in Saint Domingue were remembered by those who lived through them. The writers in question had typically not been enslaved themselves, but were instead the descendants of free, wealthy mixed-race families, often educated in France. As such, the perspective they can offer on the lives of the *Bossales*, or African-born slaves who formed the majority of new Haitian citizens in 1804, is limited. However, these early authors of Haitian independence write powerfully about the cruelty of chattel slavery in the Caribbean under French rule, and thus contribute to the collective national determination that slavery should never again be tolerated on Haitian soil. Their writings also offer an insight into the question of how colonial slavery has been remembered since 1804 in Haiti.

Less than two decades after the end of slavery in Saint Domingue, the publicist and writer Juste Chanlatte produced a passionate denunciation of plantation slavery, which he described as a horrible wound inflicted by humanity on itself. His text, dedicated to the French abolitionist Abbé Grégoire, expressed the hope that slavery would eventually be eradicated, and 'ne jamais reparaître sur la surface du globe' (Chanlatte, 1810: 9).[6] Certainly, argued Chanlatte, it would never again be able to assume the same powerful presence in the former Saint Domingue, now independent Haiti, as it had in the past, especially now that the former slaves were aware of their own power to deliver themselves from oppression: 'Que nous parle-t-on de maîtres, lorsque nos mains, cette puissance vengeresse ou conservatrice, mais surtout la marque certaine et distinctive de l'homme, peuvent nous délivrer du premier oppresseur qui osera se présenter?' (1810: 11).[7] Chattel slavery is legally invalid, he argues, making reference to the US Constitution: if liberty is an unalienable right of persons and no contract is valid without the free

---

6 Translation: 'nevermore appear on the surface of the earth'.

7 Translation: 'How can they talk to us of masters, when our own hands, avenging or safeguarding powers, bearing the sure and distinctive mark of humanity, can deliver us from the first oppressor who dares to present himself?'

consent of both parties, where is the free consent of the person who was sold into slavery in Africa? Thus, he continues, as slavery is proved to be unconstitutional, its victims should be compensated: 'Où est pour l'esclave le dédommagement équivalent à la nature et à la durée de ses souffrances?' (1810: 9).[8] First posed by Chanlatte in 1810, the question of compensation was still without a response fifteen years later, as negotiations with France for the recognition of Haitian independence began. Eventually a ruinous neo-colonial debt was imposed upon the country which compensated not the sufferings of the enslaved, but the financial losses of their former owners.

Texts by Chanlatte and his fellow state propagandist Pompée de Vastey both draw on a shared national trauma resulting not only from the experience of colonial slavery and torture prior to 1791, but also from Napoleon's attempt to re-establish colonial slavery in 1802, which resulted in some of the most sanguinary scenes of the Haitian revolution. Their writings denounce the former colonists who continued to lobby in Paris in the 1810s and 20s for a French return to Saint Domingue and for compensation for their losses in human 'property'. In response to Jean Barré de Saint-Venant, one of the louder voices calling for compensation, Chanlatte accused him of taking great enjoyment in the punishments he inflicted upon the enslaved on the plantation where he had been employed as a manager:

> Vous qui sur l'habitation Deplaa, où vous résidiez en qualité de procureur, avez ressuscité tous les genres de supplices! enterrer les hommes jusqu'au cou, les enfourner avec la bagasse, couper la langue, les oreilles ou les jarrets de vos victimes, les attacher tout vivans à des cadavres déjà putréfiés, leur fixer les jambes aux reins, jusqu'à ce que, privées de la circulation du sang, elles s'enflent, se paralysent, et tombent en pourriture; tels étaient vos passe-temps les plus doux! (Chanlatte, 1810: 15)[9]

Both authors revisit with horror how the tortures first enacted upon the enslaved were taken to new heights of refinement during the revolution against prisoners of war, including the use of imported dogs as weapons. *Le Cri de la nature* describes how dogs arrived in the colony from Cuba,

---

[8] Translation: 'Where is the slave's compensation, equal to the nature and duration of his sufferings?'

[9] Translation: 'On the Deplaa plantation where you were manager, you resurrected all kinds of tortures! Burying men up to their necks, burning them alongside the waste from the canefields, cutting out the tongues of your victims, cutting off their ears, or slashing the backs of their knees, chaining living men to putrefied corpses, tying up their legs until they lose circulation, swell, become paralysed and start to rot; these were your favourite pastimes!'

amid great jubilation from the remaining French colonists, and were then used to kill Haitian prisoners in an unheard-of public bloodbath (Chanlatte, 1810: 51). The impact of these spectacles of violence on the early Haitian national consciousness is clear, as Vastey writes years later in remembrance of their victims: 'les ombres de nos pères, de nos mères, de nos frères, de nos sœurs, victimes des français, sont sorties des cendres des bûchers, des abîmes de la mer, des entrailles des chiens dévorans, pour nous applaudir, et s'écrièrent avec nous, vengeance! vengeance!' (1815: 10).[10] However, the political usefulness of remembering the slave past also emerges in this text, as Vastey contrasts the fierce remembrance of slavery in the North with what he saw as the craven forgetfulness of the South and its leader Pétion in receiving the emissaries of France: 'Il [Pétion] est sans aigreur ni prévention contre la nation qui a fait dévorer, il n'y a pas douze ans, nos frères et nos compatriotes par des chiens' (1815: 36).[11]

By the mid-nineteenth century, the first generation of Haitians who remembered colonial slavery were almost all gone, with a few aged exceptions, and the 'bitter memories', described by Chanlatte, of this generation's enslavement under French colonial rule were already fading. The historian Thomas Madiou was himself born after the 1804 declaration of Haitian independence, but his *Histoire d'Haïti* (1847–48) drew heavily on oral sources including interviews with surviving slaves and revolutionaries in order to evoke the 'époque de souffrances et de gémissemens' ['era of suffering and cries'] of colonial slavery (Madiou, I, 1847: v). Madiou offers an interesting explanation of why plantation slavery was already fading from memory in Haiti. It was not because the memory of slavery had been made obsolete by the triumph of 1804, but rather because the African enslaved by the French colonists of Saint Domingue had never stopped being free. He was simply biding his time and awaiting his moment, before taking back the liberty that he had previously possessed: 'Il ne transigea jamais sur sa liberté' ['He never compromised on his freedom'] (Madiou, I, 1847: v). Freedom was experienced by this generation as a state to be remembered, and slavery as an aberration to be forgotten.

---

[10] Translation: 'The ghosts of our fathers, our mothers, our brothers, our sisters, victims of the French, emerged from the ashes of the pyres, from the depths of the seas, from the entrails of the ravenous dogs to applaud us and cry with us: Vengeance! Vengeance!' This passage is discussed in detail by Marlene Daut in *The Colonial System Unveiled* (2014). On the use of dogs during the Haitian revolution, see chapter one of Johnson (2012) and Lutz (2007).

[11] Translation: 'He [Pétion] shows no trace of bitterness, nor any caution against the nation which less than twelve years ago ordered our brothers and kinsmen to be devoured by dogs.'

The importance of self-determination in Madiou's interpretation of slavery's legacies in Haiti is echoed in one of the rare surviving perspectives on slavery from the first generations of the African-born majority, who were most likely to have experienced the brutal excesses of colonial slavery. Their memory of slavery and how they passed its legacies down to their children is one of the most difficult to access today. Oral history preserved through Vodou and popular songs forms one of the few ways in which historians are able to retrace the ideas of this marginalized group concerning their experiences of plantation slavery. Songs that recall the era of colonial slavery are extremely rare, but one surviving song is reproduced in Benjamin Hebblethwaite's recent anthology:

> Nou soti nan Ginen,
> Men nan men, pye nan pye!
> Nous prale yon kote, lè n rive, n a va posede!
> Anba kal negriye, nou prale yon kote
> Tou benyen, tou poudre ak Gwo Lwa a, n ape navige!
>
> (Beauvoir, 2008, cited in Hebblethwaite, 2012: 2)[12]

It is interesting to see the idea of possession evoked here: 'we'll go to a place, when we arrive, we'll own it!' The enslaved African in the Americas, who was the chattel possession of another human being, becomes here a symbolic owner, thus reclaiming some of the power lost in the hold of the slave ship. Even though the slaves are coming apparently powerless and bound, their intrinsic freedom remains uncompromised, and they will eventually triumph and reclaim power in this retrospective viewpoint.

Conclusions

It seems clear that for the official narrative, what remains of the memory of colonial slavery in Haiti is inextricably bound up with the legacies of the Haitian revolution. On a national and indeed global level, the legacy of the revolutionaries has been emphasized; for example, the UNESCO International Day for the Remembrance of the Slave Trade and of its Abolition takes place annually on 23 August in remembrance of the rebellion in northern Saint Domingue that inaugurated the Haitian revolution in 1791. The maroon, the revolutionary soldier and the named forefathers of the revolution (particularly Jean-Jacques Dessalines) have become the key figures

---

[12] Translation: 'We come from Ginen, hand bound to hand, foot bound to foot! We'll go to a place, when we arrive, we'll own it! In the hold of the slave ship, we're going somewhere, all bathed and powdered with the Great Lwa, we're sailing!'

in the national narrative of Haitian independence. Yet the legacy of the revolutionary leadership remains to some degree problematic, largely because of its inability to represent the history of the entire population of Haiti. The divisions between leadership (primarily Creole) and masses or *Bossales* (primarily African-born), and the differing experiences of slavery across this diverse population are a vital aspect of understanding not only colonial and revolutionary Saint Domingue, but also how slavery and state oppression have subsequently been experienced and remembered (and politicized) in Haiti. As Geggus points out, the significance of this cultural divide is 'far from fully understood' (2008: 41).

The multiple national memories of slavery in Haiti are tangled, transversal and turned upside down, and many have been lost entirely. The Haitian historian Louis Élie wrote that with the outbreak of revolution in Saint Domingue, the universe of the plantations was completely destroyed, eradicating everything, down to the very memory of slavery: 'ils transformeront Saint Domingue en une terre d'épouvante où le massacre, l'incendie, l'effroi de la mort déracineront jusqu'au souvenir de l'esclavage' (n.d.: 5).[13] Indeed, the question of why slavery would be remembered in a country which notoriously and successfully overthrew the global Atlantic slave system, and in which the formerly enslaved became generals, emperors and kings, making multiple declarations of their intent to remain free and independent from the French colonists, is a valid one. Yet the multiple legacies of slavery have not been entirely 'uprooted' in contemporary Haiti. They serve political purposes and are cited in national spaces. They emerge in unexpected ways in music, in oral histories and in religious practices passed down by the descendants of the African-born enslaved masses.

The cultural traces of a popular collective memory of slavery that have been identified here – including elements such as zombification, the Henri Christophe graffito and the Haitian Vodou song describing the African experience of the Middle Passage – all centre on the problem of marginality, power and control. They are surprising or even disconcerting (McAlister, 2012: 464). In these memorial manifestations of slavery, the slave can wield a considerable degree of power, whereas the master can appear as unexpectedly weak, the two roles becoming interdependent and sometimes exchangeable. Taking back power from the enslavers and in some cases symbolically assuming their role are common narrative elements in popular memories of slavery, which seek to address historic imbalances of power. Haitian writing about slavery reflects or interprets these complex power transactions, but

[13] Translation: 'They transformed Saint Domingue into a land of terror, where massacre, fire and fear of death uprooted even the very memory of slavery.'

sometimes falls short of fully accounting for them. For instance, Juste Chanlatte's claim regarding the legacy of resistance to slavery in Haiti might state that 'Our own hands [...] can deliver us from the first oppressor who dares to present himself', but it focuses entirely on the external threat to Haiti's national independence and fails to consider the internal ramifications of the complex legacies of slavery and oppression (Chanlatte, 1810: 11).

Recent work by Sara Johnson has offered an interesting perspective on the tangled interconnections between freedom and slavery within Haiti's national story, particularly relating to the question of gender in the post-independence period:

> As with emancipation enterprises throughout the hemisphere, freedom was contingent and partial, different from, yet all too chillingly familiar to, life under slavery and patriarchy more generally. It was a compromised freedom, and the Haitian case is no different, however much we hold Haiti to a higher standard because of its revolutionary struggle and official claims of black equality. (2012: 73)

The concept of a 'compromised freedom' can be understood by taking into account not only patriarchal forms of oppression and historic forced labour practices of the Haitian state, but also the contemporary 'conditions of slavery and servitude' which have affected the Haitian people (McAlister, 2002: 103). Haiti's position at number two in the Global Slavery Index in 2013 and the prevalence of the 'Restavek' system of child labour as a form of contemporary slavery can only be evoked briefly in this context, but they raise difficult and necessary questions about the legacies of slavery in Haiti today.[14] 'Taking charge' of a problematic history, as McAlister terms it, remains one of the most important and enduring aspects of these multiple legacies of enslavement and oppression, and represents an active, ongoing collective process of coming to terms with the past (McAlister, 2012: 464). In Haiti, instead of the legacies of slavery it is perhaps then the legacies of freedom in all of its myriad forms that should form the focus of continued scholarly attention.

---

14 A system of child labour known as 'Restavek' (to 'stay with', in Haitian Creole) is well established in Haiti, whereby brokers arrange for children from poor rural families to be sent to work as domestics for wealthier Haitians. Although this labour is sometimes recompensed by a chance at an education, this promise often goes unmet – 80 per cent of Restaveks do not attend school and many suffer abuse (Walk Free Foundation, Global Slavery Index, 2013).

Works Cited

Archives and Databases

Letters of Henri Christophe 1805–1806 (reel 71), Edmund Mangonès Collection, Special and Area Studies Collections, George A. Smathers Libraries, University of Florida, Gainesville, Florida.

Marronage in Saint-Domingue (Haiti) Database. Available at http://www.marronnage.info/en/index.html (consulted on 5 February 2014).

Transatlantic Slave Trade Database. Available at www.slavevoyages.org (consulted on 5 February 2014).

Walk Free Foundation, Global Slavery Index 2013. Available at http://www.globalslaveryindex.org/ (consulted on 5 February 2014).

Printed Sources

Averill, Gage (ed.). 2009. *Alan Lomax's Recordings in Haiti: 1936–37.* San Francisco: Harte Recordings.

Barthélemy, Gérard. 2004. 'Réflexions sur deux mémoires inconciliables: celle du maître et celle de l'esclave: Le cas d'Haïti'. *Cahiers d'Études Africaines* 44: 127–39, 173–74.

Beauvoir, Max. 2008. *Le grand recueil sacré: ou repertoire des chansons du vodou Haïtien.* Port au Prince: Presses Nationales d'Haiti.

Béchacq, Dimitri. 2006. 'Les parcours du marronnage dans l'histoire haïtienne: entre instrumentalisation politique et réinterprétation sociale'. *Ethnologies* 28.1: 203–40.

Bongie, Chris. 2008. *Friends and Enemies: The Scribal Politics of Post/colonial Literature.* Liverpool: Liverpool University Press.

Césaire, Aimé. 1995. *Notebook of a Return to My Native Land.* Trans. and ed. by Mireille Rosello. Newcastle upon Tyne: Bloodaxe Books.

Chanlatte, Juste. 1810. *Le cri de la nature ou Hommage haïtien au très-vénérable abbé H. Grégoire.* Au Cap: P. Roux.

Daut, Marlene. 2014. 'Monstrous Testimony: Baron de Vastey and the Politics of Black Memory'. In Baron De Vastey, *The Colonial System Unveiled.* Trans. and ed. by Chris Bongie. Liverpool: Liverpool University Press.

Dayan, Joan. 1995. *Haiti, History and the Gods.* Berkeley: University of California Press.

Debien, Gabriel. 1962. *Plantations et esclaves à Saint-Domingue.* Dakar: Université de Dakar.

Dubois, Laurent. 2004. *Avengers of the New World: The Story of the Haitian Revolution.* Cambridge, MA: Harvard University Press.

Duvalier, François. 1969. *Hommage au Marron Inconnu.* Port-au-Prince: Presses Nationales d'Haïti.

Élie, Louis. N.d. *Le Président Boyer et l'Empereur de Russie, Alexandre Ier (Une Mission diplomatique à Saint-Pétersbourg en 1821).* Port au Prince: Imprimerie du Collège Vertières.

Fick, Carolyn. 1990. *The Making of Haiti: The Saint Domingue Revolution from Below.* Knoxville: University of Tennessee Press.

—. 2008. 'Slave Society in the Sugar Plantation Zones of Saint Domingue and the Revolution of 1791–93'. *Slavery & Abolition* 20.2: 31–46.

Hall, Gwendolyn. 2005. *Slavery and African Ethnicities in the Americas: Restoring the Links.* Chapel Hill, NC: University of North Carolina Press.

Hebblethwaite, Benjamin. 2012. *Vodou Songs.* Philadelphia: Temple University Press.

Hurbon, Laënnec. 1979. *Culture et dictature en Haïti: L'imaginaire sous contrôle.* Paris: L'Harmattan.

Johnson, Sara. 2012. *The Fear of French Negroes: Transcolonial Collaboration in the Revolutionary Americas.* Berkeley: University of California Press.

Lovejoy, Paul (ed.). 2000. *Identity in the Shadow of Slavery.* London: Continuum.

Lutz, Georges. 2007. 'Un avatar de la domestication des animaux: les chiens à esclaves "Buscadores" de Cuba et de Saint-Domingue'. In Marcel Dorigny (ed.), *Haïti première république noire.* Saint Denis: Société Française d'Histoire d'Outre-Mer: 61–82.

Madiou, Thomas. 1847–48. *Histoire d'Haïti* (vols I–III). Port-au-Prince: J. Courtois.

McAlister, Elizabeth. 2002. *Rara! Vodou, Power and Performance in Haiti and Its Diaspora.* Berkeley; London: University of California Press.

—. 2012. 'Slaves, Cannibals, and Infected Hyper-Whites: The Race and Religion of Zombies'. *Anthropological Quarterly* 85.2: 457–86.

Métraux, Alfred. 1958. *Le Vaudou haïtien.* Paris: Gallimard.

Price-Mars, Jean. 2009 [c. 1928]. *Ainsi parla l'Oncle.* Montréal: Mémoire d'encrier.

Thornton, John. 1993. '"I am the subject of the King of Congo": African Political Ideology and the Haitian Revolution'. *Journal of World History* 4.2: 181–214.

—. 1998. *Africa and Africans in the Making of the Atlantic World, 1400–1800.* Cambridge: Cambridge University Press.

Trouillot, Michel-Rolph. 1990. *Haiti, State against Nation: The Origins and Legacy of Duvalierism.* New York: Monthly Review Press.

Vastey, Pompée de. 1815. *Le Cri de la Conscience, ou Réponse à un Écrit, imprimé au Port-au-Prince, intituled: Le Peuple de la République d'Hayti, à Messieurs Vastey et Limonade.* Cap Henry: P. Roux.

Beyond the Abolitionist Moment: Memories and Counter-Memories of Labour Exploitation

Cette île n'est pas une île: Locating Gorée

Charles Forsdick

Celui qui vous dit 'Gorée est une île'
Celui-là a menti
Cette île n'est pas une île
Elle est continent de l'esprit.[1]

Just less than half a mile away from the International Slavery Museum in Liverpool's Albert Dock, in the shadow of the buildings on the Pier Head known as the Three Graces, is a sign for the area known as the Gorée Piazza. This was originally the site of the Gorée Warehouses, built in 1793 and demolished in the late 1940s after they had suffered significant damage during the Second World War. In his semi-autobiographical novel *Ultramarine* (2005 [1933]), the Wirral-born poet and novelist Malcolm Lowry alludes to a local tradition according to which the iron hoops on the walls here had once been used to restrain the enslaved. He writes of the 'Goree Piazzas where they used to chain the slaves: Father showed me a bill of lading for one before he went mad' (Lowry, 2005: 67). This reference has more to do with legend than with history, for by the time the Gorée Warehouses were built, the Somersett case of 1772 had already established a pre-abolitionist precedent according to

[1] Translation: 'If anyone says to you "Gorée is an island" / That person has lied / This island is not an island / It is a continent of the spirit.' Quotation by Jean-Louis Roy on a plaque unveiled in the garden of the Maison des Esclaves, November 1999. Cited in Bocoum and Toulier (2013). This and all subsequent unattributed quotations were translated by the author of this article.

which, in theory at least, any enslaved Africans who reached England could not be removed from the country against their will (Nadelhaft, 1966).

Irrespective of the historical veracity, the naming of this site nevertheless relates directly to Gorée Island, a centre of slave embarkation off the coast of Dakar in Senegal, with which slave traders and sailors of the time would have been familiar. The continued and problematic presence of Gorée in the cityscape of central Liverpool encapsulates the central thesis of this chapter: that Gorée, through a series of representations including fictions, films and political speeches, has long been unmoored from the West African coast, having been granted a symbolic existence in a wider Black Atlantic space.[2] In the terms of Kinsey A. Katchka, '"Gorée" is no longer a uniquely historical location, but an historical abstraction that can be relocated elsewhere' (2004: 3). Developing the logic of such an observation, Jean-Louis Roy, in the epigraph cited above, elevates the island to the status of a 'continent de l'esprit' ['continent of the spirit']. The purpose of the following chapter is to illustrate the ways in which the meanings of Gorée – whilst including strands of the utopian idealization that Roy's phrase implies – are ultimately much more entangled and ambiguous. What follows is an attempt, more suggestive than in any way comprehensive, to locate Gorée and understand the symbolic, cultural and political meanings with which it has been, and continues to be, associated. It thus offers an introduction to the representation and instrumentalization of this island space – a topic that requires a much more sustained study in the future.

Central to understandings of Gorée is an acknowledgement of the slippage between the histories of the site and the memorial functions it has subsequently played. Gorée is an eloquent illustration of the tensions between these two phenomena, and the complex dynamics that characterize their interaction. Engagement with the lived past of the island – archaeological, historical, social, cultural and political – also reveals it to be a site of historiographical tension, as interpretations of Gorée in western (and especially North American) slavery studies often diverge from Senegalese and, more generally, West African interpretations. Such a divergence between symbolic and memorial traditions became startlingly apparent in 1995, when Gorée became the subject of major controversy as the US historian Philip Curtin used the newly launched 'Slavery and H-Africa' discussion list to assert the statistically minor role of Gorée in the Atlantic trade: 'though [it]

---

[2] Gorée Piazza remains one of those street names targeted by campaigners who have sought to re-baptize a number of locations, including perhaps most famously Penny Lane, which are seen as a lingering reminder of the city's slaving past.

is a picturesque place,' he noted, 'it was marginal to the slave trade'.[3] As such, Curtin continued a tradition of questioning the historical place of Gorée in the Black Atlantic, evident in earlier work such as Raymond Mauny's *Guide de Gorée* (1954), while venturing more critically into the realm of (false) memory by describing the Maison des Esclaves as a 'hoax' and the wider site as the focus of the 'Goree scam'. The journalist Emmanuel de Roux repeated these accusations in *Le Monde* the following year (1996), thereby bringing what had previously constituted a primarily academic spat into the public eye. Curtin dismissed Gorée as 'an emotional shrine to the slave trade, rather than a serious museum', and accordingly summarized a clash between quantitative historiography and a series of concerns, less empirical but nevertheless fundamental, relating to ethics, memory and ownership of the past.

What the Gorée controversy makes clear is that discussions about statistics can no longer offer satisfactory responses to debates about the afterlives of slavery in the Atlantic world. Achille Mbembe responded to Curtin, dismissing his supposed obsession with statistics as 'a strategy of guilt and exoneration', and suggesting the impossibility of comprehending the significance of Gorée 'if one considers it' quantitatively as 'only a matter of numbers'.[4] As this dispute reveals, Gorée's status as what UNESCO has dubbed an *île-mémoire* ['memory-island'] raises significant questions about the extent to which its construction in the history of transatlantic slavery – as a site of pilgrimage, as a tourist destination, as a location of political significance and as a *lieu de mémoire* – interrogates the relationship of the island to its actual history and archaeology. Viewing multiple representational techniques as key to such divergence, this chapter has three main sections – 'Fictionalizing Gorée', 'Visualizing Gorée' and 'Politicizing Gorée' – and uses these to offer an initial exploration of a complex corpus of creative material (including fiction and film), political speeches delivered on the island (by, among others, George W. Bush, Bill Clinton and François Hollande) and museums (the Maison des Esclaves itself, and other related sites). The subject is potentially vast, and the material discussed is accordingly selective. The aim, however, is to present Gorée as a particularly rich and complex case study for those interested in multi-layered memorialization, as well as in the more general representation of key sites of Atlantic slavery, suggesting in the process possible lines of enquiry for future research.

---

[3] See http://www.h-net.org/~africa/threads/goree.html (consulted on 2 October 2014).

[4] As with Curtin's comments, this is from Mbembe's contribution (4 August 1995) to a discussion on the H-NET List for African History on 'Goree and the Atlantic Slave Trade': http://www.h-net.org/~africa/threads/goree.html.

Gorée: Between History and Memory

The proliferation of geographical locations and of historical contexts in which Gorée has been represented raises searching questions about where, symbolically, the island is located and what it signifies. This chapter takes as its starting point the manifest iconicity of Gorée Island and the sedimentation of meaning that this betokens. It explores the centrality of the site in the memorialization of the Atlantic slave trade, and the role it has played in the political and cultural practices to which this memorialization is related. The island – located, in Roger Atwood's terms, 'like a moored barge in Dakar's harbour' (2012: 47) – was a commercial *comptoir* ['trading post'] during the slave trade era. Now seen as a predominantly French Atlantic site, at certain moments in its history it was equally subject to Dutch, Portuguese and British domination. Shortly after Senegalese independence in 1960, Léopold Sédar Senghor consolidated the 1941 classification of the island as a historical site, and designated Gorée as an official slavery memorial. It was during the 1970s, however, under the stewardship of a former *tirailleur*, Joseph Ndiaye, that the central building, the Maison des Esclaves, was restored to become one of the key tourist locations (and pilgrimage centres) of the Black Atlantic, allowing the site to mobilize its potential to gain revenue from international visitors.[5] Named as a World Heritage Site in 1978, Gorée then attracted scores of visitors, including prominent travellers such as Pope John Paul II, Nelson Mandela, Bill Clinton and George W. Bush.

Key to the attraction was the performance of Ndiaye himself. Until several years before his death in 2009, he provided an animated account of the many victims of slavery who, having been held in the building's cramped underground dungeons, had finally passed through its 'Door of No Return'.[6] Ndiaye's presentation was a clear example – seen within the field of thanatourism more generally – of what Chris Ryan has described as a shift from a more traditionally passive 'sight-*seeing*' to a more actively affective and participatory 'sight-*involving*' approach (2005: 188). This observation highlights the affective dimensions of certain strands of slavery-related travel and raises questions regarding the role of spectacle and even sensationalism in such practices. The controversy created by Curtin and popularized by de Roux was, therefore, not necessarily a new one (despite attempts made by the media to dress it up as such). Already, a number of Senegal-based and primarily French scholars, such as Mauny, had questioned the relative role of

---

[5] On the transformation of Gorée into a 'museum island', see Thiam (1980). On roots tourism and the concept of pilgrimage, see Davis (1997) and Ebron (1999).

[6] See also Ndiaye (2006).

Gorée Island in the Atlantic slave trade. Central to more recent critiques of Gorée was, however, Joseph Ndiaye, who was accused by authors of developing a contemporary myth of the Maison des Esclaves as part of an attempt to manufacture a tourist industry on the island. The novelist Jean-Luc Angrand (author of *Céleste ou le temps des signares* [2006]), for example, claimed that Ndiaye had exploited ideas initially elaborated by a French naval doctor and local historian, Pierre André Cariou, whose unpublished manuscript 'Promenade à Gorée' (1951–52), which describes the Maison des Esclaves in detail, was allegedly produced as the basis for an unwritten novel (see Bocoum and Toulier, 2013: 23, n. 17).

What is clear is that the construction of Gorée as a site of memory follows a clear logic that is shared by other sites: the focus on the 'Door of No Return' in the Maison des Esclaves echoes, for example, a similar feature at Elmina, and can be associated with the symbolism of a similar monument built at Ouidah as part of the UNESCO Slave Route project. In a study of the place of Gorée in school textbooks and wider pedagogical cultures in contemporary Senegal, Ibrahima Seck describes a specific 'syndrome de Gorée' (2009: 111–14) that is focused less on the wider claims to veracity and legitimacy raised by Curtin, and more on raising questions regarding the ways in which an emphasis on the island may be seen to contribute to what others have dubbed a 'maritimization' of the history of the slave trade (see notably Beech, 2001: 103–04). Seck suggests that an emphasis on sites such as Gorée, Elmina and Ouidah – evident, he claims, not only in international visits, but also in the 'tourisme de poussière' ['dust tourism'] that brings pupils from the more remote parts of Senegal to the capital – has eclipsed the attention that might otherwise have been paid to more interior locations such as Galam, Kumasi and Abomey (Seck, 2009). The result is that the geographical complexity of enslavement is no longer fully apparent.

Given Senegal's financial and political investment in the post-independence recognition of the site's historical significance, responses to the 1990s questioning of the relative importance of Gorée in the Atlantic slave trade were nevertheless robust. A seminar was organized in Dakar, bringing together historians who sought to challenge Curtin's claims, whilst underlining the continued significance of Gorée in discussions of slavery and the slave trade. Commenting at this event on Gorée's symbolic role in understandings of the slave trade, Ibrahima Thioub and Hamady Bocoum noted concisely that 'ce tragique succès s'est imposé avec tellement d'évidence qu'on a peu songé à questionner scientifiquement l'importance de la place et du rôle de Gorée dans le trafic négrier' (1997: 199).[7] They subsequently nuanced this comment

---

[7] Translation: 'this tragic success was asserted as being so grounded in evidence

by concluding that 'le discours qui commémore cette fonction de l'île n'a jamais prétendu obéir aux règles universitaires de production du savoir et, en conséquence, ne peut être mesuré à cette aune' (Thioub and Bocoum, 1997: 200).[8] As such, they maintain an ambiguity that suggests a very different approach to historiography, and even epistemology, than that deployed by Curtin in the interventions that had initially sparked the debate. As Ibrahima Thiaw notes: 'the island is a forum where memories and representations are constantly "contested"' (2008: 45). There is a need, therefore, to supplement historical and archaeological approaches – to which Thiaw, as a researcher at the IFAN (now the Institut fondamental de l'Afrique noire), has devoted much effort – with a more open acknowledgement of other forms of representation. What the Curtin incident, and the Senegalese response to it, made clear was that locating Gorée depends on an engagement with an eclectic range of representations. To begin this process, this chapter now turns to literary engagements with the island that have been published in the two decades since the controversy emerged, a corpus that reflects the site's continued role in discussions of Atlantic slavery, the slave trade and their contemporary afterlives.

Fictionalizing Gorée: The Literary Functions of the Island

The textual representation of Gorée dates back several centuries, not least because the island was a regular port of call for travellers to Senegal. It features in many eighteenth- and nineteenth-century travel narratives (Delcourt, 1982), but the increasingly symbolic importance of Gorée as a key site of the Black Atlantic means that it has, more recently, become the focus of a number of contemporary fictional texts. In several of these works, the island is elevated to the status of a Black Atlantic crossroad, a site of potential meeting of sub-Saharan Africans and those of the African diaspora in the Americas, at which historical differences may be addressed and contemporary convergences become possible. Not all the narratives of Gorée demonstrate such reverence: the Franco-Togolese writer Georges Holassey's short story 'Gorée: les esclaves y pleurent encore', which forms part of a collection with the same title, describes instead the tensions that arise from this situation. His protagonist is an African-American nicknamed

---

that little attention has been paid to any scholarly questioning of the importance of the place and role of Gorée in the slave trade'.

[8] Translation: 'the discourse commemorating this function of the island has never claimed to obey the rules of academic knowledge production and, consequently, cannot be measured by this yardstick'.

Donovan, whose visit to Gorée two years previously results in him deciding to return to settle there permanently:

> J'avais découvert l'Afrique dans une émotion indescriptible. La nature paraissait nue, crue; et la vie semblait différente de la nôtre en Amérique. Mais c'est la visite de Gorée qui m'avait poussé à prendre la décision de venir vivre en Afrique. J'étais bouleversé par cette maison des esclaves [...]. Une maison dont je garde toujours l'impression que les pleurs et les lamentations des esclaves y sont toujours entendus par les visiteurs. Gorée, je vous assure, a tout changé dans ma vie... Un peu de vin de palme, s'il vous plait. (Holassey, 2010: 11)[9]

The affective dimensions of visits to the Maison des Esclaves, associated with the guide Joseph Ndiaye, are central to the story, although with the reference to 'un peu de vin de palme', the satirical note that dominates the rest of the narrative creeps in. Donovan proceeds to describe his visit to the island. He presents it as an aestheticized experience ('avec chacun son appareil photo pour capturer quelques silhouettes de l'île'), with a light exposure to history ('des guides nous racontèrent quelques bribes d'histoire') and a blending of pilgrimage with tourism ('une petite collation dans un restaurant-bar') (Holassey, 2010: 13).[10] What emerges is an incredulity on the part of the local narrator, who underlines the very different perspectives that exist on historical sites relating to the slave trade: 'Pourquoi est-il autant torturé par cette visite de Gorée dont l'histoire écrite dans les livres n'émeut plus grand monde autour de nous?' (Holassey, 2010: 13).[11] The response is multi-layered, reflecting the tensions between past and present, underlining the ways in which place is historicized through more abstract academic interventions and, of course, suggesting the different responses to traces of the history of the slave trade experienced by Africans and African Americans. Ultimately, however, it is Donovan's insensitivity towards his hosts that is underlined, for Gorée is seen, not as a trigger for any reconciliation, but instead as a stage

[9] Translation: 'I discovered Africa in a state of indescribable emotion. Nature seemed bare, raw; and life seemed different from ours in America. But it is the tour of Gorée that pushed me to take the decision to come and live in Africa. I was overwhelmed by this slave house [...]. I always retain the impression that it is a house in which visitors can still hear the weeping and wailing of the slaves. Gorée, I assure you, changed everything in my life... A little palm wine, please.'

[10] Translation: 'each with a camera to capture some silhouettes of the island'; 'guides told us a few snatches of history'; 'a little snack in a bar.'

[11] Translation: 'Why is he so tortured by this visit to Gorée, whose history written in books no longer moves many people around us?'

for temporary self-performance: 'Nous apprenons par le propriétaire de la maison où il logeait, que Donovan est parti. Il est retourné dans son pays pour travailler parce qu'il a fini ses économies' (Holassey, 2010: 18).[12]

Holassey's short story is an acerbic reflection on the differing, even mutually incomprehensible meanings of Gorée in Black Atlantic space, whereby meanings shift according to the axis by which the island is approached and the motivations underpinning a particular journey. Gorée is desacralized and the mechanics of roots tourism satirized in the form of a dialogue of the deaf over the site's possible meanings. As such, the story may be seen to perform the rupture, evident in many pan-Africanist narratives of the black diaspora, between Africa and the Americas, against which philosophers such as Ki-Zerbo have nevertheless warned.[13]

Other texts approach the symbolism of Gorée in a more nuanced way, exploring the role of the island in contemporary Senegal and presenting it in more positive terms as a potential meeting place. The Nigerian author Gideon Prinsler Omolu, in *Deux Gorée, une île* (2004), eschews focus on external visitors to the island in order to present the island as the site of a passionate struggle between two sisters (Aïcha and Soukeyna) for one man (Oumar), in which a local *marabout* (Ibou Konaté) plays an exploitative and ultimately destructive role. Gorée, the location for the wedding of Soukeyna and Oumar, is described in idyllic, aestheticized terms: 'une belle rade, très hospitalière à l'ancrage solide'; 'les murs portaient une palette de teintes à dominantes rouge, rose et ocre' (Omolu, 2004: 55).[14] But as the narrative unfolds, this version of the island slowly fades. In a *mise-en-abîme*, the historian Soukeyna – whose marriage proves short-lived – is commissioned to write a book called *Gorée, paradis perdu et reconquis*, the launch of which involves a visit to the Maison des Esclaves. Far from the dismissive attitude evident in Holassey, Omolu describes a persistent legacy of slavery on the island: 'Au cœur de la maison, la cruauté des esclavagistes était encore plus visible' (2004: 123),[15] a legacy that seems to be reflected in the tragedies by which the novel is punctuated. However, the concluding reconciliation of the

12 Translation: 'We learn from the owner of the house where he was staying that Donovan has left. He has returned to his own country to work because he has exhausted his savings.'

13 On this potential rupture and sites such as Gorée, see Bocoum and Toulier (2013: para 20).

14 Translation: 'a beautiful harbour, very hospitable with solid anchorage'; 'the walls had a range of colours with dominant red, pink and ochre'.

15 Translation: 'at the heart of the house, the cruelty of the slave traders was yet more visible'.

sisters is associated with another reading of a more resilient Gorée, 'petite île au milieu de l'océan, triomphante à l'assaut des vagues' (Omolu, 2004: 159),[16] which suggests a refusal of any predetermined, historical meanings and a recasting of the island as a site of hope.

Such an approach also underpins the Congolese novelist Pie Tshibanda's *Rendez-vous sur l'île de Gorée* (2007), which offers an account of the efforts of the Martiniquais character Monsieur Vassard to prevent his daughter Allegra from marrying Willy, or 'ce Noir d'Afrique' ['this black man from Africa'] (5). The narrator is Willy's mother, who observes this interethnic prejudice with distaste. Visiting Martinique, she describes transatlantic axes that are absent from the other narratives: 'Tout, en Martinique, me renvoie à l'Afrique, non seulement à Ouidah ou sur l'île de Gorée, "portes du non-retour", mais aussi à tous les villages qui ont connu l'insécurité suite aux razzias esclavagistes' (Tshibanda, 2007: 11).[17] Addressing the hostility in Allegra's family to marriage with Willy, she suggests a journey back to Africa, following 'la route de l'esclave à l'envers' ['the slave route in reverse'] (Tshibanda, 2007: 41), during which Allegra's father is forced to reflect on his own identity, his relationship to sub-Saharan Africa and his prejudices against sub-Saharan Africans. The symbolic conclusion of the novel takes place on Gorée, where the young couple marry before making their way to the Maison des Esclaves: 'Et de la mairie, nous voyons une procession. A la tête, Willy et Allegra rayonnants de beauté et de bonheur. Dans le cortège, des Africains, des Antillais, des Européens, des Américains, des Asiatiques... Ils défilent, vers la Maison des esclaves...' (Tshibanda, 2007: 132).[18] In the face of the persistent hostility symbolized by Monsieur Vassard, Gorée – that meeting place of people, not only from across the African diaspora, but also from elsewhere – becomes a site of reconciliation. The haunting that lurks in a text such as *Deux Gorée, une île* is thus transformed into something much more celebratory: 'Derrière la porte du non-retour, une grosse vague vient s'abattre contre le mur comme si les fantômes de ceux qui ont servi de nourriture aux requins, à l'embarquement et pendant la traverse, venaient

---

16 Translation: 'a small island in the middle of the ocean, triumphant over the assault of the waves'.

17 Translation: 'Everything, in Martinique, reminds me of Africa, not only of Ouidah or on the island of Gorée, the "Doors of No Return", but also of all the villages that have experienced the insecurity that followed slave raids.'

18 Translation: 'And from the Town Hall, we see a procession. At the head of it, Willy and Allegra radiate beauty and happiness. In the procession, Africans, West Indians, Europeans, Americans, Asians... They process towards the House of Slaves...'

participer à la fête' (Tshibanda, 2007: 132).[19] Reconciliation appears to be offered within the African diaspora, but also between cultures previously divided by the slave trade.

A similar trajectory to that described by Tshibanda appears in *Gorée: Point of Departure* (2010), by the Bermudian novelist Angela Barry. The St Lucian protagonist Magdelene meets her ex-husband Saliou Wade at JFK airport, and agrees to travel to Senegal with their now adult daughter Khadi to visit Saliou's new family. The narrative is again one of restoration, cultural, psychological and familial: 'To restore a daughter to her father. To restore a daughter to herself' (Barry, 2010: 12). Yet it is also presented via an account of culture shock and interethnic, transatlantic tension, again pitting sub-Saharan Africa against the Americas. Gorée plays a punctual, strategic role in the narrative, for it is here that Khadi, as part of the renegotiation of her relationship with both her father and her origins, decides to take her half-sister Maimouna on a day trip. The ferry to the island is characterized by a 'festive atmosphere' (Barry, 2010: 115), and the location is once again subject to the aestheticization that is evident in other texts: 'The island of Gorée was upon them, floating like a dark golden slipper in the sea' (Barry, 2010: 117). The description of the site is almost oneiric: 'the island seemed to glide by, caught in its own dream, haunted by its legion phantoms, ensnaring all who would look on its brooding fortress, its lissom palms, its houses washed in yellow and red ochre, its placid beach' (Barry, 2010: 118). The 'whirr of cameras clicked and panning' (Barry, 2010: 118) only adds to this sense of surreality and abstraction from the everyday. The half-sisters visit the Maison des Esclaves, experiencing the deeply affective tour focused on over-determined artefacts and aspects of the building's décor: 'Chains, potent despite their rust. A single twenty-five pound lead ball. Walls slick with the slat of ancient tears. Rough floors of sand and pounded excrement. No windows' (Barry, 2010: 123). The visit to the slave house precedes the accident that serves as the climax of the text, when Maimouna falls from the quay as she tries to board the ferry to return home and is recovered unconscious from the water. There follows a long sequence in which the girl's slow recovery reveals tensions between her father's western medicine and the more traditional cure from which she seems to benefit. Having fallen into a coma, Maimouna appears to travel the Middle Passage, as if the narratives of enslavement recounted on Gorée were 'imprinted on her mind... on her body...' (Barry, 2010: 197).

---

[19] Translation: 'Behind the Door of No Return, a big wave crashes against the wall as if the ghosts of those who have served as food for sharks, both during the embarkation and the crossing, were coming to join the party.'

In Barry's novel, Gorée serves as a node of encounter between Caribbean and African peoples, but far from presenting the celebratory conclusion of Tshibanda in *Rendez-vous sur l'île de Gorée* (2007), the island serves as a continuing reminder of the persistent legacies of slavery that exist beneath its current stage management as a tourist site. Khadi's return to her Senegalese family and her re-appropriation of elements of her own childhood leads, at the conclusion of the novel, to a sense of accommodation, but one that is only reached via a deeply testing re-acquaintance, via the events on Gorée Island, with the traumas of the Middle Passage.

Visualizing Gorée: The Island on Screen

The iconicity of the Maison des Esclaves, central to the international visibility of Gorée and evoked in the novels discussed above, invites closer exploration in terms of the ways in which the island has been represented in visual culture. Extensively mapped, pictured in a series of early illustrations (see Delcourt, 1982) and presented on numerous postcards throughout the twentieth century, Gorée has featured widely in visual culture, in forms ranging from stamps (most notably a collection released to mark Dakar '66) to cinema, and from comics to photography.[20] Central to many of these representations is the Maison des Esclaves itself, of which a number of key features have often been privileged, including the Door of No Return, the symmetrically curved staircases and the handwritten signage of Joseph Ndiaye. The international visibility of Gorée has grown, not least as a result of its role in recent films, on some of which this section will now focus. In a number of these, the island serves – at times anonymously – as a backdrop to the narrative. In such cases, the Maison des Esclaves appears rarely, with the director privileging other locations, such as the cathedral or town hall, as if there is a refusal to reduce the island to a single, iconic site. When it is revealed in the film's credits that the filming occurred on Gorée, viewers recognizing the location are able to reflect on the significance of this choice.

It is not surprising, for instance, that much of Djibril Diop Mambety's *Hyènes* (1992) – an adaptation of Friedrich Dürrenmatt's *The Visit* (*Der Besuch der alten Dame*, 1956), set in the village of Colobane – is filmed on

[20] Warnauts and Raives include a *bande dessinée* entitled *La Nuit de Gorée* (1999), an account of political and sexual intrigue on the eighteenth-century island, in the 'Suites vénitiennes' series. The photography of Chester Higgins and Carrie Mae Weems, which focuses on sites of the African diaspora, contributes to an aestheticization of the iconic Maison des Esclaves. For a discussion of both of these photographic works, see Salamishah (2009).

Gorée. The director uses the island's historical connection with slavery to support an ironic critique of postcolonial African politics and consumerism, neo-colonialism and the tendency for patterns of oppression to re-emerge in new forms.[21] This critique works in parallel to the story of Linguere Ramatou, a former prostitute and now aging, wealthy woman, who revisits her home to take revenge on Dramaan Drameh, a local shopkeeper, who abandoned her after a love affair when she was sixteen. More attenuated perhaps is François Truffaut's decision to film the final scenes of *L'Histoire d'Adèle H.* (1975) on Gorée, with the island standing in for Barbados. It is on Gorée (not Barbados), therefore, that the historical narrative on which the film depends reaches its actual *dénouement*. Having followed her former lover to French Canada, the film's heroine, Adèle Hugo, eventually finds herself destitute on the Caribbean island. By, in effect, relocating the action somewhat surprisingly to Gorée, Truffaut not only underlines the entanglements apparent in a Francophone Black Atlantic space, but also suggests the symbolic flexibility of the island as it stands in for a Caribbean location.

Such manoeuvres are clearly ambiguous and remain relatively rare. Perhaps more pertinent are those films that firmly situate their action on Gorée itself. One of the best known of these is Michel Renaudeau's *Les Caprices d'un Fleuve* (1996), an account of the banishment of Jean-François de la Plaine to West Africa following the death of a rival (and friend of Louis XVI) at his hands in a duel. Named governor of the *comptoir* ['trading post'] of Cap Saint-Louis, de la Plaine passes his time playing his *épinette* ['spinet'], and is drawn into the amorous intrigue of this claustrophobic environment. He engages in relationships with Anne Brisseau, a signare and slave trader, and one of his own slaves, Amélie, whom he had earlier treated as his adopted daughter and who ultimately dies in childbirth. Called back to France during the Convention (1792–95), Jean-François finally returns to Senegal to raise the child he has had with Amélie. Released in a cinematic context of colonial nostalgia – epitomized by other works such as Régis Wagnier's *Indochine* (1992) – the film luxuriates in the sparse yet stylized interiors of Gorée, which are seen via an exoticizing western gaze. The island, which foregrounds its associations with the slave trade, nonetheless disrupts the ideological backcloth of the film and its referencing of Enlightenment abolitionism, revealing instead the persistence of French involvement in

---

[21] Mambety also uses the symbolism of Gorée in his final film, *La Petite Vendeuse de soleil* (1999), in which, during one scene, the disabled protagonist Lili is seen in a dock identified by a sign marked with 'Gorée', making the viewer aware, as Michael Davidson notes, of 'the relationship between disability and market-driven poverty' (2008: 183).

slavery in West Africa as the French Revolution was radically reshaping France itself. Produced in the context of the imminent French preparations for the sesquicentenary of abolition (1998), the film attempts to locate the then contemporary debates about *droit à la différence* ['right to difference'], as well as a more general celebration of cultural hybridity, through its historical representation of Gorée. Ostensibly anti-racist in intention, and striving to present a protagonist who seeks – albeit selectively – to humanize the enslaved characters with whom he comes into contact, the film is ultimately, however, 'permeated by unwitting colonialist thinking' (2011), to borrow Alyssa Sepinwall's phrasing.

Other films seek to reflect more actively on contemporary Gorée, situating it in relation not only to its historical past, but also to a wider contemporary Black Atlantic frame. Perhaps most prominent among these is Pierre-Yves Borgeaud's *Return to Gorée: A Musical Odyssey* (2007), which offers an exploration of the legacies of Atlantic slavery through musical culture. Focusing on the travels of Senegalese singer Youssou N'Dour and of the pianist Moncef Genoud, the documentary film begins on Gorée but proceeds on a journey through place (Western Europe and North America) and musical genres (jazz, blues, gospel, and rock and roll), before returning to a concluding concert in the Maison des Esclaves itself. The outward and inward movement of *Return to Gorée*, as well as the concluding celebration involving musicians from the various locations that the film visits, describe a process of reconciliatory synthesis and homecoming. The site on Gorée, most symbolically linked with the slave trade, now becomes a site of renewal through joint creativity. The musician emerges as *conteur* ['storyteller'] and cultural commentator, tracing a post-slavery identity that is at once rhizomatic and characterized by a common point of reference focused on an island off the West African coast. The appearance of the African-American writer and activist Amiri Baraka in the film also underlines a political dimension that reminds viewers of the role of sites such as Gorée in the search for African-American identity.

This is a theme also evident in Rachid Bouchareb's *Little Senegal* (2001), a film that similarly begins in Gorée and traces trajectories through Black Atlantic space, picking up on the themes of migration, rootlessness and intercultural friction that characterize many of the directors' other works. The protagonist Aloune, played by the late Sotigui Kouyaté, is loosely based on Joseph Ndiaye. Having worked for many years as the curator of the Maison des Esclaves on Gorée, where he has daily watched the arrival of, and greeted parties of, African-American tourists, he decides one day to travel to North America in search of enslaved ancestors deported two centuries earlier. After a journey through the southern states of the US, where he visits a former plantation and consults plantation records that have now been confined to an archive, he travels to New York, where he stays with his nephew Hassan, who lives in Harlem's Little Senegal district. Undaunted by the social divide between black Africans and African-Americans, he manages to find a 'cousine', Ida Robinson, owner of a newspaper stand, and gradually gains her confidence. Disrupting any celebratory narrative about transatlantic relations, *Little Senegal* inscribes Gorée into Black Atlantic space by overturning its traditional role as a destination for African-American tourists, and by transforming it into a point of departure for a Senegalese traveller who seeks to repeat the Atlantic crossing of his enslaved ancestors. The result is a reflection on the fragmented afterlives of slavery, seen in particular in the fraught relations experienced in New York between Africans and those in the diaspora. As such, Gorée is symbolically linked to a wider set of political and identitarian debates in a way that points to the instrumentalization of the site in both domestic and international politics, as examined in the following section.

Politicizing Gorée: The Island in a Global Frame

Following the national independence of Senegal, Gorée Island rapidly became a symbolic site in the construction of Senegal as a postcolonial nation, and was seen most notably as a means of locating the country (and indeed of providing it with a privileged location) in the political space of the Black Atlantic. Whereas during the later colonial period the island had been home to a number of French institutions, Senegal's first president, Léopold Senghor, sought to highlight the site's earlier function in the Atlantic slave trade. As has already been noted, the Maison des Esclaves was designated a slave memorial, preparing the way for formal international recognition of the historical significance of the building. The importance attached to Gorée – a key site in Senghor's politics emphasizing 'enracinement et [...] ouverture' ['roots and openness'] – is particularly apparent in its choice as one of the focal points of Dakar '66, the 'Premier Festival Mondial des Arts Nègres' ['First World Festival of Negro Arts']. As Hamady Bocoum and Bernard Toulier note, 'Gorée est un laboratoire idéal pour le projet post-colonial de la Négritude' (2013: para 26).[22] The scheduling of key events on the island, such as the 'Spectacle Féérique de Gorée' ['Magical Spectacle of Gorée'] – which presented an account of the history of Senegal, and a reflection on Gorée Island and the slave trade, with a concluding section on the growth of Dakar

[22] Translation: 'Gorée is an ideal laboratory for the postcolonial project of Negritude.'

and Senegalese independence, scripted by the Haitian exile Jean F. Brierre – not only stressed the place of slavery and its afterlives in discussions of postcolonial, pan-African, Black Atlantic identity, but also staged exhibitions that demonstrated the creative potential of black culture. In this way, they galvanized a sense of Negritudinist solidarity in a site associated with the trauma of historical suffering.[23]

The visible role of Gorée in the 1966 festival meant that the status of the island as tourist destination was firmly consolidated, although such a shift predated the popularity of 'roots tourism' and, more recently, 'dark tourism', with which other locations, such as the Gold Coast slave castles in Ghana, would be associated from the following decade onwards. In itself, this attraction was not new, and numerous colonial postcards of the site reveal its popularity with visitors in an earlier, pre-independence period. However, the location of Gorée within a Black Atlantic frame means that its status, at least with international audiences, was inextricably bound up with its former role in the slave trade. As has already been made clear, instrumental in this transformation – or perhaps, more accurately, this recovery of traces of the island's former function – was Joseph Ndiaye, whose performative interpretation of the history of enslavement and deportation associated Gorée with an affective impact that can be seen as a shift from a 'sight-*seeing*' to a 'sight-*involving*' approach (Ryan, 2005: 188). Central to Ndiaye's project was communication to and with an international audience, and overseas visitors play a prominent role in his accounts of the Maison des Esclaves. Entries in the site's visitors' book are included in his publications (Ndiaye, n.d.: 32–34), while the reflections on the meanings of Gorée by a striking roster of international figures underline the increasing politicization of the island, translated into shorthand for the trauma not only of the slave trade, but also of the phenomenon of Atlantic slavery more generally.

The list of statesmen who have visited Gorée is an impressive one, and includes spiritual as well as political leaders. Prominent among them, however, have been visitors from France and the United States, for whom the island often serves as an international stage on which more domestic issues are addressed. Not surprisingly given Senegal's continuing postcolonial relationship with its former colonizer, numerous French presidents and prime ministers have visited the island. Most recent among these has been the current head of state, François Hollande, for whom a tour of Gorée

[23] See the Archives Nationales du Sénégal, FMAN 33: Commission des spectacles. *Spectacle féerique de Gorée. Opéra populaire en huit tableaux créé à l'occasion du premier Festival mondial des arts nègres.* 1–24 April 1966. Dakar. Cited in Bocoum and Toulier (2013: n. 55).

in October 2013 served a dual purpose. On the one hand, it allowed him to distinguish himself, in a positive light, from his predecessor Nicolas Sarkozy, who notoriously enflamed Franco-Senegalese relations with the 2007 *discours de Dakar* (included in Konaré, 2008: 343–55), a speech in which he acknowledged the existence of Atlantic slavery, whilst simultaneously trivializing its significance in current debates. On the other hand, Hollande used comments at Gorée to contribute to the discussions about reparations, regarding which black activist groups in France, such as the Conseil Représentatif des Associations Noires [Representative Council of Black Associations] (CRAN) were then becoming increasingly vocal.[24] The choice of Gorée was strategic, for Hollande was able to demonstrate compassion for the victims of Atlantic slavery, whilst denying the feasibility of any economic compensation for its legacies in the present.[25]

The subject of reparations was also central to three American presidential tours of the island, those of Bill Clinton (1998), George W. Bush (2003) and Barak Obama (2013). Clinton's and Obama's visits were relatively uncontroversial. Clinton made a widely reported speech in the courtyard of the island's history museum, during which he commented on the strategic and pivotal location of the site: 'on this tiny island in the Atlantic Ocean, Africa and America meet' and 'Goree Island, still today, looks out onto the New World, connecting two continents'. He used this connection to reflect on the place of slavery (or more specifically 'the struggle to overcome slavery and its legacy') in US history. The speech allows Clinton not only to speak to an African-American audience (described problematically and counterintuitively as 'Africa's gift to America'), but also to celebrate what he calls (picking up on the term first coined by Cheikh Anta Diop, and given added contemporary resonance in the context of the end of South African apartheid) the 'African Renaissance'.

For Obama, the tour of Gorée was presented in more personal terms, as a 'pilgrimage', with accounts in the press linking the visit to previous accounts of the slave ancestry of both the president and his wife. This contrasts with Bush's earlier visit, scrutinized closely as it was part of the first visit to Africa by a serving republican leader, the logistics of which were highly controversial. In a situation of heightened security, the majority of the population of the island were confined on a local football pitch, which was transformed for the duration of the visit, as Michael Ralph (2007) notes in a highly perceptive

24 On the subject of Hollande's response to the CRAN's calls for reparations, see Frith (2015).

25 On the *discours de Dakar*, see Chrétien (2008) and Gassama (2008). On Hollande's visit, see Wieder (2012).

article on the event, into an open-air *captiverie* ['slave prison']. Alluding to the controversies surrounding the role of Gorée in the slave trade, Ralph writes that 'the technique of coercion used to subdue Senegalese peoples in that moment reproduced the way enslavement historically occurred on Gorée Island more faithfully than any event that has ever occurred at the *Maison des Esclaves*' (2007: 204).[26]

The speech delivered on that occasion has itself been subject to forensic attention, not least because it failed to include a direct apology for the US role in the history of slavery, despite the focus on questions of freedom and democracy.[27] Moreover, the removal of the people of Senegal from the 'scene' highlights the fact that the intended audience was located elsewhere. The slave trade is described as a 'sin', and Bush draws out the theme of brutality, endorses the legitimacy of resistance and acknowledges – as he did in the speech at his inauguration – the place of slavery in the foundation of the United States. Martin J. Medhurst, for whom Bush's address had the potential to be 'the most important speech on American slavery since Abraham Lincoln' (2010: 258), sees the occasion as a missed opportunity. In a detailed analysis of its content, Medhurst claims that the president 'accepts and confesses the guilt of American slavery', but then fails to pursue the logic of his speech by ignoring its implications for justice in the domestic context of the US (2010: 272). Bush's open acceptance that slavery should be seen as 'one of the greatest crimes in history' was subsequently deployed by lawyers to support legal actions relating to reparations (Carrillo, 2003: 2; Medhurst, 2010: 277 and n. 61). The speech remains, however, a carefully orchestrated performance of atonement ('an elaborately staged and internationally anticipated ceremony') during which – in Bradford Vivian's compelling analysis (2012: 8) – the history of slavery is simultaneously remembered and forgotten, and an expression of regret is substituted for any formal apology.

For Michael Ralph, the 'lyrical gymnastics' (2007: 212) of Bush's speech are to be read in the light of what Trouillot called an 'abortive ritual' (2000), in other words, a superficial evocation of the past that fails to address its implications in the present. Bush began the speech by sketching out the location of Gorée in terms of history and geopolitics, focusing clearly on geographical specifics ('on this island'; 'at this place'). However, the choice of site remained overwhelmingly symbolic, not only providing personal

---

26 The visit and speech are also analysed by Walter Johnson (2007).

27 As Ralph notes, the same was true of Clinton's speech, which similarly 'helped a U.S. president cultivate foreign policy in Africa while strategically evading the social consequences of the United States' historic participation in the Transatlantic slave trade' (2007: 212).

and political legitimacy, but also permitting a performance of what Vivian calls 'national political authority' and (in the context of the invasion of Iraq) 'international moral credibility' (2012: 23). In the process, Bush reveals both an instrumentalization of Gorée in the context of a US president's international, geopolitical self-positioning and a displacement of the North American domestic discussion of slavery and its afterlives onto another continent. Adam Goodheart reflects on this uncomfortable paradox: 'Despite the frequent attention given to the subject, slavery is still somehow held an arm's length, even an ocean's breadth, away' (cited in Vivian, 2012: 29).

Conclusion: Gorée, *île-mémoire*

The stream of prominent international visitors passing through Gorée provides a fascinating case study in the politics of national, international and transnational memory. By choosing Gorée as the location for his speech, Bush simultaneously, and in the face of a certain historiographic scepticism, legitimated the role of Gorée in the history of slavery whilst avoiding, or even evacuating, the political implications of such a memorialization in the present. The progressive transformation of Gorée into a *lieu de mémoire* is nevertheless an ongoing process. This is exemplified, most recently, in the as yet unrealized plans for the Gorée-Almadies memorial and museum, a complex whose situation on the mainland, facing the island, eloquently demonstrates the ways in which 'Gorée has become so synonymous with the history of slavery that the name can be displaced geographically to a site conceptually more convenient and current' (Katchka, 2004: 10).[28] The French colonial authorities may be seen to have begun this process, particularly through the activities of the IFAN and the opening of the Musée historique de l'A.O.F. in 1949, through which Gorée was drawn into what Agbenyega Adedze calls 'the colonial museum complex in French West Africa' (2002).[29] The role of UNESCO in the subsequent transformation of the island itself was an equally active one, representing an intervention that aimed to protect the island against the possible effects of urbanization – not least of which

[28] Katchka adds: 'Perhaps it is not coincidental to the slave house's disputed veracity, then, that the history associated with that site has been abstracted, and relocated to the mainland' (2004: 11). It is certainly clear that, at least under the presidency of Abdoulaye Wade, the Senegalese state has been much less visible on Gorée.

[29] For a full discussion of what they call the '"fabrique" de ce patrimoine mémoriel' ['"factory" of this memorial heritage'] across the twentieth century, see Bocoum and Toulier (2013).

was its metamorphosis into 'a museum-piece or a luxury dormitory suburb' (UNESCO, 1980: 38). UNESCO also sought to underline the potential of the island as what the organization's Director General Amadou Mahtar Mbow described in 1980 as 'one of those rare places where the younger generation of Africa and the Americas can refresh their memories while [...] renewing the sources of their inspiration' (1980: 12). As Bocoum and Toulier note, there is a need for this symbolic discourse relating to memory and the afterlives of slavery to be 'progressivement renouvelé' ['progressively renewed'] (2013: para 61). However, as this chapter has demonstrated, the ownership of any such process remains highly fragmented – it operates at local, national and international levels; its reflects official, semi-official and unofficial contexts; it has aesthetic, historiographical and memorial implications – meaning that the evolution of discourses around the island remains relatively unpredictable:

> l'île de Gorée est un forum permanent où le patrimoine, les mémoires et l'histoire, les commémorations et les mémoriaux, les discours muséaux, les souvenirs et les représentations, imaginées, entretenues ou construites sur la Traite atlantique sont soumis à une remise en cause perpétuelle, s'adaptant aux découvertes et aux connaissances historiques et aux messages culturels, idéologiques et politiques délivrés par les communautés patrimoniales, l'Etat du Sénégal et l'UNESCO. (Bocoum and Toulier, 2013: para 62)[30]

Approaching Gorée as a palimpsestic site of multi-directional representations, and as a progressively constructed *lieu de mémoire* of Atlantic slavery, allows us to understand how the island has been progressively represented, instrumentalized, politicized and memorialized. Such an approach thus expands Pierre Nora's concept of the site of memory, not least by underlining its potential pertinence for the field of Atlantic slavery. Moreover, studying Gorée reveals the different dynamics of history and memory that emerge in this context, challenging the singularized (and predominantly national) memory and historiography that Nora seems to imply. This chapter has sought to explain the ways in which such representations have contributed to the transformation of Gorée into a heavily over-determined site whose

---

[30] Translation: 'Gorée Island is a permanent forum where heritage, remembrance and history, commemorations and memorials, museum discourses, memories and representations, imagined, nurtured or built on the Atlantic slave trade, are subject to perpetual questioning, adapting themselves to historical discoveries and knowledge, as well as to cultural, ideological and political messages issued by heritage communities, the State of Senegal and UNESCO.'

meanings resonate at a number of historical moments and in a number of overlapping contexts (national and transnational, sub-Saharan African and pan-African, European and African-American). The persistence and wide circulation of the iconic imagery of the Maison des Esclaves remains deeply ambivalent. It is, on the one hand, an encapsulation of the historical traumas that Gorée has been conscripted to represent – but on the other, a reflection of the ambiguities inherent in a site whose undeniable symbolic power overshadows its historical function not least through the historical controversies it has provoked. During the colloquium organized in Dakar in the context of Curtin and de Roux's challenge to Gorée's status, Thioub and Bocoum stated that the island could no longer be subject – or, at least, exclusively subject – to the benchmarks of empirical western historiography. In other words (and as suggested at the opening of this chapter), Gorée could only be fully understood in the terms of the varied and symbolic transformations it has undergone in a proliferation of representations in multiple media, which locate the site somewhere on a continuum between history and memory, or in what Paulla A. Ebron sees as an interlocking of '*history* and *memory* scapes' (1999: 910; emphasis in original). This is a process perhaps best encapsulated by the Haitian poet, resident in Senegal, Jean F. Brierre, who, in one of his later texts, 'Un noël pour Gorée', succinctly describes the ongoing transformations of Gorée:

> Dans la sanie des plaies
> depuis tant d'années cicatrisées
> dans la chair des ancêtres
> et qui se rouvrent
> – crucifixion des insomnies –
> dans la chair des petits-fils,
> des perles auront mûri.
> Le sang n'aura laisse aux parois des murs
> qu'une écriture en incuse d'oracles (1980: 14)[31]

---

[31] In the pus of wounds
healed over for so many years
in the flesh of ancestors
and which reopen
– crucifixion of insomnia –
in the flesh of grandchildren
pearls have matured.
The blood will leave on the partitions of the walls
only writing stamped from oracles

The impact of the slave trade and of Atlantic slavery – inscribed within Africa, throughout the Middle Passage and via the enforced labour of the Americas – is presented in terms that echo the affective presentation of the Maison des Esclaves made famous by Joseph Ndiaye. There is an emphasis on progressive scarring, and also on the transgenerational re-opening of wounds, or rather processes whereby traces of the past are simultaneously eroded and yet appear to persist. Brierre concludes, however, by focusing on the transformation of Gorée into icon and symbol – on the ways in which the island, through the representations of novelists, filmmakers and others, has the potential to serve as a reminder of the systematic racism and brutality of the past, but also as a means of imagining possible futures in the present.

Works Cited

Adedze, Agbenyega. 2002. 'Symbols of Triumph: IFAN and the Colonial Museum Complex in French West Africa'. *Museum Anthropology* 25.2: 50–60.

Angrand, Jean-Luc. 2013. 'Petite note sur la fausse "Maison des esclaves de Gorée"'. *Huffington Post* (France) 22 February. Available at http://www.huffingtonpost.fr/jean-luc-angrand/maison-des-esclaves-goree_b_2709281.html (consulted on 2 October 2014).

Atwood, Roger. 2012. 'Senegal's Forgotten Slaves: The Untold Story of Gorée Island'. *Archaeology* September/October: 47–51.

Barry, Angela. 2010. *Gorée: Point of Departure.* Leeds: Peepal Tree.

Beech, John G. 2001. 'The Marketing of Slavery Heritage in the United Kingdom'. *International Journal of Hospitality & Tourism Administration* 2.3–4: 85–106.

Bocoum, Hamady, and Bernard Toulier. 2013. 'La fabrication du Patrimoine: l'exemple de Gorée (Sénégal)'. *In Situ* 20. Available at http://insitu.revues.org/10303 (consulted on 18 October 2014).

Borgeaud, Pierre-Yves (dir.). 2007. *Return to Gorée: A Musical Odyssey.*

Bouchareb, Rachid (dir.). 2001. *Little Senegal.*

Brierre, Jean F. 1980. 'Un noël pour Gorée'. In *Un noël pour Gorée.* Paris: Silex: 13–16.

Carrillo, Karen Juanita. 2003. 'Reparations Movement Looks to Gain from Bush's Goree Island Slip'. *New York Amsterdam News* 17–23 July: 2.

Chrétien, Jean-Pierre (ed.). 2008. *L'Afrique de Sarkozy: un déni de l'histoire.* Paris: Karthala.

Davidson, Michael. 2008. *Concerto for the Left Hand: Disability and the Defamiliar Body.* Ann Arbor: University of Michigan Press.

Davis, Olga Idriss. 1997. 'The Door of No Return: Reclaiming the Past through the Rhetoric of Pilgrimage'. *Western Journal of Black Studies* 21.3: 156–61.

Delcourt, Jean. 1982. *La Turbulente Histoire de Gorée*. Dakar: Editions Clairafrique.

de Roux, Emmanuel. 1996. 'Le mythe de la Maison des esclaves qui résiste à la réalité'. *Le Monde* 27 December.

Ebron, Paulla A. 1999. 'Tourists as Pilgrims: Commercial Fashioning of Transatlantic Politics'. *American Ethnologist* 26.4: 910–32.

Frith, Nicola. 2015. 'Saving the Republic: State Nostalgia and Slavery Reparations in Media and Political Discourses'. *Modern & Contemporary France*, 23: 213–32. Available at http://www.tandfonline.com/doi/pdf/10.1080/09639489.2015.1006124 (consulted on 8 April 2015).

Gassama, Makhily (ed.). 2008. *L'Afrique répond à Sarkozy: contre le discours de Dakar*. Paris: Philippe Rey.

Holassey, Georges. 2010. 'Gorée: les esclaves y pleurent encore'. In *Gorée: les esclaves y pleurent encore*. Le Coudray: Editions Le Mono: 7–18.

Johnson, Walter. 2007. 'Slavery, Reparations and the Mythic March of Freedom'. *Raritan* 27.2: 4–67.

Katchka, Kinsey A. 2004. 'Re-siting Slavery at the Gorée-Almadies Memorial and Museum'. *Museum Anthropology* 27.1–2: 3–12.

Konaré, Adame Ba (ed.). 2008. *Petit précis de remise à niveau sur l'histoire africaine à l'usage du president Sarkozy*. Paris: La Découverte.

Lowry, Malcolm. 2005 [1933]. *Ultramarine*. New York: Overlook Press.

Mambety, Djibril Diop (dir.). 1992. *Hyènes*.

Mauny, Raymond. 1954. *Guide de Gorée*. Dakar: IFAN.

Mbow, Amadou Mahtar. 1980. 'For the Safeguarding of the Island of Gorée'. In *Gorée: Island of Memories*. Paris: UNESCO: 1–14.

Medhurst, Martin J. 2010. 'George W. Bush at Goree Island: American Slavery and the Rhetoric of Redemption'. *Quarterly Journal of Speech* 96.3: 257–77.

Nadelhaft, Jerome. 1966. 'The Somersett Case and Slavery: Myth, Reality and Repercussions'. *Journal of Negro History* 51.3: 193–208.

Ndiaye, Boubacar Joseph. N.d. *The Slave-House of Gorée-Island*. Gorée: Maison des Esclaves.

Ndiaye, Joseph. 2006. *Il fut un jour à Gorée: l'esclavage raconté à nos enfants*. Neuilly-sur-Seine: M. Lafon.

Omolu, Gideon Prinsler. 2004. *Deux Gorée, une île*. Paris: L'Harmattan.

Ralph, Michael. 2007. '"Crimes of History": Senegalese Soccer and the Forensics of Slavery'. *Souls: A Critical Journal of Black Politics, Cultures and Society* 9.3: 193–222.

Renaudeau, Michel (dir.). 1996. *Les Caprices d'un Fleuve*.

Ryan, Chris. 2005. 'Dark Tourism: An Introduction'. In Chris Ryan, Stephen Page and Michelle Aicken (eds), *Taking Tourism to the Limits: Issues, Concepts and Managerial Perspectives*. Amsterdam; San Diego, CA; Oxford: Elsevier: 187–90.

Seck, Ibrahima. 2009. 'Esclavage et traite des esclaves dans les manuels de l'enseignement secondaire du Sénégal: des programmes de domestication coloniale aux programmes dits d'enracinement et d'ouverture'. *Historiens-Géographes du Sénégal* 8: 69–78.

Sepinwall, Alyssa. 2011. 'Classroom Classics: *Les Caprices d'un fleuve* and *Burn!*'. *Fiction and Film for French Historians: A Cultural Bulletin* 3. Available at http://h-france.net/fffh/classics/les-caprices-dun-fleuve/ (consulted on 2 October 2014).

Thiam, Alassane. 1980. 'Gorée – The Museum Island: Creation of a History Museum'. *Museum International* 32: 119–29.

Thiaw, Ibrahima. 2008. 'Every House Has a Story: The Archaeology of Gorée Island, Sénégal'. In Livio Sansone, Elisée Soumonni and Boubacar Barry (eds), *Africa, Brazil and the Construction of Trans-Atlantic Black Identities*. Trenton, NJ: Africa World Press: 45–62.

Thioub, Ibrahima, and Hamady Bocoum. 1997. 'Gorée et les mémoires de la Traite atlantique'. In Djibril Samb (ed.), *Gorée et l'esclavage, Actes du Séminaire sur Gorée dans la traite atlantique: mythes et réalités*. Dakar: IFAN-CAD: 199–218.

Tillet, Salamishah. 2009. 'In the Shadow of the Castle: (Trans)Nationalism, African American Tourism, and Gorée Island'. *Research in African Literatures* 40.4: 122–41.

Trouillot, Michel-Rolph. 2000. 'Abortive Rituals: Historical Apologies in the Global Era'. *Interventions: International Journal of Postcolonial Studies* 2.2: 171–86.

Truffaut, François (dir.). 1975. *L'Histoire d'Adèle H.*

Tshibanda, Pie. 2007. *Rendez-vous sur l'île de Gorée*. Brussels: Le Grand Miroir.

UNESCO. 1980. *Gorée: Island of Memories*. Paris: UNESCO.

Vivian, Bradford. 2012. 'The Paradox of Regret: Remembering and Forgetting the History of Slavery in George W. Bush's Gorée Island Address'. *History & Memory* 24.1: 5–38.

Wagnier, Régis (dir.). 1992. *Indochine*.

Wieder, Thomas. 2012. 'Couacs entre l'Elysée et Matignon sur les traites négrières'. *Le Monde* 14 October.

Multiple Memories: Slavery and Indenture in Mauritian Literature in French

Srilata Ravi

The history of Mauritius, an island with no indigenous populations, is the history of sequential colonialisms and successive immigrations. The Portuguese are credited with the discovery of Mauritius in the early sixteenth century, but they showed little interest in colonizing the island. The Dutch came later, but were unsuccessful in their efforts to found a colony. After their withdrawal in 1710, French colonists, adventurers and merchants transformed the island into a prosperous and flourishing sugarcane-producing colony with the help of slaves who came mainly from Madagascar and East Africa (Addison and Hazareesingh, 1999: 25). General Decaen's capitulation in 1810 transformed the island into a British-administered colony where the French, as plantation owners, maintained their economic status and cultural presence by continuing linguistic and religious practices. When slavery was abolished in 1835, slaves constituted over two-thirds of the entire population of Mauritius. After abolition, the British brought in indentured immigrants from India to work on the plantations. The Franco-Mauritian plantocracy's demand for labour was so important that by 1911 the island's demography had completely changed – from a Creole island it was transformed into a Hindu-dominated plantation society (Addison and Hazareesingh, 1999; Miles, 1999; Vaughan, 2005). Political independence in 1968 established the Hindu-Mauritian majority (almost 52% of the total island population) as the ruling elite, effectively marginalizing mixed-race Creoles and descendants of African slaves.

Even if the island has no 'natural' founding memory by way of indigenous populations, a double colonial heritage and successive free and forced migrations from Africa and Asia have generated complex memorial registers that shape Mauritian identities in the present. According to the Mauritian Constitution (1968), the population of Mauritius includes a Hindu community, a Muslim community and a Sino-Mauritian community. Anyone who does not appear to belong to one of these communities is regarded as belonging to what the Constitution terms the 'General Population', which effectively includes Europeans and mixed-race and African Creoles, who are for the most part Catholics (Miles, 1999).

As reference to a shared past, memory reassures the members of a society of their collective identity and supplies them with an historical consciousness. In Mauritius, the notion of a shared past is difficult to forge. Boudet and Peghini (2008: 13–36) distinguish three different memorial registers that define Mauritian pasts and which correspond to ethnic distinctiveness in the present: the memory of colonization as the foundation with which Franco-Mauritians and the lighter skinned members of the mixed-race bourgeoisie identify themselves; the memory of slavery as the foundation to which Afro-Creoles (descendants of African slaves) relate; and the memory of indenture as a point of origin with which the Mauritians of Indian origin identify.[1] This fragmentation of foundational memories produces fractured narratives of the nation that enter into conflict with a collective memory of colonial domination on the island. Importantly, this has led to an ethnicization of memory and the realization that access to memory in Mauritius is unequally spread between different ethnic groups. For example, unlike Indo-Hindu Mauritians, African Creoles are descendants of slaves, whose connections with their countries of origin had been brutally severed, meaning that they cannot claim direct diasporic links. In terms of commemoration in the present, plural and unevenly available memorial registers have led to the establishment of opposing processes of memorialization. Thus, Franco-Mauritians, who see themselves historically as the first creators of a founding memory, have tried to rewrite the past and become a part of the national story by erasing the more exploitative aspects of colonial history. For example, the Mauritius sugar museum, L'aventure du sucre, located in the former Beau Plan sugar factory, glorifies the island's plantation legacy. The construction of a national narrative around the sugar industry involving European colonialism

[1] Boudet and Peghini are quick to add, however, that this division cannot be categorical since not all Muslims of Indian origin identify themselves with indenture (some of their ancestors had arrived as traders), and the arrival of Sino-Mauritians relates to both slave and indenture histories (2008: 15).

overrides the horrors of slavery and the trauma of indenture. Simultaneously, Hindus use their political dominance within the state's infrastructure to exploit the symbolic power generated by the collective memory of slavery and indenture. Meanwhile, Afro-Creoles, uncomfortable with their imposed compartmentalization within the 'General Population' and marginalized as a minority ethnic group, seek to rewrite and re-appropriate the memory of slavery to forge their separate identity within the nation, since they have no 'homeland' to refer back to (Boudet and Peghini, 2008).

State policy on multiculturalism in Mauritius is based on what Paul Ricœur would call 'manipulated memory' or 'instrumentalized memory' (2004: 69), being 'the mobilization of memory in the service of the quest, the appeal, the demand for identity' (2004: 81). Ricœur asserts that the manipulation of memory involves abuses of both remembering and forgetting. As a result, the construction of identity and the public expression of this identity, both of which call for the mobilization of memory, become problematic exercises (Ricœur, 2004: 448). The recent consecration of public memorials at Le Morne and at the Aapravasi Ghat (Ravi, 2010b) illustrates how the Mauritian state's pluralist policies on managing multiculturalism rely on such processes of remembering and forgetting, which invariably result in reinforcing Hindu and Creole divisions through a public separation of the histories of indenture and slavery. In the making of a national story, collective memory preserves, selects, eliminates and invents. The Mauritian policy of encouraging the formation of links to different diasporic groups in order to manage ethnicity (Eriksen, 1994) effectively transforms memory-making into a political and strategic business, and leads to interethnic divisiveness in the present. On the one hand, an affirmative preservation of memory tends to become a form of tyrannical nostalgia (as in the case of the postcolonial Hindu-dominated bureaucracy) or colonial reminiscing (as in the case of the sugar museum at Beau Plan). On the other hand, memory as suffering can lead to marginalization and amnesia (as in the case of Creole alienation, which is also known as *Creole malaise*).

Like many forms of memory preservation – including museums, memorials, rituals, symbols and ceremonies – literature is also a medium of remembrance. However, in its double capacity as object of remembrance and medium for observing the production of cultural memory it can play an important role in problematizing versions of the past. What is of central interest to this chapter is how literature, as a form of cultural memory, remembers and/or forgets Mauritian histories of slavery and indenture in ways that are different from the other forms of public memorialization listed above. It questions whether literature contributes to a process of constructive remembering and/or forgetting, or whether it reinforces an ethnicization of the past in the present. In other words, in the course of remembering certain histories of migration, do these literary memorials forget the histories of other forms of migration?

Since I will be investigating literature in the French language – which is in itself a cultural memorial to French colonization – it is important to note that French language in Mauritius remains the dominant literary and cultural practice (Jean-François and Kee Mew, 2012), even if English is the official medium of education chosen for its perceived political neutrality (Aumeerally, 2005). In an effort to overcome ethno-religious divisions, which have arisen as a direct consequence of Mauritian policies encouraging diasporic linkages, activists have fought to institutionalize Mauritian Creole as a national language. However, in doing so, they have produced contrasting versions of Mauritian linguistic nationalisms. In one version, the Creole language is ethnicized by highlighting the contribution made by French colonialism and links to the Francophone world, whilst in another version, Mauritian Creole is nationalized in opposition to what is often perceived as the hegemony of French linguistic and cultural traditions (Eisenlohr, 2007).[2] Writing in the French language, especially in the context of literary memorialization, forces us to rethink questions that link language, identity and memory in the present of Mauritian modernity.[3]

The present study covers the Mauritian literary landscape from the 1960s to the present and includes Marcelle Lagesse, Ananda Devi, Nathacha Appanah, Barlen Pyamootoo and Amal Sewtohul. It exposes the multiple ways in which literature as a locus of mediation between history and memory remembers Mauritius's slave and indentured pasts in conjunction with the island's *aventure du sucre*. It questions whether literature contributes to a process of constructive remembering and/or forgetting, or whether it reinforces an ethnicization or 'modularization'[4] of the past in the present.

Does literary memorialization in French challenge the ethnicized memorial registers that have contributed to the communalization of Mauritian society? Does it 'modularize' memory, does it creolize memory or does it efface

[2] This perception is changing, especially amongst the more educated Hindu majority, as is illustrated by the growing number of internationally recognized Mauritian writers of Indo-Hindu origin.

[3] See Ravi (2015) for a more detailed analysis.

[4] Shipping containers are made to standard measurements and, as such, they provide modular elements that can be combined into larger structures. In this way, they bear a striking analogy to the multicultural idea of nation in Mauritius. As we will see, this analogy is exploited in an ingenious fashion by Amal Sewtohul.

'manipulated pasts' of free and forced labour? Can literature in French in Mauritius be read as a narrative of experimentation with memory-making? These are some of the questions that this chapter will address.

Sweetened Memories

Before the works of Marie-Thérèse Humbert and Ananda Devi appeared on the Mauritian literary landscape, Marcelle Lagesse had already made a name for herself as a woman writer of some acclaim. Her *La diligence s'éloigne à l'aube* (1958), a murder mystery set in the early nineteenth century, was followed by another historical novel, *Le vingt floréal au matin* (1960).[5] Written prior to independence, the re-publication in the 1990s of a novel whose thematic relevance exceeds its literary qualities is ample evidence to illustrate what Boudet and Peghini (2008) define as 'l'edulcoration de la mémoire coloniale' ['the sweetening of colonial memory'] – a process of commemoration that softens the harsher aspects of French colonization, in this case by showcasing feminine loyalties between a mistress and her slave.[6] Marcelle Lagesse's historical romance narrates the history of the Champelair family, French settlers on Île de France, through the perspective of Félicité Champelair, Creole matriarch of the plantation named Maison Blanche. The novel is an account spanning almost fifty years of her arduous experiences as a settler wife and mother, and is set during France's post-revolutionary naval struggle against the British in the war-torn Indian Ocean of 1798. Lagesse's heroine is 'une grande figure où bien des Mauriciennes se reconnaissent, auxquelles elles s'identifient par les qualités de cœur, le sens du dévouement, d'enracinement et de combativité' (Fanchin, 1993).[7] Félicité Champelair's life depicts the unrecognized role of French women in the making of the colony. During these turbulent times under the French revolutionary government on Île de France, it is clearly she who conducts and keeps strict control over the routine of everyday life both at home and on the estate. In fact, war and domesticity are an integral part of Félicité's life, reflecting that of the colony. Félicité herself lives through four of the major Anglo-French wars of the eighteenth century, including the Guerre de Succession d'Autriche (1740–46), the Guerre de Sept Ans (1756–63), the Guerre de l'indépendance américaine

5 All references will be quoted from the 1994 edition.

6 See A. Toussaint's Preface in Lagesse, 1994 (no page numbers).

7 Translation: 'a great personality in whom many Mauritian women recognize themselves, identifying with her kind-heartedness, sense of devotion, stability and fighting spirit'. This and all subsequent quotations were translated by the author of this article.

(1778–83) and the Guerres de la Révolution (1793–1802), all of which were played out in the Indian Ocean. While men like Bruni Champelair, Félicité's husband, were battling for honours on the high seas, women were fighting to save the island from epidemics, cyclones and locusts, thereby ensuring the success of the French colonizing mission. Alongside these brave women were the slaves, who also played an important role in the functioning of a colony whose position was being dictated by the exigencies of war. The novel's historical frame therefore becomes crucial because the family drama of a white Creole woman, Félicité Champelair, is set precisely at a time when the island is politically isolated, the Colonial Assembly in Mauritius having decided to resist the revolutionary government's decree to abolish slavery without compensation.

The narrative of the family of Rosélia, Félicité Champelair's slave, and that of Rosélia's children and grandchildren living in their *campements* on the plantation, unfolds at the same time as that of the Champelair family inside the Maison Blanche. The lives of the two families are interlinked. Félicité's slave is married to L'Intrépide, Bruni Champelair's slave, and they have founded a slave family on the plantation. This fictional backdrop notwithstanding, Félicité's story of settler romance, or the grand narrative of a Creole matriarch's self-empowerment on Île de France, not only pre-dates the story of indenture or 'coolie' romance as the foundational story of the island (Ravi, 2007), but also effaces the family drama of slavery. At one point, Félicité reveals her dependence on her loyal slave: 'J'aurai toujours besoin de toi, Rosélia et tu le sais bien [...] Que ferais-je sans toi?' (83).[8] However, such declarations are few and far between and Lagesse's textual remembering thus fails to fully recognize both the extent of Félicité's reliance on Rosélia and the significance of the link between slavery and domesticity. Even if domesticity on the Maison Blanche plantation involves the participation of the slaves in the daily agricultural, commercial and household routines, Lagesse's literary memorial to French colonialism in Mauritius never fully acknowledges their presence. When Félicité says, 'il faudra que je m'en occupe ... seule' (in reference to the estate or the plantation) ['I must look after this ... alone'] (115), she excludes the slaves who form the backbone of this enterprise, yet ironically includes the absent patriarch. In the eyes of Félicité, slavery is not an economic necessity, but a benevolent institution that rewards loyal service. Textual commemoration of a Mauritian past edifies kindness towards slaves at a time when the island was most renowned for its cruelty towards them (see Allen, 2005: 26). Félicité proudly recalls

[8] Translation: 'I will always need you, Rosélia, and you know it well [...] What would I do without you?'

that, since the purchase of the Maison Blanche property, they had not bought any more slaves, but had only kept those slaves that came with them, including Rosélia, L'Intrépide and some ten others. Félicité remembers with pride that the slaves, their children and grandchildren belonged as a family to the owners (37–38) and none of the members had ever been sold. She also notes that all the children born on the property were baptized and that, even if the slaves were strong believers in the traditions of 'la Grande Terre', they were prepared to make a transition to the culture of their masters.

In reality, as scholars have noted, the slave institution allowed little room for the slaves to develop their own diverse customs and culture. In their transition from Africans of heterogeneous ethnic origins to slaves they were stripped almost completely of their cultural identity (Vaughan, 2005: 91–122; Alpers, 2001: 117–56). Even if Félicité prides herself on her civilizing mission's success, the fact of the matter is that Rosélia and L'Intrépide had no cultural identity except that of being agents of servility and devotion to their colonial masters. Even slave children were perceived in terms of their eventual contribution to everyday progress on the *domaine*: 'A mesure que nous étendions nos activités, les enfants de nos gens en grandissant suffisaient à la besogne' (38).[9] Furthermore, Félicité's narrative does not include accounts of slave–master intimacy. As Vaughan points out, slave mothers often nursed Creole children (Vaughan, 2005: 123–51), and it is likely that Félicité herself relied on a slave mother to nurse her three children while she was devoting herself to 'manly' duties, like managing the estate, dealing with local colonial agents and overseeing slave labour on the plantations. Rosélia is always conscious of her social limits as a bonded slave. Moments of shared history permit Rosélia to take certain trivial liberties, like cautioning her mistress against working too hard or taking on too many responsibilities at her age (83), but she is never given the same kind of attention that Félicité gives Quettehou, her French *Intendant*. Félicité opts to remain the benevolent mistress of 'des humbles' ['humble slaves'] (85), and therefore never considers them her equal.

Thanks to the superficial complicity between Rosélia, L'Intrépide and their overtly benevolent mistress, Félicité, the text acts as an apology for slavery. But Félicité's Christian conscience cannot override the fact that, as slave owners, settlers like herself did have the 'right of life and death' over their slave possessions: 'Quarante années de patience avaient réussi à éveiller chez ces noirs une sorte de reconnaissance et de fidélité envers ceux qui leur avaient prouvé qu'un maître n'était pas nécessairement quelqu'un

[9] Translation: 'As and when we expanded our activities, the children of our slaves provided the labour as they grew older.'

prêt à punir et ayant droit de vie et de mort' (38).[10] In this way, Marcelle Lagesse's novel, like the sugarcane museum in Beau Plan, mitigates the past by obliterating the fact that the local slave regime in Mauritius was an oppressive one (Allen, 2005: 26). In doing so, it also modularizes French settler memories.

Unpromising Memories

Recent scholarship on forced and unforced labour in colonial Mauritius has revised traditional notions of continuities between slavery and indenture. In her work on the history of indentured labour in Mauritius, Marina Carter notes that the reasons for indentured emigration were highly complex and that the composition of immigrant populations depended on several factors:

> Individual explanations for migration reveal an intriguing blend of economic necessity, chance encounters, trickery, and traditions of labour mobility in defining causative factors. However these decisions or circumstances cannot be considered in isolation from the broader defining features of indentured migration. The characteristics of overseas Indian populations depended on the location and networks of recruiters, the level of influence of returnees in the targeting of specific villages, externally imposed restrictions on migration of certain caste or ethnic groups, and gender requirements, to name only some. (Carter, 1996: 41)

Such historical realities notwithstanding, the Indo-Hindu Mauritian narrative of nation homogenizes the indenture narrative to provide an emancipatory reading of 'coolie' history as a foundational romance of nationhood (Ravi, 2010b). Nathacha Appanah's *Les rochers de Poudre d'Or* (2003) reads indenture against the grain of this political interpretation. The history of *marronage* as resistance in the Indian Ocean islands of Mauritius and Réunion is associated primarily with the slave populations. While the Aapravasi Ghat memorial is a reminder of the dreaded 'Kala Pani' ['Black Waters'] crossing for Hindus,[11] Le Morne recalls acts of slave *marronage* and has become the memorial territory of the Creole community. Appanah's novel pluralizes the memories of indenture by alluding to

---

[10] Translation: 'Forty years of patience had finally opened the minds of the slaves to a kind of gratitude and loyalty towards those who had proved to them that a master was not necessarily someone who punishes or who has the right of life and death over them.'

[11] In the context of the colonial history of indenture, 'Kala Pani' refers to the Hindu labourers' fear of losing their caste if they crossed the seas.

indenture vagrancy, being another form of *marronage* that runs counter to the ethnicized commemorative symbolism of slave *marronage* in the present. Furthermore, in line with Marina Carter's claims (1996), Appanah's literary memorial focuses on the diverse origins – geographical, social and cultural – of the embarking Indians and their varied reasons for leaving their homes. It reveals that it was not just colonial exploitation, but also poverty, caste and gender discrimination that drove thousands of Indians to undertake the 'Kala Pani' crossing. Exploitative recruiters and success stories of returning 'coolies' also contributed to mass emigration. *Les rochers de Poudre d'Or* recounts the narratives of four different protagonists, each with individual stories to tell. There is Badri, the village simpleton, who after losing stolen money in a game of cards, flees the wrath of his father and heads for Calcutta in the hope of finding work as a 'coolie' overseas. Unknowingly, the simpleton walks straight into the trap laid out by the clever and unscrupulous *maistris* (recruiting agents), who benefit from the misery of their compatriots in order to collect labour for the colonies. This is how Badri finds himself duped into signing a contract for five years as a 'coolie aux champs' ['field labourer']. Then there is the story of Chotty Lal, a *kamiati*, labourer bonded to the *zamindar* ['landlord'] of Ranigunj as repayment for debts incurred by his father. In order to avoid his miserable fate as a bonded worker, Chotty Lal follows *maistry* Boodhoo Khan to Calcutta in search of work in 'Merich' ['Mauritius'] (28). There is also Vythee, who, like Badri and Chotty Lal in the north of India, flees poverty and his famine-stricken village in the south of India to join his brother in Mauritius. Finally, there is Ganga, a widowed princess who flees her husband's funeral pyre by boarding a ship bound for Mauritius, which provides her with an escape from death and the promise of a new start. The novel exposes the huge gap between the imagined voyage and the reality of the departure – the dirty and crowded departure depots, the inhumanity of the agents and the indifference of the British officers. After following the protagonists in their oceanic crossing, the novel narrates their hardships upon their arrival on the island. The unfortunate Chotty Lal flees the *zamindar*, only to die on board the ship and be buried at sea. Vythee realizes that the dream of being reunited with his brother may not be fulfilled. Princess Ganga, who has fled the cruel tradition of widow burning, is reduced to doing menial tasks and realizes that she cannot avoid the sexual advances of the plantation owner. Whereas the naive and frightened Badri, appalled by conditions on the plantation, runs away, only to be betrayed by a group of liberated African slaves.

In contrast to these individual narratives, nationalist discourse in Mauritius has tended to reinforce 'coolie' heroism and to romanticize the struggle of the indenture diaspora by privileging stories of sacrifice and resettlement over tales of trauma and dislocation. Attachment to ancestral traditions and beliefs was perceived as playing a crucial role in this success story. While Appanah's novel demystifies this 'coolie romance', it also calls into question the very basis on which the Mauritian policy of diasporic links has been constructed. In a poignant confrontation between a poor but free African Creole and a runaway contract labourer from India, the African asks: 'Hé, couillon! Nous n'avions pas de contrat, nous! [...] Sans racines, nous sommes un peuple sans racines mais la mer nous appartient. La lumière nous appartient' (214–15).[12] The symbolism of 'des sacs avec plein de trucs inutiles dedans' ['bags filled with plenty of useless stuff'] (214) from elsewhere is devalued, while the here and now of the island geography is acknowledged. William Miles points out that despite their marginalized status and their ancestors' forced exodus to Mauritius, the Creoles still regard themselves as the only genuine Mauritians:

> Unlike Hindus whose culture remains strongly Indian, Muslims whose anchor is world Islam, Chinese who emigrate according to opportunity, and Franco-Mauritians whose cultural reference of course, is France, the Creoles' attachment to their land of birth is complete and unequivocal. (1999: 219)

Appanah's literary cenotaph subverts romanticizing versions of an indentured past and makes an ironic reference to another memorial in the village of Poudre d'Or: the statue that commemorates the island's most infamous wreckage, the *Saint-Géran* in 1744. The tragic fate of the passengers of the shipwrecked *Saint-Géran* was the inspiration for Bernardin de Saint-Pierre's 1788 novel, *Paul et Virginie*. The beach at Poudre d'Or is where Paul finds the body of his beloved Virginie, who was travelling back from France on the ill-fated *Saint-Géran*. It has been argued that Bernardin de Saint-Pierre's novel is the foundational matrix that forms both a nostalgic and a critical basis for Mauritian literature in French. This subtle cross-referencing in Appanah's narrative shows that while it directly and indirectly refers to Mauritian's multiple histories of settlement, it is not a modularized or ethnicized memorial to the survivors of colonial exploitation. Rather, it presents the tragedy of the human condition, of the enormous gap between dream and reality, between desire and fulfilment, and between the vagaries of life and the inevitability of death. While the novel does not seek to creolize memories of slavery and indenture, it nonetheless uncovers the

[12] Translation: 'Hey, dolt! We people do not have a contract! [...] Without roots, we are a people without roots, but the sea belongs to us. The sky belongs to us.'

plurality of an indentured past to reveal unpromising memories so that remembering these traumatic moments of the island's indenture history in the present can be transformed into a constructive exercise in shared humanity.

Creolized Memories

Appanah's narrative not only recognizes that the presence of slaves pre-dates the arrival of Indo-Mauritians on the island, but also hints at the fact that the African Creoles are probably the only 'genuine' Mauritians, since their sole point of reference is the island. In this respect, *Les rochers de Poudre d'Or* does not seek to creolize Mauritian pasts, but suggests a common story of suffering without conflating the histories of slavery and indenture. In contrast, Ananda Devi's modernist retelling of the island's colonial history in *Pagli* (2001) involves a fictional creolization of indenture and slavery articulated in the form of an interethnic relationship.[13] The novel is centred on the life of a young Hindu woman, Daya, raped at the age of thirteen by her cousin and then married off to him when she is older. Rejecting submission to such indignation, she revolts by refusing to conform to the image of a dutiful wife and submissive daughter-in-law when she arrives in Terre Rouge as a new bride. Through her friendship with a local prostitute, Mitsy, she meets and falls in love with Zil, a Creole fisherman. Her social and sexual transgressions transform her into 'Pagli', or the mad one. The textual remembering of the island's violent past of labour exploitation is reflected in the intertwined experience of exclusion and discrimination experienced by Daya (who is a descendant of Hindu indentured labourers) and her lover, Zil (who is a descendant of African slaves). When their relationship is discovered by the community, Pagli is punished by her family, locked up in a hen coop and left out in the cold. Violence breaks out between the two communities (Hindu and Creole) and the entire village is torn apart by ethnic riots, before being devastated by a cyclone that simultaneously strikes Terre Rouge.

[13] In *L'Arbre-Fouet* (1997), Devi organizes her account of remembering indenture and slave histories around the 'arbre-fouet' ['whipping tree'], a living testimony to the violence of Hindu patriarchy (whose origin is located in indentured immigration) and slave oppression (whose origin is located in colonialism). The tree stands for the creolized histories of suffering. During colonial times, disobedient and runaway slaves were tied to the 'arbre-fouet' and flogged. Later, Hindu girls and women who defied patriarchal conventions of chastity and fidelity were also tied to this tree and whipped.

Devi's *Pagli,* which is a mixture of genres (prose and poetry), of textures (real and imagined) and of languages (Creole and French), illustrates Devi's literary project of creolizing memory. As such, her text seeks to oppose the national project of ethnicizing memory described earlier. The creolized narrative of the past is executed in multiple temporalities – the slave and indenture time of Terre Rouge, Daya's lived time of transgression and social exclusion, and the imagined time she spends with her lover, Zil. As the text moves rapidly between the traumatic memories of sexual and domestic violence inflicted on Daya/Pagli and the fragmented images of forbidden love-making with Zil, it transforms Daya's anamnesis (where she recalls her love for Zil on the one hand, and recalls the island's history of violence on the other) into 'constructive amnesia', or what Paul Ricœur terms a 'reserve' of forgetting (2004: 448). Ricœur draws our attention to the fact that forgetting is directly implied in the process of narrative configuration. He considers forgetting as a 'memorial trace', which gives a positive meaning to the notion of forgetting. By reading forgetting as a 'trace', we are able to understand the idea of the past as *having-been* and not as a past that is *being no longer* (Ricœur, 2004: 443). Ricœur believes that 'memorial traces' transform forgetting into a past that preserves (2004: 442). In Devi's fictionalization of the island's violent history, Pagli and Zil embody 'the memorial traces' of oppression and brutality of the Mauritian past, and consequently become emblematic of the vulnerability of their historical condition (see Ricœur, 2004: 412). In Terre Rouge, where both slaves and indentured labourers have suffered under a colonizing regime, the postcolonial ethnicization of memory has given rise to more bloodshed. As Daya/Pagli watches the racial hatred that explodes around her, she appeals to the descendants of the different ethnic groups to remember and accept common histories of sacrifice, instead of separating them in the present (29). Through an astucious mixing of real and imagined (narratively justified as the ramblings of a feverish Pagli, who has been incarcerated and left to die in a hen cage), Ananda Devi interweaves past and present, Creole and Hindu, and histories of slavery and indenture in a creolized narrative of remembering that subverts the multiple memorial registers exploited by politicians and opportunists from different ethnic groups on the island. While the image of 'Pagli in a cage' suggests the idea of an island-prison, the imagined and forbidden interracial relationship between Daya and Zil stands as the embodiment of this creolization of 'coolie' and Creole memories, which will ultimately liberate Daya from both Hindu patriarchy and island communalism.

In Daya's narrative, Zil does not come back to save her. He remains, nonetheless, engraved in her mind as the source of her 'madness' and her revolt. The persistence of this trace is an acknowledgement that Daya and the reader accept the past as a form of creative forgetting, or a 'having been' that allows healing in the present. By showing remembering as 'un interminable balbutiement' ['an endless stammering'] (37), *Pagli* destabilizes the manipulated memories of slavery and indenture to create a creolized narrative of constructive forgetting.[14]

Meaningless Memories

While the narratives analysed so far participate in a literary memorialization of forgotten pasts and/or suggest alternative readings of the island's histories, Pyamootoo's minimalist novel *Bénarès* (1999) questions the very significance of memory-making in the present. *Bénarès* is the story of a once prosperous Mauritian village of the same name, now desolate since the sugarcane mill shut down in the 1970s as part of the young nation's plan for economic diversification. The refurbished chimney, which has been transformed into a village landmark, signals the death of an era and the birth of a modern globalized Mauritius. The villagers, however, are deprived of their source of livelihood, most of them having been forced to look for odd jobs while the village has become 'une île à lui seul, hors du monde' ['an island unto itself, existing beyond the world'] (47). The village of Bénarès is home to Mayi, a small-time fisherman, Jimi, who does odd jobs to support himself, and the narrator, who is an apprentice mechanic. The plot's principal action is the trip to Port Louis undertaken by Jimi, the narrator and Mayi, who has won some money at cards and wishes to spend it on a night of sexual pleasure. Firstly, the narrative reduces the capital city of Port Louis, gateway to the island's global ambitions, to a place of illicit gratification. More importantly, by juxtaposing tropes of absence and immobility against the chronotrope of the road journey, the author questions the connections between past and present, and history and memory, by deliberately effacing the significance of the practice of memory itself.[15]

The text systematically subverts the road as a conventional metaphor for movement, connection and progress. It is described as ruined and derelict, and therefore as not serving any purpose. Instead, images of immobility, silence and inescapability – reinforced in the narrative by the phrase 'c'est trop loin Bénarès' ['It is too far away, Bénarès'] (13) – dominate the description of the landscape. As an 'absent' metaphor of the link between past and present, the journey questions the act of memory-making and its manipulating tendencies. The road, which is meant to connect the Mauritian

[14] See Ravi (2013) for a comparative study of *Pagli* and *L'Arbre-Fouet*.

[15] See Ravi (2010a) for a comparative study of the novel and its film adaptation.

heartland to the capital of Port Louis – a portal to the island's global modernity – is represented as an isolated, and isolating, deserted path that takes the traveller through 'une plaine étendue, sans relief' ['an endlessly flat stretch of landscape'] (88). People on the streets are represented as 'des silhouettes effilées' ['shadowy figures'] (62) and passers-by are 'indifferents à tout' ['indifferent to everything'] (57). The sense of abandonment outside on the road and the sentiment of disaffection amongst the passengers in the van create a complete sense of dislocation from the 'here and now' of modern Mauritius. The conversation of the young people in the vehicle, described as 'un bourdonnement délicat, dénué de sens' ['a delicate buzz devoid of any significance'] (63), reinforces this idea. Only Jimi the chauffeur seems to have any nostalgic connection with a historical Mauritian identity, recollecting the time when the sugarcane mill was still in operation. In its current oversized form, 'grotesque dans sa démesure' ['grotesque in its immoderation'] (43), the chimney of the sugarcane factory, just like the road to Port Louis, is nothing more than a dead link between the past and the present. Referred to as a 'monument aux morts' ['monument to the dead'] (43), it obliterates its own historical symbolism. The narrative's accent on the immediate (the physical sensation of being on the road), the lack of causal links between dialogues (the complete absence of social purpose in the conversations) and the erasure of any form of affectivity (the lack of emotional references holding the narrative together) deny the narrative any closure and hence any commemorative readings of the nation as a unified signifier of belonging in the collective imaginary. In the same vein, the lifeless conversation about the Indian city of Bénarès – a city that mythifies the sacred homeland for the descendants of Hindu indentured labourers in Mauritius – and the listless evocation of the old people waiting to die on the banks of the Ganges evoke the futility of sharing memorial links with this diasporic past. The unwillingness of the van's passengers to engage with the reality of Mauritius's indentured past – the link between Mauritius and India is 'trop vieux pour qu'on se souvienne tout à fait' ['too old to be clearly remembered'] (79) – and the invented nature of the reference itself (the narrator invents a tale about a journey to Bénarès in India for the sake of starting a conversation) destabilizes all links between memory and identity. If Devi's *Pagli,* which is effected in multiple temporalities, creolizes the memories of the past in order to break ethnic distinctiveness in the present, Pyamootoo's minimalist narrative freezes time and blocks memory altogether in an empathetic experience of collective amnesia. The narrative ends with the return to the interior of the island and to the village of Bénarès, a hollow reminder of an indentured past, which has no link to the present of the narration. What I am suggesting here is that in trying not to fall into the trap of ethnic distinctiveness, as imposed by the Mauritian model of multiculturalism, which confines ethnic identities within identifiable and fixed modules, in *Bénarès*, Pyamootoo, through an act of textual indifference to a Hindu symbol, paradoxically obliterates all references to the island's slave past. Through its anti-memorial register, the text may have blocked out the memory of indenture, but in writing slavery out completely, it re-'modularizes' memory through a process of double erasure.

Container Memories

It seems that even when literature seeks to remember differently, or even not remember at all, it can still end up 'modularizing' memory – that is, breaking it up into modular or containable registers. In a bid to find a solution for the problem of *Creole malaise* or Creole alienation in Mauritius, William Miles suggests that the Creoles take a step back to recreate 'a unifying genesis and identity with an uncomplicated African essence' (1999: 228). Reinforcing memorial modularization of Creole Africanity only echoes the imposed compartmentalization of Indo-Mauritianness and invented modularization of Franco-Mauritianness. Such memorial manipulations exclude other less visible cases. Amal Sewtohul's *Made in Mauritius* (2012) reminds us that the act of remembering one foundational story of nation is inevitably bound up with the forgetting of other foundational narratives of forced and free mobilities. The story of Chinese migrations to the island of Mauritius has yet to be configured within the multiple memorial 'modules' of national consciousness, as *Made in Mauritius* shows. Through the ingenious use of the metaphor of a freight container moving Chinese goods (and people), Sewtohul subverts the idea that memory can be separated using ethnicity as a defining boundary. *Made in Mauritius* is a story of 'humble fugitifs, partout dans le monde, entrant par la petite porte dans le monde des riches' (20).[16] We will see in the concluding section how the novel *Made in Mauritius* provides a more liberating interpretation of the shipping container.

Laval, the novel's protagonist, is born on board a container ship, which brings his Chinese parents to Mauritius from Hong Kong. The offloaded container becomes an extension of the family shack in Port Louis, a warehouse for unsold goods and abandoned family objects, and at one point a platform for a political rally. After completing his secondary education in Mauritius, Laval leaves for Australia on a scholarship to study art in Adelaide with the container, now transformed into a piece of artwork. History repeats itself in strange ways, and it is now Laval's turn to use his parents'

16 Translation: 'humble fugitives all over the world, entering the world of rich people through the back door'.

container to smuggle his friend Feisal into Australia. The Chinese 'module' reconfigures itself to become a 'trans-Mauritian' container. Once in Adelaide, the container becomes an illegal bar and public art exhibit until such time as Ayesha, Laval's childhood sweetheart, who is studying law in Adelaide, warns them of the consequences of their unlawful situation. Leaving Laval behind, Feisal appropriates the container, now transformed into 'an illegal immigrant module', and disappears into the Australian outback, where it becomes part of a commune of marginalized people from all over the world. Several years later a cynical Laval, an art teacher in a school for the underprivileged, divorced from Ayesha and estranged from his son, sets out to look for Feisal accompanied by Frances, his friend. After a long trek, during which Laval recollects his life story to Frances, he eventually discovers his friend and 'comes home' to his container. Laval, 'à la fois libre et immensément seul' ['all at once free and terribly alone'] (260), dies in his mobile and transposable 'memory module' – his 'capsule aux murs transparents' ['capsule with transparent walls'], which can 'se déplacer dans l'espace et dans le temps' ['move through space and time'] (173). The module may have confined his parents to a fixed Sino-Mauritian identity in Mauritius, but its transparent walls and unhindered mobility had allowed Laval to create his own memory far away from the place where it had first been offloaded, just as it would for Feisal.

Laval's memory, symbolized by the multi-functional and mobile container, resists all forms of ethnic determinism and challenges memory-making as a tool for boundary marking in the present. Bruno Jean-François notes that Sehtowul's text 'se débarrassera ainsi graduellement des repères historiques fixistes du passé pour s'ouvrir au monde' (Jean-François, 2012).[17] The concept of 'chain migrations' encapsulated in the image of the indefatigable container – 'cette boîte de métal' ['this metal box'] (260), or Laval's passport to a borderless identity – resists all manoeuvres to manipulate memory in a 'mobile' present. Kumari Issur (2012) notes that Sewtohul's novel 'nous installe dans la vision d'un temps transgénérationnel et d'un espace transnational et plaide pour une identité liée à la migration en chaîne'.[18]

As shown here, cultural memory produces a diversity of memorial forms. Literature remembers through narratives and, in terms of genre and textual conventions, through images and metaphors that reshape our views of the past. This chapter has shown that literary memorialization in

[17] Translation. 'will rid itself gradually of its deterministic historical references to the past in order to open itself up to the world'.

[18] Translation: 'presents us with a vision of transgenerational time and transnational space, and argues for an identity tied to chain migration'.

Mauritius challenges the ethnicized memorial registers that have contributed to the communalization of Mauritian society by mitigating, demystifying, creolizing and even deliberately effacing these manipulated pasts of free and forced labour in the postcolonial and post-national present of Mauritian modernity. It demonstrates that the story of Mauritian literature in French is in itself an experimental narrative of memory-making. Redemptive for a generation of authors like Marcelle Lagesse writing around the time when the island achieved independence, literary memorialization becomes an inventive exercise inspired by Euro-modernist aesthetics for Ananda Devi, whose towering presence in contemporary Mauritian writing since the 1990s almost overshadows the likes of Barlen Pyamootoo and Nathacha Appanah, who embrace the rules of literary minimalism to great effect in their anti-memorial narratives. Finally, representing a new crop of young writers, Amal Sewtohul, through the image of the 'homeless' container, turns the very act of memory-making on its head. *Made in Mauritius* offers a completely different perspective – Laval's *identité-conteneur* is 'home' to all and is home anywhere. It thus subverts the conventional idea of memory-making as an exercise that is tied to a single place and, more specifically, it breaks the rules of ethnic containment in Mauritius. The image of the container, 'made in Mauritius', as it moves through space and time, and shifts in function in its journey from Hong Kong to the Australian outback, foregrounds the production and significance of transgenerational and transnational memories. Perhaps Amal Sewtohul's novel can be seen, therefore, as the textual culmination of Mauritian writers' experimentation with memory-making.

Works Cited

Addison, John, and K. Hazareesingh. 1999 [1984]. *A New History of Mauritius*. Rose-Hill: Éditions de l'Océan Indien.

Allen, Richard. 2005. 'A Serious and Alarming Daily Evil: Marronage and Its Legacy in Mauritius and the Colonial Plantation World'. In Edward Alpers, Gwyn Campbell and Michael Salman (eds), *Slavery and Resistance in Africa and Asia*. London: Routledge: 20–36.

Alpers, Ed. 2001. 'Becoming Mozambique: Diaspora and Identity in Mauritius'. In Vijaya Teelock and Edward Alpers (eds), *History, Memory and Identity*. Port Louis: University of Mauritius: 117–56.

Appanah, Nathacha. 2003. *Les rochers de Poudre d'Or*. Paris: Gallimard.

Aumeerally, N. 2005. 'The Ambivalence of Postcolonial Mauritius: Policy versus Practice in Education: A Reading of Official and Popular Multiculturalism'. *International Journal of Cultural Policy* 11.3: 307–23.

Boudet, Catherine, and Julie Peghini. 2008. 'Les enjeux politiques de la mémoire du passé colonial à l'île Maurice'. *Transcontinentales* 6: 13–36. Available at http://transcontinentales.revues.org/397 (consulted on 16 November 2013).

Carter, Marina. 1996. *Voices of Indenture*. Leicester: Leicester University Press.

Devi, Ananda. 1997. *L'Arbre-Fouet*. Paris: L'Harmattan.

—. 2001. *Pagli*. Paris: Gallimard.

Eisenlohr, Patrick. 2007. 'Creole Publics: Language, Cultural Citizenship, and the Spread of the Nation in Mauritius'. *Comparative Studies in Society and History* 49.4: 968–96.

Eriksen, Thomas Hylland. 1994. 'Nationalism Mauritian Style: Cultural Unity and Ethnic Diversity'. *Comparative Studies in Society and History* 36.3: 549–74.

Fanchin, Gérard. 1993. 'La Littérature francophone de 1984 à nos jours'. *Notre Librairie* 114: 44–55.

Issur, Kumari. 2012. 'Nationalisme, transnationalisme et postnationalisme dans *Made in Mauritius* d'Amal Sewtohul'. In *Loxias-Colloque*. Proceedings of the conference 'D'une île du monde aux mondes de l'île: dynamiques littéraires et explorations critiques des écritures mauriciennes'. 23 July 2012. Université de Maurice. Available at http://revel.unice.fr/symposia/actel/index.html?id=392 (consulted on 14 November 2013).

Jean-François, E. B. 2012. 'De l'ethnicité populaire à l'ethnicité nomade: Amal Sewtohul ou la "fabrique" d'une nouvelle mauricianité'. In *Loxias-Colloque*. Proceedings of the conference 'D'une île du monde aux mondes de l'île: dynamiques littéraires et explorations critiques des écritures mauriciennes'. 23 July 2012. Université de Maurice. Available at revel.unice.fr/symposia/actel/index.html?id=411#bodyftn58 (consulted on 19 November 2013).

Jean-François, E. B., and Evelyn Kee Mew. 2012. 'Les auteurs de l'ombre du champ littéraire mauricien: entre critères de légitimation et stratégies de reconnaissance'. *Loxias* 37 (Arts et Littératures des Mascareignes). Available at http://revel.unice.fr/loxias/index.html?id=6983 (consulted on 26 September 2013).

Lagesse, Marcelle. 1985 [1958]. *La diligence s'éloigne à l'aube*. Rose Hill: Éditions de l'Océan Indien.

—. 1994 [1960]. *Le vingt floréal au matin*. Rose-Hill: Éditions de l'Océan Indien.

Miles, William. 1999. 'The Créole Malaise in Mauritius'. *African Affairs* 98: 211–28.

Pyamootoo, Barlen. 1999. *Bénarès*. Paris: Editions de l'Olivier.

Ravi, Srilata. 2007. *Rainbow Colors: Literary Ethno-topographies of Mauritius*. Lanham, MD: Lexington.

—. 2010a. 'Between Words and Images: A Comparative Study of Barlen Pyamootoo's Bénarès and Its Film Adaptation'. *International Journal of Francophone Studies* 13.3–4: 401–16.

—. 2010b. 'Indo-Mauritians: National and Postnational Identities'. *Esprit Créateur* 54.2: 30–46.

—. 2013. *Rethinking Global Mauritius: Essays in Mauritian Literatures and Cultures*. Trou d'eau douce: L'atelier d'écriture.

—. 2015. 'Island Hinduism: Religion and Modernity in Francophone Indian Ocean Literature'. In Chantal Zabus (ed.), *The Future of Postcolonial Studies*. Abingdon and New York: Routledge: 85–100.

Ricœur, Paul. 2004. *Memory, History, Forgetting*. Trans. by Kathleen Blamey and David Pellauer. Chicago: University of Chicago Press.

Sewtohul, Amal. 2012. *Made in Mauritius*. Paris: Gallimard.

Vaughan, Meghan. 2005. *Creating the Creole Island: Slavery in Eighteenth-Century Mauritius*. Durham: Duke University Press.

Speaking of Slavery: Representations of Domestic Slavery in the Oral Epics of Francophone West Africa

Sotonye Omuku

The institution of slavery and the practice of slave trading in Africa have been the subject of increasing debate over the past few decades, with historians and anthropologists considering the relationship between domestic slavery and the trans-Saharan and transatlantic slave trades, as well as the impact of these external trades on the traffic of slaves within Africa. Forced migration patterns across the Atlantic form the majority of the commemorative discourses on slavery in West Africa. Conversely, domestic slavery, which not only pre-dated and co-existed with the transatlantic and trans-Saharan trades, but has also outlived both, is often relegated to the background. Yet domestic slavery remains inscribed in the social, economic and political codes of everyday life through which its memory is perpetuated negatively, forcing slave descendants to actively dissociate themselves from their past by hiding their slave ancestry and creating new identities. The attribution of a generic ethnic identity to denote people of slave origin, as in the Gando of Benin, the unwillingness to marry slave descendants and the challenge to their political authority all constitute contemporary forms of discrimination against people of slave ancestry (Hahonou and Pelckmans, 2012: 93–97).

These contemporary memories of domestic slavery form a social narrative rooted in historical practices through which hierarchical boundaries were defined and the distinctions between slave and freeborn were maintained. Similarly, the oral epic tradition is a social memory through which identity and hierarchical structures are perpetuated across generations. By accessing the past through royal lineages and geography, epic accounts of foundation myths explain origins, migrations and the current geographical location of a people. Whether in the context of a myth of origin or through socio-political accounts of historical events, the epic serves as a reaffirmation of identity through its recourse to the past. This literary form, however, indicates a bias towards the socio-political centre and a neglect of those at the margins, characterized as it is by the presence of larger-than-life heroes, legendary rulers of vast empires and mythological figures with supernatural powers.

The epic idealizes historical and mythical symbols and the ideologies of the socio-political centre, of which the slave is seldom a part. As the criterion for inclusion within the social memory is belonging to a social, political or religious centre, the slave who is on the margins of society is rarely the subject of the epic. This is with a few exceptions, such as Ngolo Diarra the slave king in the Segou epic; Poullôri, slave of the Fulani prince Silamaka, whose bravery and friendship with his master is celebrated in both the Segou and Fulani epics; and Amar Zoumbani the slave prince in the Songhay epic of Askia Mohammed. It is clear that even though boundaries exist within the hierarchical order of these societies, inscription of a select few slaves into the social memory is based either on merit within the context of military conquest or membership of the royal family. The majority of slaves, however, constitute the nameless invisible masses, relegated to the realm of forgetting in the oral epic.

As the oral epic usually recounts historical events related to a specific community, the question is not so much the historicity of these accounts, but what these social memories represent for the societies from which they originate. Why are they repeatedly brought to the fore of public consciousness, and what is their function within African society, and specifically within the African novel, which will be our focus here? In a study on social memory, Fentress and Wickham state that

> Social memory is a source of knowledge. This means that it does more than provide a set of categories through which, in an unselfconscious way, a group experiences its surroundings; it also provides the group with material for conscious reflection. This means that we must situate groups in relation to their own traditions by asking how they interpret their own ghosts, and how they use them as a source of knowledge. (1992: 26)

The performance of the epic within society invites *conscious reflection* upon the events and ideals that define a society's past. Thus, any epic in which the slave is not merely a secondary figure, and emerges as a dominant voice, is of great importance to understanding the memory of slavery in such an oral culture.

Literary representations of slavery and the slave trade in Francophone sub-Sahara are characterized as much by the intermittence of their production across the sub-region as they are by the narrative gaps that exist in between and alongside such work. Achille Mbembe's assertion that 'there is, properly speaking, no African memory of slavery' refers not just to the absence of a memory of slavery and the slave trade within African society, but also to the non-existence of a uniform collective memory of slavery that is characterized by a singularity of experience (2002: 259). He instead suggests that if a memory of slavery does exist, it is defined by its diffraction (2002: 259). The African writer is confronted with the multiplicity of the memories of slavery, in which Africans were both practitioners and victims of domestic slavery, a system which still bears its own stigma in the form of continued discrimination against slave descendants. Similarly, the victimhood and agency of Africans in the export slave trades, which were operated over centuries first by Arabs and then by Europeans, constitute legitimate yet controversial memories of the slave trade. This diffraction of memory exposes the multiple and diverse experiences of domestic slavery and the trans-Saharan and transatlantic slave trades, resulting in divergent and often conflicting memories, which may account for the paucity of novels on the subject of slavery and the slave trade.

In an attempt to return to a pre-colonial moment, the historical novel draws heavily on oral tradition as both a stylistic and a historical source of memory. Oral tradition bears a particular significance within the Francophone West African novel as a manifestation of a nostalgic desire for a traditional pre-colonial past, as a reimagining of contemporary Africa and, conversely, as the deconstruction of the myth of an idyllic past, and as a tool for critiquing the present. Orality forms the basis of the work of such prominent authors as Ahmadou Kourouma in *Monné, outrages et défis* [*Monnew, Outrage and Defiance*] (1998), Boubacar Boris Diop in *Les tambours de la mémoire* [*The Drums of Memory*] (1990), Yambo Ouologuem in *Le devoir de violence* [*Bound to Violence*] (1968) and Aminata Sow Fall in *Le Jujubier du patriarche* [*The Jujube Tree of the Patriarch*] (1998). Notably, Ouologuem and Sow Fall have been preoccupied with the form and content of the oral epic as source and/ or subtext for their work on the memory of slavery.

The recurrence of the epic as a narrative of social memory within the West African historical novel on slavery raises questions, such as the relevance of that which is remembered and verbally recounted on the subject of slavery, as well as the significance of that which is omitted from this narrative of the past. I will therefore focus on two of the rare epics in which slavery is a central theme and the slave voice is dominant: namely, the epic of the slave-raiding state of Segou and the Songhay epic of Askia Mohammed. I hope to investigate the representation of slavery in both these epics whilst also considering the ways in which Ouologuem's *Le devoir de violence* and Aminata Sow Fall's *Le Jujubier du patriarche* highlight the epic's historical, cultural and political value as a social construct through which the memory of slavery is both explored and marginalized within the group. I will look at the devices employed in recounting Segou's history of slave raiding and the threat that slavery poses to the kingdom, before moving on to Ouologuem's use of the epic of Askia Mohammed as a source for his novel and the parallels that exist between these two works. I will conclude by examining Sow Fall's creation of the epic of Fouta Djallon in *Le Jujubier du patriarche* within the context of contemporary discrimination against slave descendants.

The Epic of Bamana Segou

The Bamana Empire of Segou, which is located in what is currently south-central Mali, was founded in 1712 by Biton Koulibaly. The epic of the Bamana of Segou focuses on two historical aspects of the city-state of Segou: its kings and the record of its warfare. First the epic provides a vaguely chronological list of kings – vague because the focus is primarily on outstanding historical personalities, such as Biton Koulibaly, the founder of the empire, Ngolo Diarra the slave king, Monzon, his son, and Da Monzon, whose story forms the bulk of the epic. The majority of the events recorded in the epic of Bamana Segou occur during the eighteenth and nineteenth centuries. They depict the rise to power of Biton Koulibaly, the founder of the empire, and his transformation of the *ton* (voluntary group of young men) into his own personal army, with which he carried out raids on the neighbouring villages, and captured and enslaved their inhabitants.

The epic also gives an account of wars that were fought between Segou and its rivals: the Fulani chiefs Basi of Samaniana, Dibi of Niamina, Diétékoro of Kârta, along with the Fulani of Kounari and the Fulani of Macina. These episodes reveal a culture of warfare and the resultant capture of hordes of slaves, who were either absorbed into the kingdom or sold to the slave trade. Upon arrival in Segou, such slaves were usually taken into the homes of nobles and warriors or used for agricultural labour. Although they existed at the bottom of a hierarchy that consisted of nobles, freeborn, occupational caste groups and slaves, some slaves played a significant role within the political corridors of Segou. The *tonjon* or slaves of the *ton* were unlike house or farm slaves. They were a part of the *ton*, the elite group which led Segou's military exploits. The institution of captives as slaves of the *ton* occurred during the reign of Biton Koulibaly, after the battle against Bina of Fabugu:

> They shaved the men's heads
> Leaving only a big tuft of hair.
> The women were shaved in the ordinary way,
> But the men were left with a big tuft.
> So they were recognised as slaves among the other people.
> This was the origin of the tònjònw, council slaves. (Conrad, 1990: 99)

The slave was thus differentiated by his physical appearance, as well as by his name. Slaves of the *ton* were given distinctive proverb names, such as Sini Ye To Alama [Leave tomorrow to God], Nyuman Tilè Tè [It is not time for good things] and K'i Bila I Yèrèma Segu O Mago Tè Nya [To be left alone in Segou, goals are never achieved] (Conrad, 1990: 161). In addition to their physical difference, slaves were also noticeable within the social space for a lack of knowledge of socio-cultural norms. Thus the slave was seen to act outside of acceptable Bamana behaviour because he was an outsider:

> They did foolish things in the village,
> They did foolish things in the house,
> But nobody paid attention to them.
> They said 'Leave him alone,
> He is just a council slave'. (Conrad, 1990: 99)

Although the epic does not overtly reference Segou's slave trading, there are multiple accounts of warfare and the capture of slaves through the recurring theme of the honey beer tribute, which is paid by Segou's tributaries. There is a reference to the fact that Koulibaly's mother produces honey beer, a theme which becomes significant throughout the epic, as the capture of slaves occurs only as a result of a neighbouring community's inability or refusal to pay the honey beer tribute demanded by Koulibaly's and, subsequently, other rulers' emissaries.

> Since Biton came to power,
> His mother gave us beer and honey liquor
> We spend the day drinking at their house and come home after,
> But we do not plough for her or clear her field.
> Let us see about this. (Conrad, 1990: 96)

As a result, the Bamana institute a custom in which money is raised from their tributaries in order to pay for the honey liquor. This honey price, or soul price, is given to the ruler of Segou. Thus honey beer becomes a metaphor for the slave-raiding lifestyle of the *ton*, as villages that cannot pay the honey price are carted away into slavery.

Quite early on in the epic we see such a raid as providing a low-scale forum for people to be exchanged peacefully in the absence of the complete monetary value of the honey beer tribute, as in the case of Ngolo Diarra, who is sold into slavery as a child. Ngolo Diarra's brothers give him to Biton Koulibaly's men as part of the honey price owed by their town, Nyola. As Meillasoux notes, within the context of slavery in a single community, 'the existence of a debt presupposes a hierarchization of lineages based on the acquisition of wealth, and thus the disappearance of the principles of equality and solidarity between families; this can take place only through contamination by the merchant economy' (1991: 40). Although this is historically relevant, Ngolo's case is a result of his brothers' jealousy, as opposed to an inability to pay the honey price. They say:

> Let us make a plan of what to do against Ngolo [...]
> When the honey-price collectors come this year,
> Let us plan not to pay the full amount of cowries.
> We will give two hundred cowries less twenty,
> And say our hands cannot reach.
> We will send our brother with the cowries to Biton Kulubali the man-killing hunter. (Conrad, 1990: 107)

This exchange of a human being as payment for a debt is not unusual within the context of domestic slavery, but what becomes problematic for Segou is the fact that the slave Ngolo Diarra eventually rises to become ruler of the kingdom, and this in spite of various schemes to murder him.

If slavery is at the heart of Segou's military exploits and political and economic dominance, the social impact of the influx of captives into the city-state of Segou is equally a threat to its stability. Running alongside the theme of the honey beer tribute as a metaphor for war and slave raiding is, therefore, the insult to the king in the person of Ngolo Diarra when recalling his slave status. This insult to Ngolo Diarra and the kings who descend from his line, including Da Monzon, often instigates war between Segou and the offending village. Such insults are seen throughout the cycle with references to Ngolo Diarra's slave status following subsequent generations, especially Da Monzon, his grandson. When Da Monzon asks Basi Samaniana, the Fulani chief, for his daughter's hand in marriage, the latter sends this reply:

> Eh, does Da not know about his grandfather Ngolo?
> That he was added to the honey-price from Nyola?

Does he not know that Ngolo was given to Biton Koulibali in Sekoro?
Does he not know that all his ancestors were slaves?
Oh, that a slave should come to a noble such as me, asking for my daughter! [...]
He should ask for a weaver's stool, comb and shuttle.
He should ask for a basket and hoe so he can collect termites and feed the chickens.
A slave's work is to collect termites or to weave. (Conrad, 1990: 203)

This is the standard formula for the insult against Da Monzon, to quote his lineage and his origins in Nyola and to emphasize his slave status. The verbal insult against the king of Segou brings to the fore his slave origins, brands him as a foreigner in Segou and ultimately challenges the legitimacy of his rulership. Basi rejects Da Monzon's request to marry his daughter because he is unwilling to enter into a marriage alliance with a slave descendant, even though the slave descendant is Da Monzon, king of Segou. The war that occurs in response to this insult, along with other wars in the name of the honey price, results in entire villages being taken captive by Segou.

Along with warfare, other modes of capture in Segou included brigandage and mounted raids, the latter of which is not directly referenced in the epic (Belcher, 1999: 120). Biton Koulibaly led bands of raiders made up of outcasts from the small, decentralized villages of the Niger basin (Meillasoux, 1991: 143). These warriors, as mentioned earlier, raided neighbouring villages in return for protection and immunity. In addition, individuals or small groups preyed on vulnerable travellers and children from Segou, and kidnapped them for sale. The most significant example of brigandage within the epic is the case of Bilisi, who kidnapped children from Segou and gave them as payment in exchange for his honey beer. The theme of honey beer thus returns to the cycle in the story of Bilisi. Where it had earlier been used to depict the wanton slave-raiding lifestyle of Segou's soldiers, the desire for honey beer becomes a threat to the security of the state, in particular to the vulnerable children of Segou. Bilisi is shown as an all-consuming ogre figure who inspires fear in Segou's warriors. He creates a great sense of insecurity in Segou and its surrounding villages by threatening the people and exacting a tribute of a portion of meat from them every week, as well as kidnapping their children to pay for his honey beer:

The next time he went out for a drink,
Whoever's virgin daughter he met,
He would capture and sell her.
The family of that child would go to Faama Da.

> They would say 'Eh, what about this matter of Bilisi?
> If this matter of Bilisi does not change,
> He will make Segou a city without children. (Conrad, 1990: 271)

For the first time in the epic cycle, the association between honey beer and the acquisition of slaves constitutes a threat to the security of Segou as parents of captured children appeal to Da Monzon to end Bilisi's reign of terror.

The mnemonic device of honey beer recurs as a motif throughout the epic, with reference to wars, the *ton*'s slave raids and Bilisi the slave raider's reign of terror over the city-state. With each repetition of this theme, its significance appears to evolve, so that honey beer encapsulates slave acquisition in its different forms. In spite of its military and economic strength through slave raiding as represented by the honey beer metaphor, Segou is not impenetrable, as seen in the Bilisi episode. Alongside this is the notion that the most powerful person in Segou, the king, can be subject to discrimination because of his slave status. In fact, by incorporating the insults against the slave king within its narrative, the epic presents a critical account of the kingdom of Segou, a social memory that not only is focused on the victories of the kingdom, but is self-critical enough to recall the vulnerability of Segou because of the legacy of domestic slavery.

Sourcing the Epic: The Epic of Askia Mohammed in Ouologuem's *Le devoir de violence*

The problem of slave status is also central to Yambo Ouologuem's novel *Le devoir de violence. Le devoir* relates the history of the domestic slavery and serfdom of the fictional kingdom of Nakem, a possible anagram of the Kanem Empire, located in modern-day Western Chad (Hale and Malio, 1999: 157). The novel, published in 1968, deconstructs idealist notions of Africa by opposing Africanist romanticizing over the continent's pre-colonial past, and replacing it with what Ouologuem presents as a more realistic history of unrelenting violence, inflicted by the ruling Saifs upon their subjects. By focusing on such controversial issues as domestic slavery and its impact on the internal and external trade in slaves, Ouologuem paints a fatalistic picture of what he claims to be Africa's past. In fact, his account of this past, as encapsulated in the Nakem Empire, is so damning that the Congolese critic Aliko Songolo argues that the overwhelming European reception given to *Le devoir* was 'not surprising because the novel seems to exculpate the former metropolises for crimes for which they had, justly or unjustly, been held responsible' (Songolo, 1978–1979: 146).

For the historical account of the Nakem Empire in *Le devoir*, Ouologuem draws primarily from African sources, specifically oral and written narratives of the Songhay Empire, a state which dates from the eleventh century, and spanned an extensive geographical area covering parts of present-day Mali, Mauritania, Niger, Nigeria, Gambia, Burkina Faso, Guinea and Senegal. Ouologuem's novel is based on one of the few African epics to deal explicitly with the theme of slavery – the Songhay epic of Askia Mohammed. The epic narrative consists of proverbs, genealogy, panegyric and etiological stories about the different groups in the Songhay Empire, in particular the *jeseré* (griots), *sohanci* (sorcerers) and *sorko* (fishermen or praise singers of river spirits). The political motivation of the epic is to situate the ruler Askia Mohammed and his dynasty centrally in Songhay history and to legitimize his political and religious rule. For this reason, the bulk of the epic is dedicated to Askia Mohammed.

Without digressing too much into the academic arguments regarding allegations of unacknowledged borrowing and plagiarism that surround *Le devoir*, it is important to note that Ouologuem borrows from both European and African sources.[19] The epic of Askia Mohammed is a primary source for the account of the Songhay Empire upon which the Nakem Empire of the novel is modelled. Ouologuem's narrator acknowledges the epic, as well as two written chronicles in Arabic – the *Tarikh el Fettâch* [*Chronicle of the Seeker*] and the *Tarikh es Sudan* [*Chronicle of Africa*] – both commissioned by the Songhay ruler Askia Mohammed. The epic, as recounted by the Nigerien *griot* Nouhou Malio in the Zarma dialect of Songhay, and recorded by Thomas Hale between 1980 and 1981, is made up of three sections: the birth and rise of Askia Mohammed, the genealogy of the Askia dynasty, and the final episode, which attributes the fall of the capital Gao to the slave prince Amar Zoumbani.

In *Le devoir*, the tendency to romanticize Africa's past within the oral epic is countered by Ouologuem's resurrection, not of heroes, but of villains of epic proportions, in particular the slave-trading Saif dynasty. Although he bases the novel on the Songhay epic, Ouologuem subverts the social function of the epic through the reconstruction of a negative memory, an anti-epic. He also challenges the exclusion of the slave memory from the oral narrative by compressing the listing of the genealogy and deeds of the Saifs into the first two chapters of *Le devoir*, dramatically shifting the focus from the predominance of the Saif dynasty to the lineage of Kassoumi, the slave, for the rest of the novel. The transformation in the epic form is seen

[19] For more on the allegations of plagiarism, see Sellin (1971, 1999) and Miller (1985).

in the sudden shift from the listing of the Saifs' lineage to the less formal narrative of the lives of the slave Kassoumi and his son Raymond Kassoumi. Thus Raymond emerges from the margins of Nakem's social hierarchy as the subject of the novel, the account of the Saifs constituting the historical and indeed the contemporary social background against which Kassoumi and his offspring are the major actors.

Ouologuem maintains the theme of the irreversibility of slave status at the crux of *Le Devoir* as a parallel to the Amar Zoumbani episode in the Askia Mohammed epic. The epic mentions the presence of captives in the homes of Songhay nobles, for example the Bargantché slave (northern Benin) owned by Askia Mohammed's mother, and the Dabay slave (Mali), Amar Zoumbani's mother, as indicative of Songhay's warring expeditions, and their role in establishing the empire as a dominant economic and political power. The foreign origins of these captives, alongside the continued reference to their status as aliens within the epic, signify the position of the slave as both foreigner and outsider. Yet in addition to the notion of the slave as existing within Songhay, while living socially on its margins, is the hierarchy that exists among slaves with relation to the probability of being sold by the master. As Stoller states,

> All slaves of the Songhay could theoretically trace their descent patrilineally to a prisoner of a precolonial war [...] a Songhay might sell his prisoner slave (benya, benyey) [...] but once the slave had produced offspring, the offspring (horso) became either farmers who tilled the soil of a noble patron, or skilled specialists (weavers, bards, blacksmiths and musicians) who are still clients of noble patrons. (1981: 767)

Thus, whilst the captured slave may be on the margins of Songhay society, he or she could attain incorporation through various means; for example a woman could integrate through marriage to a noble, and the product of such a marriage would be considered as *horso*. Although incorporation allowed certain privileges, including even the right to own slaves, there remained a distinction between incorporation, that is to say belonging, and the technicalities of actual freedom. A slave could achieve their freedom by ransom or by enfranchisement. Until then they remained the property of their master.

In Malio's account of the epic of Askia Mohammed, the mistaking of incorporation for freedom occurs with the mother of Amar Zoumbani, who, in spite of being married to a Songhay chief, has never been ransomed and so remains the property of her original owners. She is a captive of the former chief, father of Sagouma. Now married to the new chief, Soumayla Kassa, she remains Sagouma's slave because her freedom was never purchased by her husband. Even though she has been incorporated into Songhay society through marriage, both she and her son Amar Zoumbani remain the property of her original owner. For this reason, Amar Zoumbani, although a prince, unwittingly remains a slave. This unfortunate situation is at the heart of the Amar Zoumbani episode. The *griot* recounts the exchange between Amar Zoumbani and his father Soumayla Kassa in which the prince discovers the truth about his slave status:

> He came home to his father's house, he said to his father,
> So he is a captive.
> Soumayla Kassa said to him,
> 'You are a captive
> Because when I married your mother, I did not buy her freedom.
> It is the captive of someone else that I married.
> It is also the captive who gave birth to you.
> If at least I had freed your mother –
> But to tell you the truth I didn't free her.
> Everything they tell you is true'. (Hale and Malio, 1996: 44)

Amar Zoumbani's mistaken assumption that his incorporation via membership of the royal family equates with freedom, along with a persistent refusal to accept his slave status, leads to a series of incidents, culminating in the prince jeopardizing the efforts of the Songhay army by disobeying the rules of warfare. The fall of Gao, and indeed the decline of the entire Songhay Empire, is blamed primarily on Amar Zoumbani's failure to observe the mores and social hierarchy of Songhay, thus reaffirming his slave status and the behaviour that is inevitably associated with it.

Like the epic, Ouologuem's narrative illustrates the porosity of hierarchical boundaries, while simultaneously dispelling that notion by demonstrating the fragility of assimilation and therefore of belonging. He draws from the epic's theme of the irreversibility of slave status, through the parallel between the lives of Raymond Kassoumi, son of the slave Kassoumi and adopted son of the ruling Saif, and the epic's Amar Zoumbani, son of Soumayla Kassa, chief of Gao, and a captive woman. Ouologuem's narrator recounts Raymond Kassoumi's own attempts to reinvent himself by erasing his slave status through education, marriage to a French woman and his political aspiration to become the first president of Nakem. Yet at the end of the novel, the narrator emphasizes Kassoumi's helplessness as the impending president of the newly independent Nakem nation: 'Kassoumi, habile calculateur, avait mal calculé: fort de ses titres et de l'appui de la France, il s'était cru maître de l'ancien maître, alors même que seul le flambeau de Saïf, un instant assoupi pour mieux briller, plus rougeoyant que jamais, garantissait à l'esclave l'acquisition des suffrages' (Ouologuem, 1968: 191).[20] In the face of the Saif's continued oppression, Kassoumi realises that he can never escape from his status as a slave and that all attempts to elevate his position have been futile.

In both texts the idea that incorporation can be substituted for freedom is explored. The moment in which Raymond understands that he will always be a slave of the Saif is strikingly similar to Amar Zoumbani's own realisation of the inevitability of slave status in *The Epic of Askia Mohammed*. In fact *Le devoir* and Nouhou Malio's account of the epic end on a similar note – the irreversibility of slave status for the educated slave and president-elect Kassoumi and the slave prince Amar Zoumbani, respectively. Whilst Amar Zoumbani, the slave prince, is merely a minor character in the epic, his lineage and heroic deeds not being highlighted like those of the primary characters of the Songhay narrative, in *Le devoir*, the *griot* or narrator traces the life of Raymond Kassoumi from birth to the moment before he becomes the president of the Nakem nation. In Ouologuem's adaptation of the account of the Songhay Empire, the slave is not a footnote to the epic. Instead, he is central to the plot. By drawing from and indeed manipulating the epic to represent the slave voice, Ouologuem therefore confronts the mythification of Africa's past as a victim of slavery with an account of a violent history of domestic slavery and slave trade, as practised by Africans.

Creating the Epic: The Epic of Fouta Djallon in Sow Fall's *Le Jujubier du patriarche*

Aminata Sow Fall's 1993 novel *Le Jujubier du patriarche* relies on the epic form more as a narrative technique than as a source for the content of the novel. Unlike Ouologuem, Sow Fall does not borrow explicitly from previous oral epics or even from written historical accounts. Instead, by creating a convincing, albeit completely fictive, epic of the Fulani of Fouta Djallon, she uses the epic style as a platform for an interrogation of social memory within the novel. Through the epic screen of warring Fulani clans, she situates the characters and events within a realistic ethnic space, thereby exploring ancient tensions that arise from the historical co-existence of multiple ethnicities in the Senegambian sub-region. The epic and the modern-day

[20] Translation: 'Kassoumi, the skilful calculator, had miscalculated: with his wealth of qualifications and the support of France he believed that he had mastered the ancient master, when only the Saif's torch, briefly dimmed in order to shine brighter than ever, could guarantee the slave's acquisition of votes.' This and all subsequent quotations were translated by the author of this article.

account of the life of the principal characters co-exist in the novel as past and present are related simultaneously.

Whilst Ouologuem tackles the crisis of representation by adapting the epic of Askia Mohammed to focus on the slave Raymond Kassoumi as a central character against the historical background of the Saif dynasty, Sow Fall differs in her technique. Using the form of the epic as a foundation, in terms of its orality and its incorporation of prosaic narrative, poetry and panegyric, she creates her own epic by interspersing it with the contemporary narrative of the novel. The result is an epic that erupts into contemporary life, the present day being constantly challenged by the memory of the past. Unlike Ouologuem, whose central characters are based on the historical figures of the Songhay Empire, Sow Fall creates her own epic and therefore her own heroes. Yet both authors tackle the irreversibility of inherited slave status in the context of domestic slavery.

Le Jujubier tells the story of Yelli, a descendant of a ruling Fulani clan, originally from the town of Babyselli, and the tensions that exist within his family through his quarrels with his wife, his economic and subsequent social downfall, and the fragmented fictive kinship that exists between his wife, Tacko, and a slave descendant, Naarou, whose family has served theirs for generations. Parallel to, and interspersed with, the principal character Yelli's own present-day story is the epic of Fouta Djallon, which recounts the heroic deeds of Yelli's ancestors. The epic develops in the novel through song, poetry and prose, as recounted by the major characters, and by the *griot* during his annual visits to Yelli in the city. It is depicted primarily as fragments, which are interspersed with the contemporary account of Yelli's life.

Through the figure of Naarou, Sow Fall explores contemporary discrimination against people of slave descent, via the marginalization of the record of their lineage from social memory in the form of the oral epic. Naarou first learns the epic under the *griot* Naani over a period of years and, upon finding a gap in the representation of her slave lineage, she addresses their marginalization. When she asks the *griot* about the genealogy of her ancestor Biti, he states that the lineage of slaves is not the subject of the epic, indicating that this is the privilege of the aristocracy.

> Elle apprendra du griot que 'Biti, l'amazone à l'allure de guêpe et au coeur de lion' était sa lointaine ancêtre. Elle en éprouvera une fierté considérable et voudra en savoir plus:
>
> Alors c'était la grand-mère de ma mère?
> Oh! C'est plus loin que ça ma fille.
> Comment s'appelaient ses enfants?
> Sira, Dior et Lari.

> Et leurs enfants? [...]
>
> Ma petite fille [...] Quand on a Warèle et Biti, *on peut oublier le reste.*
>
> L'usage ne prévoyait pas de retenir la généalogie des esclaves. (Sow Fall, 1998: 37; my emphasis)[21]

The idea that 'one can forget the others' indicates that the consequence of the omission of the slave lineage from the epic is forgetting, and that forgetting is perpetuated within the social memory whenever the epic is repeated.

Very few epics break with this pattern. Yet by rewriting the epic for the purpose of their novels, both Ouologuem and Sow Fall challenge the marginalization of the slave in the oral epic, and therefore challenge social memory. Ouologuem achieves this structurally by relegating the deeds of the Saif to the opening two chapters of *Le Devoir* and therefore foregrounding the character of Kassoumi the slave. Similarly, Sow Fall, through Naarou, highlights the inadequacy of the epic narrative in its initial form as a construction of the socio-professional caste of *griots* to honour the socio-political elite and, therefore, to inadvertently marginalize the slave voice. Sow Fall's own creation of the epic of Fouta Jallon is mirrored in the novel by this slave who, upon discovering that her slave ancestor's lineage is largely absent from the epic, decides to compose an addition to the existing account in the form of a panegyric for Warèle and Biti, her female slave ancestors. Naarou seeks representation for her ancestors, and indeed for herself, within the epic of Fouta Djallon, claiming a legitimate stake in the social memory of the group as a member of the Babyselli community.

The catalyst for Naarou's reaction is her adoptive mother Tacko's verbal abuse in which she openly cites Naarou's slave status, thus excluding her from Yelli's aristocratic lineage. Having been rejected as a child of Yelli's family and treated as a slave, Naarou then claims her slave ancestry. She says of her slave ancestors, Warèle and Biti: 'Je descends de Warèle et de Biti qui ont joué un rôle déterminant dans l'épopée. C'est Naani en personne qui me

---

21 Translation: 'She learnt from the griot that "Biti, the amazon with the hourglass figure and heart of a lion" was her distant ancestor. She felt considerable pride and wanted to know more:

> So she was my mother's grandmother?
>
> Oh! More distant than that my child.
>
> What were the names of her children?
>
> Sira, Dior and Laru.
>
> And their children? [...]
>
> My dear child [...] When one has Warèle and Biti, *one can forget the others.*
>
> It was not customary to memorize the genealogy of slaves.'

l'a appris quand j'étais toute jeune. Je n'ai jamais pensé à une cloison entre Warèle, Biti, Sarebibi, Dioumana et les autres mais comme Mère me traite d'esclave, je revendique Warèle et Biti; je revendique leur part de l'heroïsme' (Sow Fall, 1998: 89).[22] This is a deliberate compensatory act by which the epic is transformed through the inscription of the slave past onto the social memory, so that by the end of the novel, the fictional epic is transformed from an elite male-dominated account to one in which both the slave and the woman are the central figures.

Through Naarou, Sow Fall illustrates the need for the subaltern to respond to the dominant master narrative by addressing the omission of her past through the techniques of invention and adaptation. In Naarou's outrage at the marginalization of her slave ancestors, and her subsequent response to perceived gaps within the epic, she retrospectively retrieves the silenced, in this case female, slave voice, so that it exists alongside that of the dominant master figure. Martin calls this attempt 'Une démarche proche de celle des *womanists* américaines qui, elles aussi, se penchent sur les diverses reliques d'un passé opaque afin d'y trouver les mots et la musique qui leur servira à nommer et chanter leur propre mythe-histoire' (Martin, 2000: 300).[23] With Naarou, the response is found on two fronts. Firstly, by dedicating a praise song to Dioumana, she foregrounds the female voice, subverting the vilification within the epic of this elusive figure of the wife of the Almamy, who disappears into the belly of a whale because of her husband's infidelity. Secondly, she reformulates the epic through the invention of the account of her slave ancestors, so that it commemorates the central role played by these erstwhile forgotten characters in reuniting the warring Fulani factions.

Sow Fall's creation and use of the epic of Fouta Jallon in *Le Jujubier* reveals a 'narrative structure that weaves African oral tradition around the Western-style text' (Schwartz, 2007: 57). She explores specific themes, such as the function of the epic as a social memory and an instrument of the marginalization of the slave voice within society. Her approach to the oral epic can be seen as two-fold. In terms of the invention of the epic for the purpose of the novel, Sow Fall distances herself from existing West

---

22 Translation: 'I am descended from Warèle and Biti, who played an indispensable role in the epic. Naani himself taught me the epic when I was very young. I never thought there was any distinction between Warèle, Biti, Sarebibi, Dioumana and the rest, but because Mother treated me like a slave, I claim Warèle and Biti; I claim their role as heroes.'

23 Translation: 'An approach that is similar to that taken by American womanists who also delve into the diverse relics of an opaque past in order to retrieve words and music that will help them to name and celebrate their own history-myth.'

African epic accounts, creating instead a fictive epic that explores the heroic deeds of Yelli's ancestors. Yet through the figure of Naarou, the epic of Fouta Djallon, which is authentic within the novel, forms the foundation for a questioning of the inclusiveness of social memory, thus provoking a concurrent and alternative narrative which takes into account the slave voice, albeit as a response to the master narrative. The excerpts of the epic, which are recounted throughout the novel, therefore culminate in a final section in which there is a complete break from the twentieth-century narrative as Naarou narrates the epic poem to an audience of relatives. Whilst previously the epic has only featured as a fragmented narrative within the structure of the novel, by the final section, Naarou's composition is presented to the reader as an uninterrupted passage of epic song, which she sings whilst the other characters listen with rapt attention.

Conclusion

The oral recollection of the memory of slavery in the West African empires of Songhay and Segou provides a way into understanding the complexity of the ramifications of slavery and slave trading across the sub-region. In both the Songhay and the Segou epics, one sees a memory that is as inventive as it is questioning of identity and of its nobility through the theme of slavery. Slavery and slave trading form the economic backbone of these societies. Yet these epics, which are unique in their examination of slavery, reveal the threat that slavery poses to the socio-political centre, whether through the irreversibility of slave status, as in the case of Amar Zoumbani, or through the insult to the slave king and his descendants, as well as the terror of Bilisi in the Segou Empire.

The epic's dual quality of memory and fiction forms a platform for subsequent inquiry into the nature of a social memory of slavery, as represented by the novel. By deploying the epic form in the quest for a memory of slavery, both Ouologuem and Sow Fall reconnect with the past as they challenge the ways in which remembering and forgetting are socialized through the adaptation and invention of this form within the social context. The epic is presented as a social memory of the group; but this is a group in which the members claim the right to retell their past through the epic, irrespective of their slave status. Although the fictionalization of memory that is typical of the epic form is reflected in these entirely fictional works, it no longer serves as a tool for the politically motivated white-washing of the account of heroes' lives. Instead fiction becomes the servant of the slave and a means by which their accounts can be inscribed into the oral epic. By depicting slavery through the lens of fiction, these authors attempt to navigate the contemporary stigma and shame of slave status in order to fill in the gaps that exist in oral sources.

Yet both Ouologuem and Sow Fall draw on the oral epic tradition, not for its historicity, but for its value as a *phantasm* of the past: a social construct that is an *illusion* of a group's past in order to create and affirm its collective identity. Through the use, and indeed the problematizing of, the epic, these authors situate the oral narrative at the centre of an inquiry into the past that examines the content and form of the epic by questioning its subjectivity as a curator of memory. By mirroring the fictionalization of the narrative of social memory in this body of work both stylistically and in terms of content within the novel, memory in the form of the oral epic is both imitated and disputed, affirmed and challenged. The challenging of the epic by these authors, and their transformation of the epic, albeit in different ways, therefore addresses more acutely the questions raised in the West African epic about the position of the slave in society. Through their recounting of the memory of slavery, Ouologuem and Sow Fall invite us to reflect on and challenge the portrayal of the slave past and the enduring impact of its legacy.

Works Cited

Belcher, Stephen. 1999. *Epic Traditions of Africa*. Bloomington: Indiana University Press.

Conrad, David C. (ed.). 1990. *A State of Intrigue: The Epic of Bamana Segu According to Tayiru Banbera*. Oxford: Oxford University Press.

Diop, Boubacar Boris. 1990. *Les tambours de la mémoire*. Paris: L'Harmattan.

Fentress, James, and Chris Wickham. 1992. *Social Memory*. Oxford: Blackwell.

Hahonou, Eric, and Lotte Pelckmans. 2012. '"History must be rewritten!": Revisionist Ambitions among West African Slave Descendants'. In Douglas Hamilton, Kate Hodgson and Joel Quirk (eds), *Slavery, Memory and Identity: National Representations and Global Legacies*. London: Pickering & Chatto.

Hale, Thomas, and Nouhou Malio (eds). 1996. *The Epic of Askia Mohammed*. Bloomington: Indiana University Press.

—. 1999. 'Rewriting the Songhay Past in *Le devoir de violence*'. In Christopher Wise (ed.), *Yambo Ouologuem: Postcolonial Writer, Islamic Militant*. London: Lynne Rienner: 155–74.

Kâti Ben El-Hâdj El-Mattaouakkel, Mahmoûd. 1913. *Tarikh el Fettach ou Chronique du Chercheur*. Trans. by Octave Houdas and Maurice Delafosse. Paris: Ernest Leroux.

Kourouma, Ahmadou. 1998. *Monné, outrages et défis*. Paris: Éditions du Seuil.

Martin, Florence. 2000. 'Échos et grains de voix dans *Le Jujubier du patriarche* d'Aminata Sow Fall'. *French Review* 74: 296–307.

Mbembe, Achille. 2002. 'African Modes of Self-Writing'. Trans. by Steven Randall. *Public Culture* 14: 239–73.

Meillasoux, Claude. 1991. *The Anthropology of Slavery: The Womb of Iron and Gold*. London: The Athlone Press.

Miller, Christopher. 1985. *Blank Darkness: Africanist Discourse in French*. Chicago: University of Chicago Press.

Ouologuem, Yambo. 1968. *Le devoir de violence*. Paris: Éditions du Seuil.

—. 1971. *Bound to Violence*. Trans. by Ralph Manheim. London: Heinemann.

Sa'dī, Abd al Rah'mān ibn 'AbdAllāh. 1981. *Tarikhes-Soudan* (2 vols). Trans. and ed. by Octave Houdas and Edmond Benoist. Paris: J. Maisonneuve.

Schwartz, Lucy. 2007. 'Re-valuing Traditional Patrimony'. In Ada Uzoamaka Azodo (ed.), *Emerging Perspectives on Aminata Sow Fall: The Real and the Imaginary in Her Novels*. Trenton: Africa World Press: 43–64.

Sellin, Eric. 1971. 'Ouologuem's Blueprint for *Le devoir de violence*'. *Research in African Literatures* 2: 117–20.

—. 1999. 'The Unknown Voice of Yambo Ouologuem'. In Christopher Wise (ed.), *Yambo Ouologuem: Postcolonial Writer, Islamic Militant*. London: Lynne Rienner: 67–88.

Songolo, Aliko. 1978–1979. 'Fiction and Subversion: *Le devoir de violence*'. Trans. by Jo Anne Cornwell. *SubStance (Literature and Its Others)* 6–7.21: 141–55.

Sow Fall, Aminata. 1998. *Le Jujubier du patriarche*. Monaco: Le Serpent à plumes.

Stoller, Paul. 1981. 'Social Interaction and the Management of Songhay Socio-political Change'. *Africa: Journal of the International African Institute* 51: 765–80.

From Forgetting to Remembrance: Slavery and Forced Labour in Tunisia

Inès Mrad Dali

At least since the modern period, Morocco and the Regencies of Algiers, Tunis and Tripoli were among the regions directly implicated in the enslavement and displacement of sub-Saharan African peoples, and were used either as platforms for their transit towards Europe or as territories seeking domestic and agricultural labour. In the case of Tunisia, slaves were brought overland as part of trans-Saharan business and trade, but they could also be transported by sea, the trans-Mediterranean trade completing the trans-Saharan trade. Domestic slavery concerned large urban areas, as well as the rural world, but there remained some specificities relating to certain regions. From a global perspective, the Tunisian Regency was less of a 'slave society' than a 'society with slaves', with current research suggesting that the Tunisian economy was not directly dependent on the slave trade or on the presence of slaves. If the role of slaves in society was indisputable, it was nonetheless only indirectly useful to stakeholders in the evolution of this society.

When an intellectual and moral abolitionist movement spread throughout the world in the early nineteenth century and began exercising considerable pressure on slave societies, the Regency of Tunis was also inevitably affected, with the first abolitionist measures appearing in the early 1840s. In 1841, the Bey decided to end the export and the public sale of slaves with the closure of the slave market. The following year, the decision was taken that all children born of enslaved parents would be declared free. Finally, in January 1846, the Bey ordered the promulgation of a text abolishing slavery. There was also a second abolition of slavery in 1890, hastily drafted by the protectorate authorities in the hope that this ban would restore their tarnished image after charges had been brought against, and a scandal had erupted concerning, the French resident minister, Justin Massicault (1886–92), who was suspected of having made use of slave labour (French Diplomatic Archives: docs 61, 101, 105). Generally speaking, however, the French protectorate authority (1881–1956) pursued a conciliatory policy towards the abusive detention of slaves, which led to the drafting of the text in 1890.[1]

Today, the Tunisian black minority consists not only of descendants of slaves, but also of sub-Saharan immigrants, who were encouraged by the French colonial administration in the early 1890s to come and work in the Regency of Tunis. The latter arrived mainly through Tripolitania to settle down, often definitively, encouraged by a growing need for workers in Tunisia. However, current social discourses, along with the proliferation of discriminatory images, have meant that the black population of Tunisia are collectively seen as the children of slaves, thereby eliding historic distinctions and specificities. Moreover, the history of the differences between these groups, as well as their migratory movements and the particular uses of this workforce, which became more pronounced towards the end of the nineteenth century and during the first half of the twentieth, remain totally unknown.

This leads us to question how such a process of forgetting could occur and for what reasons, especially given that the history of slavery is not only known, but also generally attached to the collective black population of Tunisia as a founding history of their presence in the region. Why does the fact of voluntary emigration, which, as we shall see, can be closely correlated to forced labour and forms of indenture, remain totally unknown and silenced, whether in Tunisia or in France, the latter of which directly benefitted from the labour of this workforce?[2]

---

1 This abolitionist law, decided by the colonial authorities, aimed at stopping the campaign of denunciations led by the press and French political opposition against the colonial administration's policies.

2 Several studies have focused on forced labour and the *Indigénat* system in French colonies in Africa, with the exception of Tunisia, which is considered by historians to have been spared from this practice. See Echenberg (1975), Manning (1982), Fall and Mbodj (1989), Coquery-Vidrovitch (1992), Fall (1993) and Touré (1996).

Contemporary Ignorance and Other Confusions

The most crucial period for understanding this gap and even denial in memory, as well as the reasons for the non-transmission of this history with specific reference to post-slavery forms of labour, is the period following the 1890 abolition. This period is notable for its desire to exclude any allusion to slavery from the vocabulary and areas of preoccupation of the colonial administration. From then on, slavery was considered outmoded. Another feature of this period was the massive influx and necessary management of 'Sudanese' immigrants.[3] While some were fleeing slavery in neighbouring Tripolitania, most migrants came directly from Sudan in response to the promise of jobs in a European colony in its installation phase.[4] Black 'foreigners', designated in the colonial administrative records as 'Tripolitains', 'Sudanese' or 'Fezzani', came into the country in large numbers to work in construction and agriculture. From then on, the preoccupations of the colonial authorities were simultaneously to reconcile security (controlling these arrivals), achieve fiscal profitability (by imposing tax demands on these people) and maintain this workforce, which was presented in the colonial administration's correspondence as 'special' and as appreciated for its 'sobriety and hard work' (Feraud, 1872: 167–76; Riban, 1895: 24). So what were the 'special' features of this policy and how did it impact upon the population? In a country where the organization of foreigners was still in flux under a new colonial administration, how was this mass mobilization of an immigrant workforce[5] – which

[3] It is important to highlight that the word 'Sudanese' is not linked here to a specific territory or culture. Black immigration was not limited to individuals from the region of Sudan. Indeed, Fezzanis from the southwest region of present-day Libya constituted a large percentage of black migrant labour, arriving as early as 1891–1892. They were sometimes named by the government as 'Sudanese', the term being used by the colonial administration both to refer to people from the Sudan region (which then included countries like Niger, Chad and Mali) and to designate the black populace in general.

[4] Due to both its agricultural labour and its mining needs (located in the Gafsa region in the southwest of the country), and later to its competitive relations with Italy, the French colonial government in Tunisia had taken measures to facilitate the entry of Tripolitans into the territory. As the only region, other than Algeria, to border Tunisia, present-day Libya was for the Regency of Tunis a large and compelling platform for exchange and transit within the sub-Saharan area. Hence, the colonial authorities generally facilitated the access of Tripolitans.

[5] No statistics are immediately available to compare population size, but administrative correspondence attests to the regular arrival of migratory groups at this time.

represented a double economic interest as both productive and taxable workers – managed? Moreover, how would this new colonial administration understand these multiple non-native identities?

One of the most important elements regarding the experiences of the black population in Tunisian post-abolitionist society lay in the new social organization set up by the protectoral authorities, whose main purpose was the levying of the *Mejba* capitation tax, for the purposes of which previously operated distinctions between Tunisians and foreigners were to be removed.[6] Indeed, as part of the French colonial administration's policy, there was no question of distinguishing the emancipated slave or the son of a slave, or even a native Tunisian, from the free black immigrant without any known slave ancestry. The distinction at the administrative level took place mainly through the phenotype ('Negro') or by an indefinite and vague designation based on their supposed origin ('Sudanese').[7]

This way of noting differences was new compared to that previously exercised under the sovereignty of the Bey, who spared foreigners from the *Mejba* fiscal tax introduced in 1856, therefore exercising a differentiation, not between blacks and whites, but between Tunisians and foreigners. Records show that, since at least the 1870s, a significant number of Tunisia's black emancipated slave populace had paid a tax as Tunisians (Ben Tahar, 2000: 669–83).

But the colonial administration practised a rather different policy. In 1891, the French colonial authorities began to make their taxation demands through a new policy relating to both the indigenous population and 'foreigners', with some exceptions. The black population of the Regency of Tunis was particularly affected. From the beginning of this fiscal campaign, several protest letters were sent by different communities relating to this

6 The capitation tax *Mejba* was instituted in 1856 by 'M'hamed bey, à titre d'ailleurs provisoire pour sortir son Gouvernement de l'embarras où il se trouvait et en attendant les jours meilleurs; c'était un secours demandé par le Souverain à ses sujets [...] Les Tunisiens seuls [devaient] donc y être astreints, c'était bien l'esprit du Bey, car un souverain manquerait à sa dignité en demandant des secours à des étrangers.' Translation: 'M'hamed bey, as a temporary measure to remove his government from the embarrassing position in which it had found itself and in the hope of better days to come; the sovereign requested the help of his subjects [...] The bey considered that the duty ought to fall only to the Tunisians, because it would be shameful for a sovereign to request aid from foreigners' (Tunisian National Archives (TNA), series E, carton 18, file 2 (1891–1913), doc. 134). This and all subsequent quotations from this and other sources were translated by the author of this article, unless otherwise stated.

7 Under the French colonial administration, they all had to pay the same tax as other Tunisians.

issue. For the French administration, all 'blacks', whether recently freed or immigrants, were to become taxable due to the equality in rights and duties. It was further argued that since the black people from the Sudan region, whether freed or immigrants, were Muslims, they all had to pay the tax in accordance with the Islamic principle of equality between Muslims. By leaning on this supposed obligation found in the Islamic scriptures, the French authorities definitively justified their refusal to exempt the black population and foreigners from taxation.[8] Moreover, the exemption of the Syrian Maronite, a Christian community (see Moosa, 2005), confirmed that the distinction between taxable and exempted was, in fact, based on religious identity. This fiscal equality between 'Muslims' and 'foreigners' reveals the authority's underlying perception or interpretation of identities. For the French colonial administration, religious affiliation prevailed over the status of foreigners by exploiting a supposed tenet of Islam. Even the reigning Bey had not applied this rule, considering it unworthy for a sovereign to charge foreigners for an established tax introduced as support from the people to its government. This new configuration of identities was also concretized by a new decision to include all of these identities (foreign and local) under the prism of one denomination – 'Sudanese' – designating a group of black individuals who, from then on, were subjected to the authority of a common Sheikh, who would act as their mediator and, notably, their tax collector.[9]

Tax collection was not an easy task because public resistance to it was relentless and the complicities of both local sheikhs and colonial farmers were important.[10] Indeed, European colonists themselves supported the cause of the foreign labourers, as they too were concerned with protecting their

---

[8] A document submitted to the resident general on 5 June 1891 that advised on the tax exemption explicitly mentioned this point: 'L'idée d'une distinction entre musulmans basée sur leur origine [...] est totalement étrangère au concept musulman. Le musulman arabe, marocain, soudanais, qui passe en Tunisie, s'y trouve donc de plano assimilé au musulman tunisien, soumis aux mêmes autorités justiciable des mêmes juges, régi par la même loi, assujetti aux mêmes impositions.' Translation: 'The idea of distinguishing between Muslims based on their origin [...] is totally foreign to the Muslim's way of thinking. The Muslim, whether Arabic, Moroccan or Sudanese, who spends time in Tunisia can therefore be fully equated to the Muslim Tunisian, and thus be subjected to the same legal system and the same judges, be governed by the same rule of law and be subjected to the same charges' (TNA, E, 18, 2 (1891–1913), doc. 68).

[9] The sheikhs were appointed by the colonial administration and were replaced when they failed in their mission to collect tax.

[10] In some cases the sheikhs did not raise the tax or overlooked the disobedience of some of their citizens.

interests.[11] Because of these new taxes, the labourers would sometimes run away. European farmers operating large properties in the north were strong advocates of anything that could contribute to increasing and maintaining immigration, and especially the presence in the Regency of this 'special' workforce. The agricultural European colonists who had settled in the Regency appreciated these migrants and the local black population, who were considered as a highly productive workforce, and a campaign to keep them in the country (and to facilitate their life by removing the tax) was actively supported by them. The French colonial authorities thus met real difficulties in implementing their taxation policy and would remain divided between the need to raise taxes and fill their vaults on the one hand, and the necessity of avoiding a conflict of interests with the colonial population on the other.[12]

From One Enslavement to Another: The Growing Scale of Forced Labour and Indenture

In the aftermath of the second abolition in 1890, other forms of degrading work, such as indenture and hard labour, took over from slavery. This abolitionist period was characterized by an accentuation and institutionalization of the *khamessat* or sharecropping contract, along with the introduction of compulsory work for all natives. The *khamessat* looks like

[11] The European foreigners were 'sheltered' and therefore not taxed by the *Mejba*.

[12] A document addressed to the resident general in November 1896 once again denounced the support of 'a part of the French colony' to the resistance movements of the black labour: 'On sait que depuis 5 ou 6 ans, une agitation, conduite avec la complaisance d'une partie de la colonie française, a pour objet de soustraire à l'impôt de capitation les étrangers musulmans Fezzani, Marocains ou autres qui viennent s'établir dans la Régence. A la suite d'une campagne de presse en leur faveur, M. Pauliat Sénateur s'est fait le défenseur des ces indigènes et a rapporté favorablement leur pétition au Sénat. La question soumise au Département, celui-ci s'est prononcé contre la prétention des intéressés (voir dépêche du 16 août 1893 no 326).' Translation: 'We know that in the last 5 or 6 years, there has been agitation, driven by the complacency of a part of the French colony, to exempt foreign Fezzani Muslims, Moroccans and others who come to the Regency from the tax. Following a newspaper campaign in their favour, the Senator M. Pauliat has come to the defence of these natives and their petition was favourably reported to the Senate. The department to which this matter was submitted has pronounced itself against the claims of these parties (see the dispatch of 16 August 1893, no. 326)' (TNA, E, 18, 2 (1891–1913), doc. 68).

the sharecropping or *colonat partiaire* in French law.[13] As Brunschvig states, it is not clear whether

> 'il relève de l'héritage de l'antique colonat romain, avec lequel on a pu dire qu'il présente les plus grandes analogies', ou plutôt s'il s'agit d'une 'survivance de la coutume berbère' – et les deux hypothèses, au reste, ne s'excluent point absolument l'une l'autre – C'est que ce contrat sui generis [...] est étranger par son origine et par sa nature au droit musulman. Il lui est même par certains de ses aspects, nettement contraire. (Brunschvig, 1986: 17–21)[14]

Unlike indenture in the Caribbean, the *khamessat* is a form of contract that existed in Tunisia before the implementation of the French protectorate. It was not a new form of exploitation established by the colonial administration, but was rather modified by the latter to serve the interests of the new settlers.

Through this contract (which was mostly verbal and was regulated and functioned according to the local customs), the *khammès* (a sharecropper) would provide, at least in theory, only his work, whereas the *fellah* (the landowner) would supply the land and all the necessary elements to cultivate it, including the capital (seeds, advances), the oxen, the plough, a few litres of oil, a pair of shoes and a yearly renewal of clothing. All of these advances were added to the *khammès*'s debt. From the revenue gained by the harvest was subtracted the salary to be paid to the workers, the tax paid by the *fellah* and finally the cost of the seeds supplied to the *khammès*. The rest would be shared out, with only one-fifth going into the pocket of the *khammès*. From this fifth, the owner would still subtract the advances that had been provided to allow him to survive up until harvest time. If the harvest was deficient and the fifth was not sufficient to pay off the owner's advances, the *khammès* would have to be rented as labour for an additional year.

---

[13] Section L462-1 of the French Rural Code states that 'Le bail à colonat partiaire ou métayage est le contrat par lequel le possesseur d'un bien rural le remet pour un certain temps à un preneur qui s'engage à le cultiver, sous la condition d'en partager les produits avec le bailleur.' Translation: 'The sharecropping lease is the contract by which the owner of a rural property temporarily gives his land to a recipient who commits to its cultivation on the condition of sharing the produce with the lessor.'

[14] Translation: '"it is a legacy from the ancient Roman colonists, which it resembles in many ways", or rather whether it is a "throw-back to a Berber custom" – in any case, the two hypotheses are not mutually exclusive since this contract is sui generis. [...] It is foreign in both its origin and nature to Islamic law, and in some respects is clearly in total opposition.'

It is possible, from this information, to begin drawing a portrait of the *khammès*. They were usually men who needed to acquire an immediate sum of money in order to pay off a debt or to marry, for example. Such a man would find a landowner, request the required sum and, in exchange, would commit to working for him. To discharge his debt, he would be required to do all the work needed on the land entrusted to him, except the harvest, for which the master had to provide assistance. With the exception of these charges, the master could not demand anything from the *khammès*, and if he employed him in other work, he would therefore be bound to pay him. There were, however, many abuses.

The problem was that, in reality, the *khamessat* had many similarities to debt slavery. For example, in the event of the *khammès*'s death, his heir would be charged with finishing the work of the deceased. Conversely, if the *fellah* died during the agricultural season, the *khammès* would have to finish the work for the heir of the deceased *fellah* (Temimi, 1999: 97). In other parts of the legal texts relative to this contract, it is stated that 'Art. 32: Le khammès ne peut abandonner son état qu'en devenant agriculteur lui-même, et s'il ne lui est pas possible de le devenir et qu'il quitte son état pour entreprendre un autre métier ou simplement pour rester oisif, etc., le caïd [regional chief] l'obligera à renouveler son contrat avec l'agriculteur chez lequel il servait ou à exercer son métier chez un autre (décrets du 29 novembre 1874 et du 12 octobre 1886)' (Chailley-Bert, 1896: 1114–15).[15] There was a kind of condemnation or penalty for those who began this type of contract and remained there indefinitely. Thus, not only could the contract be inherited and the dependency perpetuated over several generations, but the *khammès* was also required not to change activity, meaning that the commitment was doubly indelible.

Beyond the legal and theoretical aspects, in practice, several testimonies drawn from archives show that the *khammès* often suffered as a result of this dependency and the difficulty of honouring the commitment, and struggled to finally break free. Many archival documents contain complaints of *khammès* regarding their fate and status, and the abuses inflicted on them by the landowners, who subjected them to ill-treatment and humiliation.[16]

---

15 Translation: 'Art 32: The *khammès* can only abandon his state by becoming a farmer [meaning owner] himself. If this is not possible and he leaves his position to undertake another job or simply to do nothing and so on, the caïd [regional chief] will oblige him either to renew his contract with the farmer whom he served or to exercise his duty with another farmer (decrees of 29 November 1874 and 12 October 1886).'

16 In cantilenas collected during the twentieth century, there is a reference to the harsh condition of *khammès*: 'Dors! Dors, mon petit! Tu seras le khammès

There are also reported cases of abuses against the *khammès*' wives or daughters, and a number of complaints about carrying out tasks that were not related to their initial prerogatives, such as cleaning the landowner's house or doing the chores of a delivery boy (Temimi, 1999: 97).

To illustrate the difficulties for the *khammès* in getting out of this situation, let us take the case of the *khammès* Kilani ben Othman Radsi, who in 1891 wrote a letter in which he complained to the authorities about the persecution from which he was suffering at the hands of the landowner to whom he was committed. He recounts initially that he only had to cultivate the land and the crops, but that later the *fellah* began to force him to perform different kinds of works, 'comme un esclave possédé' ['just like a possessed slave']. He wrote:

> il a fait sur moi des pressions et m'a jeté en prison une première fois en prétextant que je refusais d'honorer mon contrat. Il m'en a fait sortir et m'a emmené près de la ville Sebelet al-kahia alors que j'ai laissé ma femme à Radès. Là j'ai fini le labour et suis rentré à Radès souffrant. Cet homme me redemanda de revenir travailler mais j'ai refusé, il m'a alors promis de me donner un qifz de céréales, et j'ai encore refusé en disant que c'était au naïb de cheikh el Médina [le représentant du maire] de décider. Il m'a alors ré-emprisonné. Et dire que j'ai travaillé pour lui pendant 18 ans [...] et j'ai travaillé patiemment. Je vous demande d'être le juge entre lui et moi, vous qui êtes juste. (TNA, E, 233, 11/1 (1891–1921), doc. 152)[17]

Because of the numerous abuses, the only way to leave this infernal circle was either to escape or, in a small number of cases, to enrol in the French army.

Despite the fact that this type of contract had existed since ancient times in Tunisia, and knowing the consequences that it could give rise to in terms

---

d'un maître, Dont le cœur sera noir, noir, Comme la terre que tu remueras. Et toi aussi, pour manger tu le voleras. Dors! Dors, mon petit! Car lorsqu'on dort on n'a pas faim.' Translation: 'Sleep, sleep, my little boy! You'll be the *khammès* of a master. Whose heart is black. Black as the land that you will plough. And you too will steal to eat. Sleep, sleep, my little boy! Because when you sleep you are no longer hungry.'

[17] Translation: 'he exerted pressure on me and threw me into prison for the first time under the pretext that I had refused to honour my contract. He made me leave and brought me to a place near the town of Sebelet al-Kahia, while my wife remained in Radès. There, I finished the ploughing and returned to Radès in bad shape. The man asked me to return to work again, but I refused, so he promised to give me a qifz of cereal, but I still refused, saying that it was for the *Naïb* of Sheikh el Medina [the representative of the mayor] to decide. So he imprisoned me once more. Yet I worked for him for 18 years [...] and I worked patiently. I ask you – you who are just – to be the judge between him and me.'

of the freedom of the individual, many European settlers and big agricultural companies, such as the French-African Company, resorted to this type of contract for their farms in the late nineteenth and twentieth centuries. While this led to many abuses, it meant that the settlers also suffered from the negative consequences of using such a contract, such as employing *khammès* who, being prisoners of an indelible contract, would often run away or leave before the harvest was over (notably during bad harvests) and therefore before they had honoured their commitment and paid off the sum which had been advanced to them. Repeated bad harvests could indefinitely perpetuate the debt and thus dependence.

The colonists did not easily accept the escape of these *khammès*, who, because they were Muslims, could only be prosecuted through the Tunisian courts. This then explains the settlers' support for the request that 'foreigners', including the 'Sudanese', become 'French protected', making them subject to trial in the French courts.[18] Yet the problem remained that this court had no means to legislate on the particular case of the *khamessat*, which was totally foreign to French case law.

Complaints relative to these cases of escapees were regularly sent to the French colonial authorities, in particular by colonial agricultural companies. For example, the manager of the Société Agricole et Immobilière Franco-Africaine sent a report on 3 December 1891 to Commander Cartoux, civil controller in Tunis, on cases of escapes that had occurred on one of the company's farms located in Sidi Thabet (northern Tunisia):

> Pour différentes raisons et des époques différentes, [6 khammès sur 49] ont jugé à propos de se sauver de notre domaine sans voir payé la somme qu'ils devaient non seulement comme prix de leur achat de khammès, mais encore les avances qui leurs ont été faites aux époques où sous le coup de la famine ils n'avaient rien pour se nourrir.
>
> La plupart d'entre eux sont rentrés sans difficulté alléguant pour leur

[18] Up until 1891, these requests were justified by both the black community and some of the colonists as the solution to the perpetuation of slavery despite its prohibition, as they were claimed to 'deter Tunisians from enslaving'. Such requests were, however, rejected by the French authorities, represented by the resident Massicault, who was under strong opposition from many French and European settlers. By the 1890s, it was generally only women and children who were still being illegally enslaved, whereas men had been largely emancipated after the abolition of 1846 and were able to leave their masters more easily. The post-abolitionist condition that awaited them was arguably no more comfortable, but at least it guaranteed them freedom – that is, the possibility of earning money for their own capital.

excuse les raisons de l'arabe qui n'ont pas le sens commun; mais pour l'un d'eux le cas est différent.

Le nommé Belgacem ben Ahmed el Hamami prétend deux choses:

1. qu'il a été renvoyé par mon prédécesseur [...]

2. qu'il a été acheté par le nommé Naceur Bouboucha et qu'en conséquence il n'appartient plus à la société franco-africaine. [...]

Bien que, comme société française nous ayons plus de tendance à être jugés par un tribunal Français, il me semble qu'en l'espèce, le Tribunal arabe seul puisse trancher la question.

La loi française ne connait pas le Khammès qui contre une somme d'argent, qu'il est tenu de rendre à un moment donné, doit son temps à celui qui lui fait ces avances; et de plus il n'a pas le droit de s'engager nulle part avant sa complète libération.

Il passe à cet effet devant le notaire un acte qui ne lui est rendu que du jour où il est complètement libre. [...]

Je vous prierai Monsieur le contrôleur civil de vouloir bien transmettre à qui de droit la plainte que j'ai l'honneur de déposer entre vos mains, afin de me faire rentrer en possession de ce khammès dont le travail à cette époque de l'année, me serait fort utile. (TNA, E, 233, 11/1 (1891–1921), doc. 100)[19]

---

[19] Translation: 'For various reasons and at different periods, [6 khammès out of 49] escaped from our lands without having paid the sum which they owed not only as the price of their purchase as *khammès*, but also the advances which were disbursed at times of famine when they had nothing to eat.

Most of them returned without any trouble, giving the usual nonsensical 'Arab' excuses; but for one of them, the case is different.

Belgacem Ben Ahmed el Hamami, as he is called, says two things:

1. that he was sent away by my predecessor [...]

2. that he was bought by a man by the name of Naceur Bouboucha and that consequently he no longer belongs to the French-African Society [...]

Although, as a French company, we should be judged by a French court, it seems to me that, in this case, only an Arabic court can rule on the issue.

French law does not recognize the *khammès*, who, in exchange for a sum of money, which he is required to return at some point, owes his time to the person who gives him these advances – and who furthermore has no right to make a commitment elsewhere before his liberation is complete.

An act to that effect is presented to the notary, which is then returned to him only once he is completely free. [...]

I beg of you, Civil Controller, to pass onto whomever it may concern the complaint that I have the honour to put before you and return to my possession this *khammès* whose work at this time of the year would be very useful to me.'

As this document suggests, this French company employed a rather large number of *khamessas* in one of its numerous exploitations on Tunisian territory and took advantage, in substance, of this system of quasi-serfdom. It additionally highlights the kind of vocabulary used to discuss their condition ('prices of their purchase', 'he was bought', 'he belongs', 'his liberation'), underlining the similarities between *khamessat* conditions and that of debt slavery.

The *khammès*'s condition and the reasons for his escape were connected not only to bad harvests combined with the nature of the contract, but also to other obligations, such as the required *Mejba* tax, which made it even more difficult for the *khammès* to honour his commitments.

As mentioned earlier, the settlers, especially those installed in the richer north and organized into associations, often tried to have greater control over the *khammès* in order to force them to work, particularly by insisting that the foreign workers become subject to trial in the French courts. While it was decided that only the *Ouzara* court had jurisdiction over these cases by the decree of 12 October 1886, several attempts were made to rehabilitate the demands by positing them with representatives of the colony, who forwarded them on in turn to the authorities in mainland France. Yet these requests were refused, as shown in the following letter from the French resident sent to the civil controller of Béja in June 1904: 'J'ai l'honneur de vous informer que cette question a été examinée [...]. A l'unanimité les représentants de la colonie ont déclaré qu'il est impossible de donner satisfaction au vœu exprimé [au vœu qui ne tiendrait à rien moins qu'au rétablissement officiel du servage]' (TNA, E, 233, 11/1 (1891–1921), doc. 46).[20]

This refusal was reluctantly accepted. Having failed to obtain a source of forced labour, the colonists demanded that at least the offence of fraud be recognized, which they were successful in. Given the non-solvency of the *khammès*, who were incapable of paying off their debts, this did not resolve the problem. For example, a letter written by the delegate at the main Tunisian colonial administration to the governor general of Algeria on 3 December 1905 lists the reasons for a complaint by a group of settler-farmers installed in the governorate of Zaghouan:

> Les colons européens qui traitent à l'année avec des ouvriers agricoles indigènes sont absolument désarmés vis-à-vis de ceux-ci pour l'exécution

---

[20] Translation: 'I have the honour of informing you that this question was examined [...]. The representatives of the colony unanimously declared that it is impossible to give satisfaction to the expressed wish [the wish that would be nothing less than the official restoration of serfdom].'

des contrats et recouvrement des avances qu'ils sont obligés de leur faire.

Il est d'autre part impossible, sauf à de très rares exceptions d'obtenir des indigènes une caution garantissant exécution de leurs contrats, leur insolvabilité personnelle ne leur permettant pas de trouver des garants [...] les seuls en effet qui s'engagent comme khammès, sont ceux qui n'ont aucune ressource et sont obligés pour vivre de solliciter les avances des propriétaires.

Cette situation générale des ouvriers agricoles indigènes justifie suffisamment la législation indigène qui régit les contrats de khammesat [Il est ici fait référence à la législation initiale relative au khammesat, et qui est en faveur du travail forcé].

En matière de contrats de travail la législation française est absolument inefficace pour garantir les colons européens de la mauvaise foi de certains ouvriers indigènes [...] seule la législation du pays peut assurer l'exécution des engagements contractuels de ces derniers envers les colons. (TNA, E, 233, 11/1 (1891–1921), doc. 36)[21]

Faced with the impossibility of being reimbursed, the settler-farmers demanded to re-adopt the old laws relating to the *khamessat* (those that the decree of 13 April 1874 ascribed to the indigenous owners; TNA, E, 233, 11/1 (1891–1921), doc. 62), which meant restoring compulsory labour. Instead of imprisoning them and waiting indefinitely for a refund which would never transpire (with the charges of imprisonment also to be paid by the plaintiff), it was presented as more effective to force them into returning

---

[21] Translation: 'The European colonists who deal with the native farm labourers throughout the year are absolutely powerless to execute their contracts and to cover the advances that they are required to make. [...]

It is on the other hand impossible, except in very rare exceptions, to obtain from natives a pledge guaranteeing the execution of their contracts since their personal insolvency does not allow them to find guarantors [...] the only persons to commit themselves as *khammès* being those who have no resources and are required to seek advances from the owners in order to live.

The general situation of the native farm labourers is ample justification for the use of native legislation, which governs the contracts of *khamessa* [reference is made here to the initial legislation governing the *khamessat*, which is in favour of forced labour].

In terms of employment contracts, the French legislation is absolutely ineffective in insuring the European settlers against the bad faith of some native workers [...] only the laws of the country can ensure the execution of the contractual commitments of the latter to the colonists.'

to the workplace, which meant contracting a bond for life with the colonist farmer. While this was simultaneously condemned in mainland France, it was nonetheless the French that were asking for the implementation of new legislation.

Until 1907, all the *khammès* who refused to go through with their contractual commitment were imprisoned. They were released only when they committed to fulfilling their contracts, as specified in article I of the decree of 4 August 1884. In June 1907, this article was repealed and section 257 of the Code of Obligations and Contracts was established, stating that the *khammès* could not be forced to work through imprisonment. The only remaining legal avenue left open to the colonists then was the civil courts and the unique right to ask for the condemnation of their *khammès* for damages for non-fulfilment of contracts.[22] It was decided that this abrogation of compulsory work and detention should apply only to the new contracts, thus forcing *khammès* who had entered into contracts before 1907 to submit to the old regime.

The problems relative to contracts between agricultural owners and *khamessa* were never definitively resolved. Numerous decrees were made without ever really preventing the encroachment of the rights of one or the other party. Certain workers took advantage of the high demand for labour in the north of the country to escape and to repeatedly commit to contracts with those offering the best conditions, in spite of the risks and the prohibitions. Moreover, the owners continued to deal with a workforce that guaranteed no stability.

As mentioned earlier, another route of escape for the workers, which would then become institutionalized, was to join the French army. Archival documents show that it was possible for the youngest *khammès*, under certain conditions, to disengage from their contract by joining the military. The bonus received through enrolment allowed them to pay off their debts to the landowner. The army also required a certificate of good conduct issued by the old masters, which still forced them to retain the good will of the latter. While this may have appeared an attractive prospect in some cases, it nonetheless reveals the extent of the *khammès*' difficulties and the limitations of their career prospects (TNA, G, 17, 13, doc. 1).

22 This new constraint for the landowner based on a unique possible recourse – pursuit through the civil courts – obviously provoked many protests.

Compulsory Labour, or *travaux de prestation obligatoire*

In addition to these other forms of post-abolition labour exploitation appeared a new type of forced labour: the mandatory public service, or *travaux de prestation obligatoire*. It has been widely forgotten that, as well as agricultural work and the payment of the *Mejba* tax, the native population, including the *khammès*, were also forced to undertake mandatory services or duties for the French colonial authorities. The colonial administration obliged all the natives to serve time doing hard labour, such as road construction projects, and to do so for free. In 1887, compulsory labour was introduced via a circular sent to all the civil controllers, with a decree appearing in the official journal of legislation in 1891 (TNA, E, 376, 1 (1887–) docs 4–15, 16, 19).

This obligation did not concern the colonists, but only the natives subjected to the *Mejba* tax – that is, men between eighteen and fifty years of age.[23] Initially, these works had to be realized at the same moment as the sowing or harvest season, which gave rise to much opposition and disobedience from the population concerned. The compulsory and burdensome nature of this work gave rise to numerous complaints throughout the country in the 1890s, centred on the fact that it prevented them from performing their job. The Tunisian prime minister thus declared himself against compulsory labour, a position that he outlined in a letter to the French colonial administration:

> Pour quelques journées de travail par an actuellement [...], nous recevons des plaintes [...]. La corvée a existé en Tunisie; elle était considérée par les habitants comme une charge très lourde. Aussi fut-elle abolie en même temps que d'autres impôts impopulaires et remplacée par la *Mejba* qui subsiste encore aujourd'hui. Le projet constitue un retour à l'ancien impôt, tout en laissant subsister l'impôt qui lui a été substitué. (TNA, E, 376, 1, doc. 77)[24]

Compulsory labour was nonetheless maintained and, in order to escape it, many Tunisians had recourse to the possibility of buying back their obligation to work. Repurchase prices were clearly established by a decree. For example,

[23] Article 9 of the decree of 1895 states that the colonist can, if he wishes, make voluntary contributions to 'donner le bon exemple aux indigènes' ['set a good example to the natives'] (TNA, E, 396, 2/1 (1898); E, 376, 1, doc. 82).

[24] Translation: 'For some working days of each year [...], we receive complaints [...]. When compulsory labour existed in Tunisia, the inhabitants considered it a very heavy burden. So it was abolished at the same time as other unpopular taxes and was replaced by the *Mejba*, which remains in effect today. The project constitutes a return to the old tax, while maintaining the tax that took its place.'

the working day of one man was valued at 1 franc, that of horses, mules or camels at 0.90 francs, that of donkeys at 0.15 francs and that of carts and cars at 3 francs (TNA, E, 376, 2/3 (1898–1900), doc. 2). The increase in the phenomenon of repurchase put the administration in a difficult situation: the amassed sums were significant, but the labour needed to execute these works, for which these sums were intended, was almost non-existent.

Beyond the archaic character of the compulsory labour or duties, which clearly recalls the system of medieval serfdom, several archival documents, including administrative correspondence, highlight the problems caused by this practice. One example includes a report written in 1899 on 'travaux de prestation' in the north of the country (in the region of Kef) that insists in particular on the ways in which this obligation was experienced and perceived by the Tunisian population. These included a sense of humiliation and contempt for the European surveillance agents, who were seen to treat the population as little more than servants, all of which created a lack of motivation, anger and an increase in the number of cash repurchases. Several reports insist then on the fact that it was a kind of 'impôt qui revêt aux yeux des indigènes le caractère d'une corvée humiliante' (TNA, E, 376, 1, doc. 255).[25]

The particular type of forced labour represented by 'les travaux de prestation obligatoire' or compulsory labour – which was also closely related to the *Indigénat* system that characterized French colonialism, notably in Africa and Asia – is considered by historians as having little to do with North Africa, and especially Tunisia. The facts of its existence seem to have interested neither historians nor local memory.

As a result, the historical facts relating to compulsory forms of labour during the French protectorate are today completely unknown in Tunisia. Similarly, the exploitation of the *khammesat* system of serfdom by the French colonial settlers has been largely forgotten. How then are we to interpret and understand this forgetting, or this phenomenon that consists of relegating these methods from the colonial period to the historic category of facts 'of little importance'? This bring us back to the question of whether the emphasis on the need to defend the memory of those who suffered from chattel slavery has led to a failure to recognize other forms of colonial and post-slavery exploitation. Arguably, the problem comes not from the duty of memory attached to this widespread human disaster that took on such dimensions, but from the fact that it has inadvertently contributed to concealing and eclipsing other memories that are related to forced labour and indenture. The problem may be that we have not yet gained enough distance

25 Translation: 'tax which the natives see as a humiliating duty or chore'.

from colonialism and its practices to truly understand what it was, especially since colonialism raises questions about the complex relationship between the state, its history and memory (Bonniol: 2007). Perhaps this is a result of the more widespread politics of forgetting developed in response to France's colonial and slave-owning past, as suggested by Myriam Cottias (2007) and Stiina Löytömäki (2013), as well as Christine Chivallon and Nicola Frith in this volume.

As has been seen, slavery was established in certain African countries well before their colonization, and even served as a pretext for a 'civilizing mission'. In general, slavery did come to a total and effective end in the years following these colonial occupations, even if it proved to be a dreadful tool to take over politically and diplomatically in many countries, including Tunisia. Yet if slavery had been subject to criticism since at least the beginning of the nineteenth century, forced labour and indenture would nonetheless remain acceptable forms of exploitation that were directly connected to the colonial phenomenon for the simple reason that they served the colonial economy. While slavery was judged with relative severity and largely eradicated by the colonial administration, forced labour and forms of indenture simultaneously were tolerated and constituted one of the key colonial methods used by this administration. It is for this reason that we face such difficulty, even today, in truly remembering (Saïdi, 2007) and evaluating the impact of this history.

Works Cited

Ben Tahar, J. 2000. 'Un document sur la minorité noire à Djerba au milieu du XIXè siècle', *Revue d'Histoire Maghrébine* 97–98: 669–83.

Bonniol, J. L. 2007. 'Les usages publics de la mémoire de l'esclavage colonial'. *Matériaux pour l'histoire de notre temps* 85: 14–21.

Brunschvig, Robert. 1986. 'Contribution à l'histoire du contrat de Khamessat en Afrique du Nord'. In *Études sur l'Islam classique et l'Afrique du Nord*. London: Variorum Reprints: 17–21.

Chailley-Bert, Joseph. 1896. 'Les conditions économiques et sociales de la colonisation agricole en Tunisie'. *Revue des sciences pures et appliquées* 17: 1111–18.

Coquery-Vidrovitch, C. 1992. *L'Afrique occidentale au temps des Français. Colonisateurs et colonisés (1860–1960)*. Paris: La Découverte.

Cottias, M. 2007. *La question noire. Histoire d'une construction coloniale*. Paris: Bayard.

Echenberg, Myron J. 1975. 'Paying the Blood Tax. Military Conscription in French West Africa, 1914–1929'. *Canadian Journal of African Studies* 9.2: 171–92.

Fall, B. 1993. *Le Travail forcé en Afrique occidentale française (1900–1945)*. Paris: Karthala.

Fall, B., and M. Mbodj. 1989. 'Forced Labor and Migration in Senegal'. In Abebe Zegeye and Shubi Ishemo (eds), *Forced Labor and Migration: Patterns of Movement within Africa*. New York: Hans Zell Publishers: 265–68.

Feraud, L. C. 1872. 'Délivrance d'esclaves nègres dans le sud de la province de Constantine'. *Revue Africaine* 16: 167–79.

French Diplomatic Archives (Quai d'Orsay-Paris). Political and Commercial correspondence, no. 15, file 1.

Löytömäki, S. 2013. 'The Law and Collective Memory of Colonialism: France and the Case of "Belated" Transitional Justice'. *International Journal of Transitional Justice* 7.2: 205–23.

Manning, P. 1982. 'Slavery, Colonialism and Economic Growth in Dahomey, 1640–1960'. *African Studies* 30: 415–34.

Moosa, Matti. 2005. *The Maronites in History*. Piscataway, NJ: Gorgias Press.

Riban, C. 1895. *La Tunisie agricole*. Paris: Challamel.

Saïdi, Hédi (ed.). 2007. *Mémoire de l'immigration et histoire coloniale*. Paris: L'Harmattan.

Temimi, Hedi. 1999. *'Mihnatoul-khammes fi tounes beyna-ttachri' wal waqi'*. Beit al-Hikma: Al maghiboun fi Tarikh Tounes.

Touré, A. 1996. 'L'impôt de capitation dans le Sénégal unifié: Une constante dans son rôle d'instrument de domination coloniale (1921–1936)'. *Annales de la Faculté des Lettres et Sciences humaines de Dakar* 26: 71–82.

Tunisian National Archives (TNA), series E, cartons 233, 376 and 396.

Tunisian National Archives (TNA), series G, carton 17.

Imaging the Present: An Iconography of Slavery in Contemporary African Art

Claire Griffiths

> Conceptually, what one refers to as contemporary African art indicates a clearly critical relationship with tradition, the nation, and the world.
>
> (Okele-Agulu in Aronson and Weber, 2012: 81)

Introduction

As memories of slavery re-emerge in recent historiographies of the transatlantic slave trade, contemporary visual culture from Francophone Africa is participating in this reassessment of the past as part of an on-going discussion of 'development' in present-day Africa. By engaging with the history of the slave trade and exploring its connections with the use of African labour in contemporary modes of production in West Africa, recent art works from the region that once formed the heartland of the French slave trade can be seen to offer a discursive platform on which to foreground 'alternative memorial practices and forms of memory-making' that are moving 'beyond patrimonial discourses and the nation-centredness of the abolitionist movement' (Frith and Hodgson, introduction to the current volume, 17). Two- and three-dimensional and digital works produced in the late twentieth and early twenty-first centuries by artists originating from Francophone Africa, many of whom now live and work in Europe,[1] draw on a visual imaginary that

[1] In an interview at Princeton University in 2010, the West African art historian Chika Okeke-Agulu focused on countering what he identified as an

invokes the history and legacy of the transatlantic slave trade in its contemporary relevance to aspects of development in the former French-speaking colonies of Africa.

In some cases, this body of cultural production engages with European iconographies of slavery by recreating and/or subverting the visual elements that made up the original modes of representation to offer a transnational platform from which to address the economic relationship that has bound Europe, Africa and the Americas for almost four centuries. In other examples, the works draw on textual rather than visual references to the era of the slave trade. In all the various aesthetic and conceptual modes of engagement explored here, the content analysis focuses on how these works are memorializing a past, while simultaneously redefining the history of that past and developing a critical understanding of its legacy in the present.

The works looked at in this chapter are by artists from Benin, the former Dahomey, and West Central Africa, both major centres of the French engagement in the transatlantic slave trade.[2] Key amongst them is arguably the best-known piece of installation art from the region, *La Bouche du roi*, by Beninese artist Romuald Hazoumé. In the UK, Hazoumé became known for this monumental work over the course of the bicentenary year of 2007. The British Museum commissioned this edition of the work as its centrepiece to commemorate the passage of the 1807 bill through Parliament outlawing the transportation of slaves on British vessels. A discussion of four exhibitions of this installation later in this chapter focuses on the dynamic critical narrative Hazoumé has developed, which maps the role of human labour in the oil and mineral extraction industries of West Africa today onto historic forms of exogenous wealth production based on despoliation, enslavement and forced

---

assumption in western art historical theory that an artist who leaves the African environment to work elsewhere ceases to speak and work from an authentically 'alternative' (speaking from a western location) or 'subaltern' (in philosophical terms) perspective. As he pointed out, African artists who live in the US and Europe are still 'African', and 'their work derives from and speaks to their experience of home and the world. [...] So the inordinate emphasis on the African artist's place of residence, whether she lives inside or outside the continent, speaks to the misunderstanding about why [African] people (including artists) decide where to live and work, whether by choice or compulsion' (Aronson and Weber, 2012: 88).

[2] According to the slave voyages database at Harvard University's DuBois Institute, almost two million people were embarked from the Bight of Benin during the period of the Atlantic Slave Trade, making it second only to West Central Africa in the number of enslaved Africans departing on the Middle Passage (Trans-Atlantic Slave Trade Database, 2008).

labour from the region. A second Beninese artist who is re/constructing memories of slavery within the new visual landscape of the contemporary African arts in Africa and Europe is Pélagie Gbaguidi, whose series *Code noir* evokes, rather than directly represents, the legacy of French slaving in West Africa. Since its inception in 2004, Gbaguidi's *Code noir* series has developed into a broader engagement with the legacy of colonization in Francophone Africa, involving a number of related projects, including one in collaboration with the archives department of the Belgian Royal Museum of Africa in Tervuren.

The third body of work examined in detail is *L'Union des états de 1848 à nos jours* by Moridja Kitenge Banza from the Democratic Republic of Congo, whose work is of particular significance in the reclaiming of the iconography of the slave trade. In 2010, Moridja Kitenge received the Leopold Sedar Senghor Prize, effectively the Grand Prix, at the ninth 'Dak'Art' African art biennial for a piece entitled *De 1848 à nos jours*. His winning installation of video and mixed media included a large mural constructed from sugar spoons (Figure 10). This mural evokes, as does Hazoumé's installation, the famous image produced by William Elford of the scandalous 'close packing' of slaves in the Liverpool slave ship the *Brookes*, duplicated and distributed in the British Parliament by the Society for Effecting the Abolition of the Slave Trade (SEAST) in the spring of 1789. A reproduction of the original print formed part of Kitenge's installation, reinforcing the visual reference to the slave trade in the arrangement of the sugar spoons mural and the textual reference to legal abolition in the title *De 1848 à nos jours*.[3]

Ultimately, this chapter sets out to examine how this body of work contributes to a new transnational iconography of slavery that simultaneously engages critically with the past and the dynamics of development in present-day West Africa. It considers how these contemporary works contribute to an on-going political analysis of the making of postcolonial Africa, which seeks to uncover the multiple dimensions of economic marginalization and exploitation that characterize African development today.

---

[3] As it transpired, the explicit reference to the legal abolition of slavery in the French colonies (27 April 1848) in the title, as well as the explicit use of Atlantic slave trade images in the installation, was not mentioned in the review of the biennale's Grand Prix winner in the biennale magazine *Dak'art actu – le Quotidien de la Biennale des Arts de Dakar*. The review focused on the theme of the work as 'une représentation diplomatique' ['a diplomatic representation'], where the 'artiste invite à l'unité des Etats africains' ['the artist proposes the unity of African States'] (2010: 5). This and all subsequent quotations from this and other sources were translated by the author of this article, unless otherwise stated.

Francophone African Art in the Postcolonial Period

In a bid to locate the emergence of this trope in Francophone African art both historically and culturally, the analysis will begin by briefly contextualizing the works in terms of the development of continental and principally Francophone African art in the postcolonial period. Here, they are viewed in relation to the structural landscape of production that has emerged and evolved during the period since Independence. The historical and cultural analysis of Francophone African art production draws from the dominant characteristics of the schools and movements that have formed over the past half century, and looks at the relationship that has evolved between the product, the producer and the political context of production in Francophone Africa since the mid-twentieth century. In this way the role of the artist as interpreter and communicator of contemporary social preoccupations (cultural, religious, social, political and economic) is framed within the broader critical discourse surrounding the related concepts of modernity and development in postcolonial Africa.

It should be noted that, in the context of contemporary African art, the practitioner is 'almost automatically recognised as a critic or at least a social commentator by virtue of his or her profession' (Asgarad, 2010), a role that marks a period of significant development following the constraints on artistic expression imposed by the colonial project. At the height of the colonial venture in Africa, local artistic production was viewed through a primarily anthropological lens, conflating artist with artisan, minimizing the role of individual creativity and maximizing the importance of tradition and inherited practice. As the occupying forces started to withdraw in the mid-twentieth century, colonial Francophone Africa witnessed the emergence of art schools and movements fed by alternative, if still exogenous, philosophical narratives. Drawing on notions of Jungian 'collective consciousness', formal art institutions were founded that promoted the production of an 'authentic' African art, which meant art uncontaminated by European art history.[4] The legacy of this flowering of so-called untutored or intuitive and 'authentic'

---

[4] There were many examples of such schools across French, Belgian and British Africa. They were hailed in many respects as anti-colonial bastions of African artistic production in the sense that they rejected European aesthetic norms and practices. One of the more famous and enduring examples was the Hangar, run by expat Frenchman Pierre Romain-Defossés in the Belgian Congo. The phenomenon was not restricted to Francophone Africa, as evidenced by the history of African art schools from the 1930s to 1960s in South Africa, Rhodesia and Nigeria (see Littlefield Kasfir, 1999).

African art integrated into the structural landscape of art production in the final decades of colonial rule, and, not surprisingly, has persisted into the postcolonial era. As Clementine Deliss has argued, such 'colonial' configurations endured, as 'African art exhibitions in Europe and America continued to swing unsatisfactorily between the anachronisms of "ethnographic" models and market-inspired [...] "tribal art"' (1995: 4).

During Independence, the importance of the visual arts in the construction of national identities had led to a flourishing of 'national' as well as pan-African art movements, exemplified by the Negritude-inspired Ecole de Dakar, sponsored by Senghor, and avant-gardisme, promoted by Mobutu in Zaire. Dreams of economic and cultural renaissance born of Independence faltered as the commodity crises of the 1970s hit and economic depression spread across West and Central Africa. The international 'recovery' plan (known as structural adjustment programmes, or SAPs) that followed in the 1980s decimated state spending, laying bare the minimal human and social development of the first decades of independent rule in the former Francophone colonies. As the political landscape changed, a new visual language emerged. The rural idyll of the Negritude imagination and the modernist, urban-inspired avant-gardisme that had characterized a first optimistic wave of postcolonial art production in the former Francophone colonies lost ground to competing visual narratives. New and recovered techniques, materials and modes of art production were put to the service of alternative critical discourses emerging in the Francophone ex-colonies: 'We find them [artists] re-imagining the formal parameters of traditional artistic media [...] to mediate, comment on and examine real or imagined personal and collective histories' (Enwezor and Okeke-Agulu, 2009: 30).

Since 1990 and the belated 'arrival' of African art on the global scene,[5] 'the discursive landscape of contemporary African art has been shaped according to the struggle between two fields of knowledge [...] and played out in two principal arenas: the ethnographic museum and the museum of art' (Enwezor and Okeke-Agulu, 2009: 12). It is within this increasingly globalized and transnational arena provided by art museums and exhibition space that the works explored in the next section can be located, all of them being firmly anchored in an intellectual terrain where perspectives on contemporary African development are being worked out through a renewed engagement with the past and a critical understanding of its legacies in the present.

[5] The 'arrival' is often signaled as starting with the inclusion at the 1990 Venice Biennale of Ghanaian artist and former art teacher Brahim el Anatsui (now referred to as 'El'), the first African artist to be invited to participate.

Imaging Slavery in Francophone African Art: Manifestations of a Historic Present?

The flourishing of an intellectual and critical aesthetic in the second wave of postcolonial visual culture in Africa emerged out of the multi-directional influences and cultural traffic that have flowed between and among artists located in countries in Africa, Europe and North America since 1990. It is from within these cross-continental networks and exchanges that a visual engagement and transnational iconography of the legacy of slavery in Africa has been evolving in contemporary African art. Artists working independently in former French and Belgian colonies have taken historical iconography and texts from the era of the transatlantic slave trade to engage in a discussion about the state of economic and human development in modern-day Africa. The following discussion focuses on three of these bodies of works which have been constructed around recognisable European textual and visual representations of the slave trade, and which consciously relocate these reference points into a contemporary African economic and geographic space. The works included – Romuald Hazoumé's *La Bouche du roi*, Moridja Kitenge's *L'Union des états africains de 1848 à nos jours* and Pélagie Gbaguidi's *Le Code noir* – are far from being an exhaustive review of African art engaging with the European slave trade and its connections to contemporary development issues in Francophone Africa. The works here exemplify the various conceptual narratives in which the legacy and reproduction of historical slavery in contemporary society is emerging as a trope. While each work displays a fundamentally individual creative engagement with this common trope, the two elements that unite them are an emerging iconology of the enslaved body and a narrative that conflates historical and contemporary time in referencing the history of the slave trade.

Romuald Hazoumé, *La Bouche du roi*

In the work *La Bouche du roi* by Romuald Hazoumé, the word *roi* is both a topographical reference, being a deformation of the Portuguese for river, and a reference to the French involvement in the slave trade. As Romuald Hazoumé explained in an interview for the Musée du Quai Branly in Paris (2005), 'La bouche du roi [...] vient du nom de l'estuaire du fleuve [...] que les Portugais ont appelé "a boca do rio" (embouchure du fleuve), que les Français ont plus tard transformé en "bouche du roi" par ignorance.'[6]

[6] Translation: 'The *Bouche du roi* [...] comes from the name of the estuary of a river named by the Portuguese "a boca do rio" (at the river's mouth) that the French later unwittingly mistranslated as the "King's mouth"'.

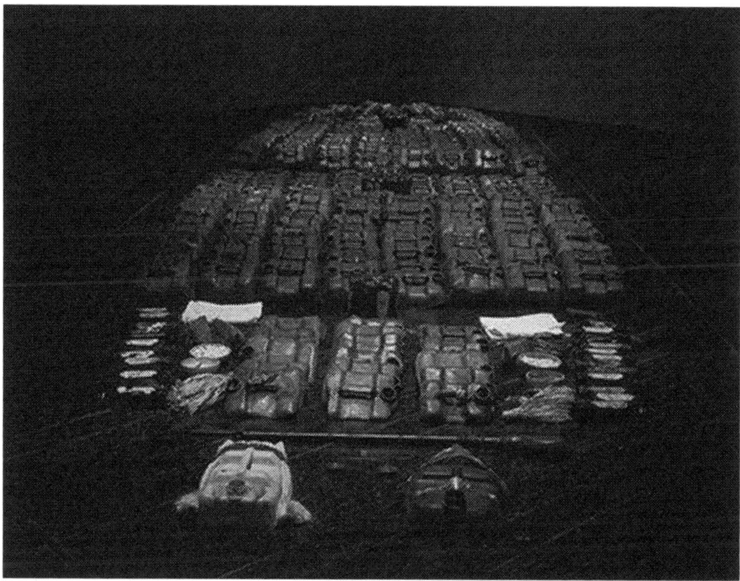

Figure 9: Romuald Hazoumé, *La Bouche du Roi*.
Original full colour image by George Hixson.

The 'Bouche du Roy', as the estuary is also referred to locally, is part of a delta system that provided several embarkation points serving local slave ports (notably Agbodrafo, known to the Portuguese as Porto Seguro) along this stretch of the Atlantic seaboard that the Europeans would name the 'Slave Coast'.

In this first example of contemporary works engaging with historic and modern slavery, the artist depicts the historically enslaved body as an absence, a disembodiment and ultimately a vanishing. In *La Bouche du roi*, the body, as the substance of individuated identity, is represented by a manufactured material plastic. This representation of enslaved people enclosed in the hold of a ship is viewed from a distance ideally above the work (as in the British Museum), enabling the onlooker to absorb the diagrammatic visual references of this massive low-level horizontal installation. From this perspective, the memory of the image of Elford's 1789 representation of close packing on the *Brookes* slave ship combines with the work.

Viewed from a distance, Hazoumé's plastic containers, representing the individual bodies of enslaved people, merge into an undifferentiated mass, bringing to the fore the historical and creative challenge of reclaiming the history of the individual enslaved and re-examining the historiography of their disappearance.

La Bouche du roi has been retelling the history of the transatlantic slave trade in Dahomey through a series of four installations that have acquired new narrative dimensions with each display. Work began on *La Bouche du roi* in 1997 in Hazoumé's studio in Porto-Novo, Benin, and it was first exhibited in 1999 at the Institut français in Cotonou. The initial audience of expats, diplomats and local elites were engaged through the piece to reflect upon France's trading history in this part of the world, as the viewer's gaze was drawn to two larger jerry-can masks positioned prominently side by side in the prow of the vessel. A yellow mask, representing the French king, and metaphorically Europe's involvement in the slave trade, lies alongside a large black mask representing the involvement of African rulers. The role of African traders in the transatlantic slave trade is thus made explicit in the installation. As the artist stated in an interview in 2007, 'I made it for my people' (White, 2007: n.p.).

By focusing on the agents of the trade, the artist adds a dimension to the narrative that is not present within the original *Brookes* diagram. Elford's 1789 image contains no explicit visual reference to the slavers themselves. The inhumanity of the slave system is felt rather than seen. It exists in the pity generated by the gaze of the sympathetic viewer confronted with the implications of the 'close packing' of slaves in the ship's hold. In the original image the African body is a cipher: it is inert and any potential for agency disappears into victimhood. As Marcus Wood has aptly described it, the African bodies of the Elford print are 'supine in perpetuity' (Wood, 2010: 263). Encountering the original image, it is the viewer who becomes the dynamic force of the piece, bringing, through his or her outrage, a moral conscience to the narrative. In contrast, the viewer of Hazoumé's work has a role both outside and within the piece. The spectator is confronted by the monstrosity and is part of it.

The 304 re-used jerry-cans that make up the structure of *La Bouche du roi* carry a significant textual load; not only are they connecting the viewer to a collective historical memory of the transatlantic slave trade, but they are also bringing the audience into contact with a contemporary human disaster originating in the same part of the world and implicating, once again, an international financial system in an era of economic globalization. Subsequent versions will gradually see this contemporary narrative coming to the fore.

A second showing of the piece took place in 2004 in Houston, Texas, in the landmark modern art museum designed by Renzo Piano to house the Menil Collection. The installation of an African work of art in an American museum founded by two French émigrés, Jean and Dominique de Menil, echoes something of the transcontinental relevance of the work.

In Houston, the contemporary narrative of the piece was underscored by an accompanying video of a scene played out across the Niger Delta on a daily basis, with a particular resonance in the capital of America's oil state. The video, entitled *La Roulette beninoise* [*Beninese roulette*], follows the hazardous journey of a local oil smuggler as he transports jerry-cans dangerously overfilled with crude oil that have been strapped to his motorbike on illicit runs over the border between Benin and Nigeria. Illegal trading of oil between countries in the Niger Delta region constitutes a significant 'parallel' market operating outside the control of the American and European multinationals that otherwise dominate the regional oil industry. While the Niger Delta is endowed with around a quarter of the production capacity of the whole of Saudi Arabia, some 2.5 million barrels a day, barely 1 per cent of the six million people living in the area benefit directly from the wealth generated from this resource, while an estimated three-quarters of the population of this region, some 4.5 million, live in poverty on less than $30 a month.[7] Oil spills have caused land, air and water pollution, decreasing fish stocks, contaminating water supplies and destroying arable land. The United Nations Environment Program estimates that the environmental damage from over fifty years of oil production in the region could take a quarter of a century to repair (UNEP, 2011: n.p.). The video draws the attention of the viewer to such issues associated with the export economy of West Africa and reminds us of its transcontinental dimensions. In the region where human beings were once subordinated to the exigencies of the transcontinental trade in sugar, European and American-led oil production has created what has been described as a new form of 'enslavement' of the local workforce.[8]

The emphasis on the human suffering being experienced in workforces holding up global industries was underlined in a third major exhibition of the work at the Musée du Quai Branly in 2005, this time through a soundtrack: 'L'objet rejoint la parole dans cette installation par la restitution d'un fond sonore qui semble émaner des masques eux-mêmes: une litanie de noms d'esclaves et une improvisation de chants alternés, des "Lamentations" ou

---

[7] As the UNDP Human Development Report 2013 indicates, Nigeria, the biggest country in the area, has 68 per cent of its population living under the poverty line, as reported from surveys undertaken between 2007 and 2011 (UNDP, 2013: 160). The other countries in the Delta, including Benin, do not have sufficiently regular and robust statistical accounting procedures to provide equivalent national data.

[8] See Karen Kellogg's (2012) analysis of the impact of oil production in the Niger Delta on the local population.

implorations aux divinités yoruba afin que cesse la souffrance de ces hommes qui "ne savent pas où ils vont"' (Musée du Quai Branly, 2005).[9] This physical bodily dimension comes to the fore in a fourth international exhibition when *La Bouche du roi* came to the British Museum to mark the bicentenary of the 1807 Slave Trade act. 'Liquor bottles, beads and cowrie shells are included [...], as are tobacco and spices, their aroma mixing disturbingly with the terrible sounds and smells of a slave ship' (British Museum, 2007: n.p.). With this ultimate sensory assault on the viewer, the dehumanization that characterized the original 1789 diptych has been replaced by both metaphysical and physical forms of reincarnation. It is precisely this reclaiming and reconstruction that becomes the key element in the dynamic visual narrative as it is being experienced by viewers engaging with Hazoumé's visual historiography of the slave trade.

Through multiple layers of references, the installation conveys the transnational character and the travelling potential of Francophone African art. The structure Hazoumé has created is endowed with a historical load that pulls together three continents articulated around a shared historical narrative of slavery, but constructed outside of historical time lines. Hazoumé describes his approach scientifically: 'my work is like a modern day archaeology' (Spring, 2008: 126). In practice, he engages in *La Bouche du roi* in cross-disciplinary techniques and succeeds in relocating a transcontinental visual iconology of slavery within an atemporal space that lies beyond the historical transatlantic slave trade and contemporary economic development.

Moridja Kitenge Banza, *L'Union des états de 1848 à nos jours*

In the work of this young artist from Kinshasa, trained in the Ecoles des Beaux-Arts of Lumumbashi, Kinshasa and Nantes, and now working in Montreal, the enslaved body is explored through an installation that takes the viewer on a journey from total disembodiment, through a process of reflection and reconfiguration, to arrive finally at a third stage of joyous individuation and reincarnation.

In the winning installation in Dak'Art 2010, the first part of *L'Union des états de 1848 à nos jours* contained a display of massive bank notes denoting a fictitious pan-African currency. The centrality of money and exchange in the past, present and future of Africa are cemented here in the viewer's mind as

[9] Translation: 'Objects and voices are united in this installation through a soundtrack which seems to emanate from the masks themselves, producing a litany of names of slaves alternating with lamentations and exhortations to the Yoruba gods to relieve the suffering of these men [sic] who "know not where they go".'

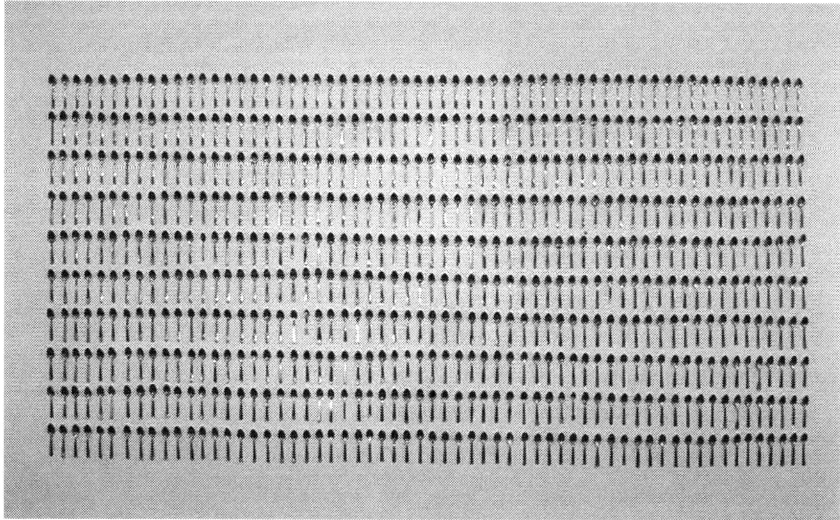

Figure 10: Moridja Kitenge, Section of *Union des Etats de 1848 à nos jours*, Prix Léopold Sédar Senghor, Dak'Art 2010. Image courtesy of the artist.

the journey proceeds to the central piece in the three-part work: a large-scale mural, composed entirely of sugar spoons.[10] At first sight, the spoons look uniformly positioned and identical; but on closer inspection they are merely similar. In fact, they are the result of a participative event that took several years to complete as the artist bartered his fictitious currency against the purchase of these sugar spoons from many locations, in restaurants and cafés, mostly in France, and from friends and acquaintances.

Drawing directly from the same diagram of the *Brookes* slave ship that inspired *La Bouche du roi*, this reconfiguration is mapped out in spoons that constitute both the print medium and the image. What Hazoumé creates from recycled jerry-cans, Kitenge creates from spoons, acting here as a human cipher that is emptied of agency and voice, disembodied and commodified. This commodification reinforces the relationship between material and narrative in both of these works. Notably, Kitenge's work also brings together a metaphysical retelling of the history of the slave trade within the physical materiality of the sugar spoon. This article of European manufacture takes the viewer directly into a tangible relationship with this enduring by-product of the primary export product of the French slave-based economy in the Americas.

[10] It was this mural that visitors encountered on entering the official exhibition housed in the Musée Theodore Monod on Place Soweto in Dakar.

Figure 11: Moridja Kitenge, *Bateau négrier*, installation, Nantes, 2011, detail. Image courtesy of the artist.

A reproduction of the original Elford 1789 image of the *Brookes*, which is located to the left of the mural, serves as a pivot for the installation as it shuttles between abstraction, materiality and temporality. In the sugar spoon frieze, this icon of the abolitionist movement has been deconstructed and transformed into an abstraction, the human cipher evolving out of its simplistic original form and forward on its journey from disembodiment to corporeality.

Developing this interim space of connection and disconnection with the history of slaving, a later installation of the work in Nantes sees the addition of a new version of the original Elford print (Figure 11) made using coffee as the print medium, and again replacing the human cipher of the slave in Elford's diagram with the sugar spoon of the *de 1848 à nos jours* frieze.

The third and final section of the Dakar triptych is a video entitled *Hymne à nous*. Here the spoon of the original frieze has become embodied in a single human form that has multiplied and then collectively breaks into song. The viewer is presented with a two-minute film of what appears to be a choir of men singing to Beethoven's 'Ode to Joy'. The human cipher has arrived at the end of the journey of reconstruction and has recovered agency and voice. In fact, the video shows a compilation of multiple takes of the artist himself singing an anthem he entitled 'Hymne à nous'. Kitenge has described the video in its purpose and content as a work of both individuation and collectivism:

> Je dirais plutôt qu'elle fait appel à une conscience collective. J'ai mixé des textes extraits des hymnes nationaux congolais, français, belges ainsi que des extraits du poème de Friedrich von Schiller dont Beethoven s'est inspiré pour composer l'Ode à la joie et d'un extrait du discours du roi Léopold II 'roi des Belges' quand il envoie les missionnaires au Congo pour la colonisation. J'ai filmé un plan fixe d'une chorale qui se dirige elle-même,

> sans maître de chœur, pour dire que c'est à nous Africains de décider de nous-mêmes et de dire ce que l'on pense. (Andriamirado, 2010: 1)[11]

The return of the 'voice' has a particular salience in this context. The 'silencing of the slaving past' that Christiane Taubira highlighted in her campaign for recognition of the 150th anniversary of the second abolition in France in 1998 has been underscored and reinforced in the work of academics and activists, such as Françoise Vergès and Myriam Cottias. Cottias, in particular, has focused on the importance of 'voice', or the taking away of voice, in the aftermath of abolition, notably in the case of Martiniquais, whose freedom after 27 April 1848 was offered in exchange for their silence (Cottias, 1997: 293–313). The incorporation of words and creation of text are key elements in the way this work can be seen to engage with the historiography of slavery and with contemporary political development in Central Africa.

Pélagie Gbaguidi, *Le Code noir*

Le Code noir is the third and final work that contributes to what is being posited here as a new visual historiography of the slave trade. It moves away from representations of the human body to focus on a visual rendition of the sensory experience of the body in the history of slavery. What the artist, Pélagie Gbaguidi, achieves in her series of works engaging with the history of the transatlantic slave trade is perhaps nearer to what has been identified as a 'biopolitical' dimension in African art – an aesthetic that has been closely explored in relation to the visual expression of the physical impact of brutalization, notably under the Apartheid regime, as seen in South African art (Enwezor and Okeke-Agulu, 2009: 49).

Born in Dakar to Beninese parents and educated in West Africa and Europe, this Beninese artist presents the human body in her work as an atomized and individuated materialization of human suffering. The human being becomes isolated from the mass, allowing Gbaguidi to reflect upon the dehumanizing logic of slavery. Several works from her series *Le Code noir*

---

11 Translation: 'I would probably say that the piece is appealing to a collective consciousness. I've mixed up extracts from the Congolese, French and Belgian national anthems, as well as the poem by Friedrich von Schiller that was the inspiration behind Beethoven's Ode to Joy and an extract from a speech made by King Leopold II ("King of the Belgians") to missionaries sent out to colonize the Congo. The film is a single angle shoot of a choir with no choirmaster. What I am saying here is that it's up to Africans to manage their own affairs and to say what we think.'

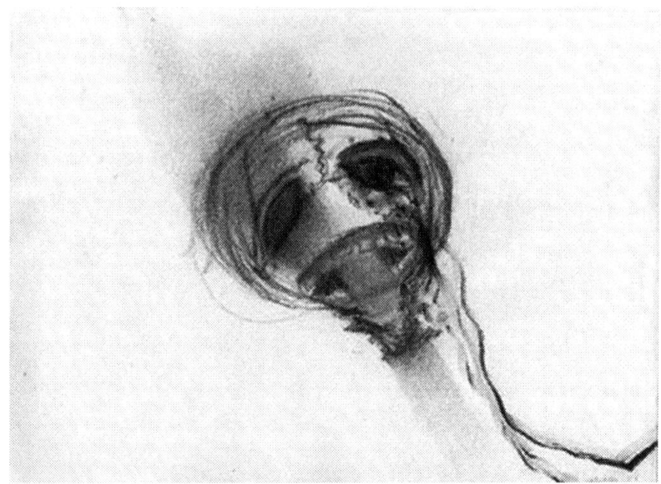

Figure 12: Pélagie Gbaguidi, *Le Code noir*, Dak'Art 2006. Image courtesy of the artist.

have been exhibited in the official selections at Dak'Art in 2006 and 2008 (Figures 12 and 13), and more recently at several venues in Europe, including Nantes.

Gbaguidi came to this subject matter in 2004 as a result of having taken up an artist-in-residency at the Centre des Arts Contemporains in Nantes. Attesting to the importance of Nantes in the French transatlantic slave trade, the city's historical museum at the Château des ducs de Bretagne houses a permanent display of slave-trade-related artefacts. Among these lies a very small leather-bound book behind thick glass in its own display unit. The book contains the official legal framework for the operation of the French slave trade. The extraordinary and inhumane impact of the contents of this book, known in French as *Le Code noir* since its promulgation by the King of France, Louis XIV, in 1685, is explored by the artist in her series of the same name. Gbaguidi's first encounter with the 1742 edition of *The Black Code* unleashed a series of visions that inspired the launch of an initial set of drawings and paintings under the title *Le Code noir*, a collection which over a period of three years grew to some 120 works (Gbaguidi, 2012).[12]

Describing her role as a *griotte*, in the sense of a historian of our times, Gbaguidi argues that 'ce travail de mémoire' ['this memory work'] is more than

[12] This and subsequent information regarding Gbaguidi's work comes from an interview with the author at the artist's studio in Belgium in April 2012, and subsequent email exchanges.

an artistic project. It is a project that works on how memory is constructed, how it is written and how it is transferred from generation to generation. It focuses particularly on what is omitted and on what has not been recognized or recorded. It is in this space that she re-finds that lost reality and reconstructs the memories of slavery. It is a project that is bringing the artist into direct contact with the on-going re-memorialization and rewriting of the history of slavery, both in Europe and in West Africa, as it is reframed within the universality of violence and relocated to a contemporary context.

In 2007, during a residency in Krems in Austria, Gbaguidi explored the *Code noir* theme in the context of its connections with Nazism and state violence. The Austrian residency gave rise to a further forty works, leading to a selected exhibition in Krems, with the series now expanding to some 160 works. Gbaguidi's description of her motivation in producing these latter works on the '*indicible*' or unspeakable aspects of the crime of slavery has precedents in Holocaust studies. In *Eichmann in Jerusalem: A Report of the Banality of Evil,* Hannah Arendt described her engagement with the trial of Adolf Eichmann as one of exposing 'the unspeakable in the banality of evil' (1964: 118). It is this dimension in the history and legacy of slavery that Gbaguidi's work articulates so effectively in her series *Le Code noir.* Among the many images, we encounter distorted faces (Figure 12), their open mouths emitting soundless screams, projecting a sense of the psychic and physical imprint that intolerable and monstrous violence leaves behind on the individual and in the memory generated in and by those individuals.

In 2008 the selection committee of the Dak'Art international biennial chose two of Gbaguidi's *Code noir* works for inclusion in the official exhibition. One of these is a textual piece, containing no visual representations of the human body. The title of the work, *Manifeste contre l'édit du code noir de Louis XIV 1685,* embroidered in red silk on white linen, encapsulates the narrative function of the piece.[13] It is a response to the *Code noir* of 1685, exposing what Abdoulaye Gueye has described as the core function of that original text: 'The *Code noir* epitomizes the relegation of blacks out of the category of human, a total estrangement from humanity by way of bondage' (2011: 93).

Gbaguidi's exposé of this function is underscored by the stark contrast between the medium and the message: the stitchery, calligraphy and surface medium are refined and delicate, redolent of an age that was both brutal and genteel, and riven with the contradictions epitomized by the slave trade. What follows in the text is a searing attack on the human cost of this legislation. The *Code* is not simply attacked as a historical crime, but rather

[13] Conversation with the author at the artist's studio, 12 April 2012. The fine stitchery was done by hand by a Belgian needlewoman.

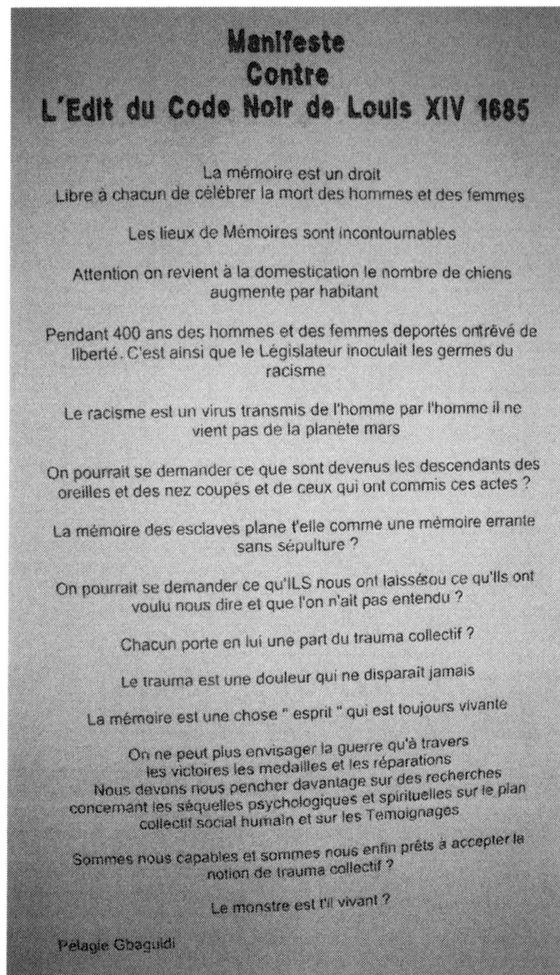

Manifeste
Contre
L'Edit du Code Noir de Louis XIV 1685

La mémoire est un droit
Libre à chacun de célébrer la mort des hommes et des femmes

Les lieux de Mémoires sont incontournables

Attention on revient à la domestication le nombre de chiens augmente par habitant

Pendant 400 ans des hommes et des femmes deportés ontrêvé de liberté. C'est ainsi que le Législateur inoculait les germes du racisme

Le racisme est un virus transmis de l'homme par l'homme il ne vient pas de la planète mars

On pourrait se demander ce que sont devenus les descendants des oreilles et des nez coupés et de ceux qui ont commis ces actes ?

La mémoire des esclaves plane t'elle comme une mémoire errante sans sépulture ?

On pourrait se demander ce qu'ILS nous ont laissésou ce qu'Ils ont voulu nous dire et que l'on n'ait pas entendu ?

Chacun porte en lui une part du trauma collectif ?

Le trauma est une douleur qui ne disparaît jamais

La mémoire est une chose " esprit " qui est toujours vivante

On ne peut plus envisager la guerre qu'à travers
les victoires les medailles et les réparations
Nous devons nous pencher davantage sur des recherches
concernant les séquelles psychologiques et spirituelles sur le plan
collectif social humain et sur les Temoignages

Sommes nous capables et sommes nous enfin prêts à accepter la notion de trauma collectif ?

Le monstre est t'il vivant ?

Pelagie Gbaguidi

Figure 13: Pélagie Gbaguidi, *Le Code noir*, Dak'Art 2008. Image courtesy of the artist.

connections are drawn between historical slavery and contemporary racism. In this way, the artist locates this work alongside others in the series by firmly embedding it in a contemporary context. For example, in a current project in the Royal Africa Museum in Tervuren in Belgium, Gbaguidi's drawings respond to works in the museum's archives and on display, notably to Edouard Manduau's *La Civilisation au Congo* of 1884. She does this by stripping history back, uncovering the 'unspeakable' and challenging the erroneous timelines that traditionally frame our references to Africa.[14]

---

14 Accessible online at http://www.africamuseum.be/collections/browsecollections/humansciences/display_object?objectid=32617.

Gbaguidi explains her engagement with the subject in these terms: 'For me outing the monster from oblivion has required my taking a stand in relation to the history of Africa; and in so doing participating in the transmission of the contemporary story'.[15]

The connection her work has with the works explored earlier in this chapter does not lie in a reclaiming of an iconography of slavery. Indeed, Gbaguidi visualizes the imprint of slavery on human consciousness and memory in her series *Le Code noir* by drawing from different aesthetic and art historical traditions. Rather, where the work of these three artists intersects is in an analytical exploration of the contemporary dimensions of the historical crime of slavery. Instead of positing slavery as a past event, the ending of which was marked by abolition, the works subvert the progressive view of the historical process by locating the historical past within the present. As such their work is contributing to a dynamic critical discourse being generated by creative, cultural and academic communities, as well as by the plethora of political organizations that make up the critically engaged civil society of Francophone Africa.

Conclusions

While not all art from the former French and Belgian African colonies is 'political', there is a widely shared assumption in the art world, from practising visual artists to curators to critics, that the focus of the African artist should be directed towards social and political issues.[16] As Moridja Kitenge observes in an interview: 'la politique impregne mon travail' ['politics infuses my work'] (Andriamirado, 2010: 2). This dimension of Francophone African art is recognized beyond the 'art world', as testified by Abdoulaye Wade's opening address to the Dak'Art biennale of 2010. The Senegalese president made great play of the close connection that exists in Africa between art, culture and development: 'l'art', he stated, 'est le baromètre de nos réalités' ['art is the barometer of our reality'] (Wade: 2010).

In the works of Romuald Hazoumé, Moridja Kitenge and Pélagie Gbaguidi, the enslaved body refers to a period in Africa's past while signifying a contemporary reality. In transforming the iconography (that is the form) of the enslaved body and placing it into dialogue with the viewer, the works are generative of a new iconology that generates a new meaning.[17] In this context,

---

15 Interview with the author at the artist's studio in Belgium, 12 April 2012.

16 Table ronde, Conference *Dak'Art et Développement*, Village de la Biennale, Dakar, 9 May 2010.

17 This difference was defined by Barry Hallen in reference to Suzanne Preston

the narrative load carried by the icon becomes dynamic, as the multiple audiences in Africa, Europe and the US engage with the works and generate more layers of meaning. As Blier (1995) has noted, meanings in African art are generated at multiple levels, and key to this is the reception of the work in these different contexts.

While there has only been space to discuss three works in detail in this chapter, it should be mentioned that there are many other artists drawing visually on the legacy of the transatlantic slave trade to explore contemporary issues in West African development.[18] Together these works can be explored as an intellectual (as opposed to aesthetic) art movement in the mapping of contemporary development issues, and particularly the exploitation of human capital, onto images of historical slavery. Collectively, these works reclaim the humanity of the enslaved, either through a refiguring of the dehumanizing cipher or through the total absence of a recognisably human body in figurative abstraction or in text. Drawing from a range of visual traditions, the works offer a critical commentary of modernity and development in a conflation of historical time. This temporal collapse proposes an alternative historiography of Atlantic slavery, where abolition ceases to exist in its traditional legal and social formulations.

As the visual narrative positions itself within a wider multidisciplinary critique of the global issues of poverty, economic exploitation, underdevelopment and emigration in contemporary Francophone Africa, these works contribute an alternative dimension in which to explore existing critical development theory in the region. In these works, history is visualized within a framework that succeeds in challenging and undermining erroneous ways of historicizing and presenting African development as continuous, 'modern' and 'progressive'. In essence, this emerging 'movement' (as it might be labelled) is making a visual contribution to displacing chronological constructions of slavery and abolition by offering an alternative aesthetic platform that is capable of accommodating a far broader, transnational history of the past and present of West and Central Africa.

Blier's work on African art and 'her reworking of the distinction between iconography and iconology, between form and meaning' (1995: 76).

[18] Notable among these are Julien Sinzogan from Benin, Guy Wouaté from Cameroon and Jems Robert Kokobi from Cote d'Ivoire, to mention just three. Other artists addressing the same themes through less explicit visual references to historical slavery include Barthélemy Toguo, Pascale Martine Tayou and Viya Dibé.

Works Cited

Published Works

Andriamirado, Virginie. 2010. 'Je m'inspire de l'histoire pour interroger ce que je vis et la manière dont je ressens le monde'. Interview with Moridja Kitenge Banza. *Africultures* 26 June. Available at http://www.africultures.com (consulted on 22 November 2012).

Arendt, Hannah. 1964. *Eichmann in Jerusalem: A Report of the Banality of Evil.* New York: The Viking Press.

Aronson, Lisa, and John S. Weber (eds). 2012. *Environment and Object: Recent African Art.* Munich, London and New York: DelMonico Books Prestel.

Blier, Suzanne Preston. 1995. *African vodun: art, psychology and power.* Chicago: University of Chicago Press.

British Museum. 2007. 'La Bouche du Roi: An Artwork by Romuald Hazoumé'. Press release. Available at https://www.britishmuseum.org/about_us/news_and_press/press_releases/2007/la_bouche_du_roi.aspx (consulted on 23 March 2014).

Cottias, Myriam. 1997. 'L'oubli du passé contre la citoyenneté: troc et ressentiment à la Martinique (1848–1946)'. In Fred Constant and Justin Daniel (eds), *1946–1996: cinquante ans de départementalisation outre-mer.* Paris: L'Harmattan: 293–313.

Dak'art actu – le Quotidien de la Biennale des Arts de Dakar 2 (10 May 2010).

Deliss, Clementine. 1995. About Modern Art in Africa. London: Whitechapel Gallery.

Elford, William. *Brookes.* Royal Museums Greenwich. Michael Graham-Stewart Collection, object identification ZBA 2745. Available at www.nmm.ac.uk (consulted on 15 February 2014).

Enwezor, Okwui, and Chika Okeke-Agulu. 2009. *Contemporary African Art since 1980.* Bologna: Damiani.

Gueye, Abdoulaye. 2011. 'Memory at Issue: On Slavery and the Slave Trade among Black French'. *Canadian Journal of African Studies/La Revue canadienne des études africaines* 45.1: 77–107.

Hallen, Barry. 1995. 'Philosophy, Postmodernism and Art in Contemporary African Studies'. *African Studies Review* 38.1: 69–80.

Kellogg, Karen. 2012. '"That is our bitterness": Enslavement by Oil in the Niger Delta'. In Lisa Aronson and John S. Weber (eds), *Environment and Object: Recent African Art.* Munich, London and New York: DelMonico Books Prestel.

Littlefield Kasfir, Sidney. 1999. *Contemporary African Art.* London: Thames and Hudson.

Musee du Quai Branly. 2005. *Romuald Hazoumé et La Bouche du Roi.* Available at http://www.quaibranly.fr/fr/programmation/expositions/expositions-passees/romuald-hazoume-et-la-bouche-du-roi.html (consulted on 6 May 2014).

Spring, Chris. 2008. *Angaza Africa*. London: Lawrence King.

Trans-Atlantic Slave Trade Database. 2008. Available at www.slavevoyages.org/tast/database/search.faces (consulted on 31 March 2014).

United Nations Development Programme (UNDP). 2013. *Human Development Report 2013, The Rise of the South: Human Progress in a Diverse World*. New York: UNDP.

United Nations Environment Programme (UNEP). 2011. 'UNET Ogoniland Oil Assessment Reveals Extent of Environmental Contamination and Threats to Human Health'. Available at http://www.unep.org/newscentre/default.aspx?ArticleID=8827&DocumentID=2649 (consulted on 6 May 2014).

White, Michael John. 2007. 'Carrying the Past into the Present: Romuald Hazoumé, "La Bouche du Roi"'. *1807 Commemorated: The Abolition of the Slave Trade*. Available at http://www.history.ac.uk/1807commemorated/exhibitions/art/labouche.html (consulted on 25 March 2014).

Wood, Marcus. 2010. *The Horrible Gift of Freedom: Atlantic Slavery and the Representation of Emancipation*. Athens, GA, and London: University of Georgia Press.

Oral Sources

Asgarad, Meskerem. 2010. Curator and director, National Art Centre, Addis Ababa, Ethiopia. Round table and subsequent discussions held at the conference 'Les Arts plastiques et le développement'. 9–10 May. Village de la Biennale de Dak'Art, Dakar.

Gbaguidi, Pélagie. 2012. Artist, interviewed by the author at the artist's home in Belgium, 12 April.

Wade, Abdoulaye, President of Senegal. 2010. Dak'Art 2010 opening address, Théatre Daniel Sorano, Dakar, Senegal, 7 May.

Cartographies of Memory, Politics of Emancipation

Françoise Vergès

Since the 1960s in Martinique, French Guiana, Guadeloupe and Réunion, and since 1998 in metropolitan France, memories of the slave trade and colonial slavery have mobilized associations, artists and scholars. After a long period of marginalization in French history and culture, colonial slavery has become a point of reference for the women, children and men who identify with those who were enslaved in the French colonies. It has been used to question the French national narrative and its pervasive inequalities, to explore the role and place of racial thinking in the making of French society and culture, and to analyse its contemporary legacies both in France and in the former colonies that became French departments in March 1946. Archaeological research, new research in the archives, the construction of memorials and monuments, the opening of galleries dedicated to the history of the slave trade and slavery in French museums, the organization of colloquiums and temporary exhibitions, the creation of spectacles (including dance, theatre and artistic performances) and the exploration of new fields (for example in law, the arts and music) have all testified to the renewed importance of this history for understanding the past and the present. The Taubira law, which in May 2001 recognized the slave trade and colonial slavery as 'crimes against humanity', marked an important turning point in this process. In 2006, the first national day for commemorating the memories of the slave trade, slavery and their abolitions was held (10 May), and in 2012 the largest memorial in the world dedicated to the struggle against slavery, the Memorial to the Abolition of Slavery, was opened in Nantes. These important acts suggest that progress has been made in the fields of education, research and culture. So how do we explain the fact that, in the wake of decolonization, such a resurgence in memories of slavery has led to official commemorations that are often emptied of social and cultural content, whether in the Hexagon or in the overseas departments? Moreover, clear discrepancies remain between official commemorations and state discourses on the one hand, and the cultural, social, economic and political situation of the territories in which slavery reigned supreme for two centuries on the other.[1] These imbalances lead us to question how the paths opened up by the struggle for recognition for France's slaving past have been diverted away from their radical promise to lead us to social justice, and thus to examine the context in which these memories were revived and whether they can ever escape instrumentalization.

It is not surprising that the ways in which memories are activated reflect the political and cultural contexts in which they emerge. In the 1970s, as memories resurfaced within the context of decolonization, it was the resistance of the enslaved – marooning, insurrection and rebellions – that was celebrated, becoming the source of anti-colonial struggle. Historiography of the time insisted on the importance of this resistance and the role of slavery in European imperialism. Nowadays, French historiography is more diverse. One approach seeks to challenge the focus of the 1970s on resistance and to look at forms of complicity or arrangement within the plantation nexus. The plantation is seen as a 'grey zone' – a notion proposed by Primo Levi, who challenged the tendency to over-simplify and gloss over unpleasant truths concerning the inmate hierarchy that inevitably developed in the camps, and that was exacerbated by the Nazi methodology of singling some out for special privileges. But Levi also insisted on the *responsibility* of a system that sought to brutalize human beings to the extent that only the strong could survive (Levi, 2013). Another approach argues that the abolition of slavery was incomplete and it did not question racial hierarchy or economic inequalities (Schmidt, 2009). But few works have tackled the centrality of slavery in the French experience and its connection with a weak abolitionist movement. Arguably, this is because French historiography still marginalizes the role and place of colonialism in the making of France.

To understand contemporary memories of slavery, it is important to analyse how the anti-colonial struggles of the 1960s and 70s that took place in the French overseas territories were quashed, and how a subsequent reconfiguration of the Republic's former 'civilizing mission' has contributed

---

[1] Data from the overseas territories (IEDOM and INSEE) consistently reveals these disparities in terms of unemployment, industry, social malaise, and so on.

to a new form of cultural hegemony. I refer here to Antonio Gramsci's notion, which explains the process of moral and intellectual leadership whereby dominated or subordinate classes *consent* to their own domination by ruling classes, as opposed to simply being forced or coerced into accepting inferior positions (1971). Too often, historical research into the memories of slavery has neglected to examine the political context in which these memories emerged after the 1946 law had transformed the former colonies into overseas departments. The social, cultural, economic and political mutations that have occurred in the past sixty years have changed these overseas societies in unprecedented ways, and they provide the backdrop for the emergence of memories of slavery and their marginalization. Some elements of these mutations deserve to be listed, including the postcolonial struggle; the development of a culturally and socially powerful middle class constituted of civil servants; the end of the rural world; increasing social inequalities and unemployment rates (the unemployment rate having remained for the last five decades between 20% and 30%); the arrival of consumer society with its destruction of local enterprises and its construction of large malls and dependency on importation; the lack of connections with surrounding countries and of local opportunities; not to mention the legacies of racism. Arguably, it is impossible to analyse how and why memories of slavery have emerged and evolved, as well as who have been the main actors within this revival, without also looking at these important mutations.

In the 1960s and 70s, memories of slavery constituted a point of reference within the decolonization movement and the affirmation of a culture, history and language inherited from conflicts, tensions and encounters in a context of brutal exploitation, racism and inequality. These memories served as a counter-discourse, or a decolonial rhetoric, for the women and men whose lives had been made invisible by the colonial regime. It led to creative expressions in culture, arts, images, poetry, music and literature. An intellectual and artistic generation learned about the heroes and heroines of the anti-slavery struggle – Mulâtresse Solitude, Louis Delgrès, Cimendef, Dimitile, Héva and many others – and about the anticolonial struggle through which they could analyse and understand the postcolonial present. Memories of slavery were then associated with the political parties of the anti-colonial Left, as well as social and cultural movements that were turned towards decolonization struggles throughout the world.

In 1998, the call to remember the slave past reached the Hexagon during the 150th anniversary of the abolition of slavery in the French colonies.[2] That

[2] The focus on French abolitionism over the slaves' revolts and resistance led to protest and to the 23 March 1998 march through the streets of Paris, when

year, the first demands for the recognition of the slave trade and slavery as 'crimes against humanity' were presented to the National Assembly. One proposition was finally discussed and led to the adoption of the Taubira law (10 May 2001). In May 2006, the Chirac government followed a number of propositions made by the Comité pour la mémoire de l'esclavage [Committee for the Memory of Slavery] (CPME), then presided by Maryse Condé, including making 10 May the 'National Day for Remembering the Slave Trade, Slavery and their Abolitions'.[3] There were frictions and tensions around the choice of the national date. In 2009, the association CM98 obtained the recognition of 23 May as the 'Remembrance Day for the Victims of Slavery'.[4] In the overseas departments, 10 May comes after local remembrance days (22 May in Martinique, 27 May in Guadeloupe, 10 June in French Guiana and 20 December in Reunion).[5] Since the Taubira law demanded an official ceremony with the highest representatives of the state, the format had to be negotiated with the state. It thus depends on the capacity of the Committee and of actors within civil society to influence the government, and on the government's political approach. There are also broader socio-political contexts that weigh heavily on the decision-making process, such as whom to invite, what to say, whom to please and what amount of money the government agrees to spend. Official speeches have varied widely from one year to the next, some being purely formal, while others have sought to reach further than the familiar and highly moralizing rhetoric condemning slavery. Although 10 May has taken hold in society – associations, schools, cities and universities all organize their own ceremonies – its success remains dependent upon the commitment of official institutions, which lend space and logistical support to the commemorative events. The reconciliation of officialdom with popular expressions

30–40,000 'descendants of slaves' celebrated their ancestors (see Vergès, 2006, for more on the sesquicentenary).

[3] Article 4 of the 2001 law required the creation of a committee of twelve personalities. Presided by the writer Maryse Condé, the first committee held consultations with politicians (notably Taubira), artists, scholars and associations about the choice of a national date of commemoration. Between 2004 and 2008, I was vice president of the Committee, and I became its president in 2008, following Maryse Condé's resignation. I was then president from 2009 to 2012.

[4] Serge Romana, president of CM98, was a former member of the Committee. He resigned from the Committee over their choice of 10 May.

[5] These dates reflect the local applications of the 27 April 1848 decree (Loi no. 83-550, 1983), with the exception of Martinique, where the enslaved forced the colonial governor to declare emancipation on 22 May, before the decree's official arrival.

has remained difficult. The process of remembering the slave trade, slavery and their abolitions remains fragile and is far from being inscribed in French consciousness. Not only do the national media barely mention the 10 May ceremony, but, until now, the official event has been held on an invite-only basis.

In 2006, the decision was taken to hold the official ceremony in the Jardin du Luxembourg, which is the property of the Senate. With the exception of 2009, when it was held in Bordeaux, the official ceremony has always been held there and has involved both the State and the Senate. Between 2006 and 2012, the Committee tried to influence the content of the ceremonies, pushing for the inclusion of artists to foreground the cultural legacies of the enslaved. There is now a monument in the Jardin, inaugurated in 2007, entitled 'Le Cri, l'Écrit', created by the artist Fabrice Hyber, and a stele was unveiled in 2011 for the ten-year anniversary of the Taubira law which celebrates the specific contributions of slaves' struggles to human rights. In 2013, the ceremony under the presidency of François Hollande centred on the laying of wreaths by children in front of the monument, but in both 2011 and 2013, ceremonies were marred by the brutal expulsion of members of the Brigade Anti-Négrophobie from the Jardin. Set against this heterogeneous context, this chapter considers how memories of slavery can support and enrich renewed struggle for social and cultural justice, and how they might escape the processes of reification whereby they become an empty shell for official commemoration.

It is important to begin by looking anew at the situations of Martinique, French Guiana, Guadeloupe and Réunion. For the sake of clarity, I will refer to these as overseas territories, even though this terminology is problematic since it perpetuates a cartography in which the Hexagon acts as the central reference for its satellites. Today, the cartography of the French national narrative is contained within the borders of the Hexagon. But throughout history, this cartography has been both mutilated and mutilating, as it has passed through different phases of contraction and expansion. Indeed, the borders of French history have gone through many different configurations. What is of interest here are the ways in which the 'end of the colonial empire', which came to a close in 1962 with the end of the war in Algeria, has led, as Kristin Ross (1996) and Todd Shepard (2006) have separately argued, to a period of contraction. Decolonization meant that France reconfigured itself within the borders of the Hexagon and Europe. This has meant that the demands and needs of the societies living in the overseas departments have slowly become irrelevant. Though France wants to keep them within its administrative and political space because of geopolitical and economic interests, it does not integrate them into its national consciousness. Data and statistics concerning the overseas departments are never added to national data. Hence, information about work, health, education, housing and demographics does not enter national statistics. The works of Aimé Césaire and Frantz Fanon are still not taught in school, and it would be exceptional to find a French schoolchild capable of naming a hero of the anti-slavery struggle. As Maryse Condé has said, 'Pour les Français, ces endroits se résument à ces lieux de vacances où ils boivent du punch et mangent du boudin' (Vergès and Sesquin, 2011).[6] But this ignorance is not exclusive to the Hexagon, since even in these territories, young people barely know their history and culture and it is therefore left to willing teachers to educate them.[7]

The members of the caste of civil servants within these territories became active agents in maintaining the status quo, despite the degradation of their social and economic conditions. Originally, during the colonial empire, French civil servants were lured to the colonies with higher salaries and greater benefits than they would have received in France for the same position. Their resettlement in the colony was fully covered – they received an indemnity of 40 per cent for being far from France, an indemnity of 25 per cent for accepting to go to the colony and six months' salary to help them settle – and they could travel back to France every two or three years with their family. After the Second World War, the government did not abolish these privileges and thereby created a marked difference between metropolitan and local civil servants, leading to protests by the latter. In 1948, strikes occurred throughout the overseas departments, but to

---

6 Translation: 'For the French, these places are simply holiday resorts where they drink punch and eat blood sausage.' This and all subsequent quotations from this source and others were translated by the author of this article, unless otherwise stated.

7 In a 2011 report, the Institut national de recherche pédagogique (INRP) revealed that teachers privilege the *leçon de morale* (moral of the story) when they speak of colonial slavery. Teachers declare that they want to give a civic lesson to the future 'white' citizens by showing them that 'blacks' must be treated with respect. The racialization of colonial slavery is explained as a failure of moral values and the struggle against racism becomes a lesson about respect and humanistic tolerance, and the brutality of the search for immediate profit based on brutal human exploitation is marginalized. Observations in classes by the researchers of the INRP show that students do not quite comprehend why slaves did not 'revolt' and put an immediate end to the slave trade and slavery, which in turn pushes teachers to emphasize punishment and death. The agency of slaves and their voices, as well as those of other actors – namely, slave traders and slave owners – are minimized.

no avail.[8] In 1950, a second wave of strikes led the government to adopt a 25 per cent rise in salaries for local civil servants, but inequalities between civil servants from France and local civil servants continued to increase. In the National Assembly, Aimé Césaire denounced the status of the 'local cadre' by arguing that it was a remnant of colonialism and racism.[9] These disparities were justified in a report in 1951 to the government by metropolitans serving in Martinique, who argued that 'Si l'Européen veut garder son autorité indispensable au bon accomplissement de sa tâche, il doit veiller particulièrement à son vestiaire, d'où frais supplémentaires' (cited in Anonymous, 2013).[10] The report added that 'le métropolitain, astreint à subir ce climat tropical, ne peut, par ses conditions de vie antérieures, ses difficultés d'adaptation, supporter de vivre lui et sa famille dans la case, habitat normal de la grande masse de la population' (cited in Anonymous, 2013).[11] Following the report's proposal, the government increased the indemnity for the metropolitan's spouse. Local unions saw it as a further expression of racism and contempt. They struck in all four departments from 15 May to 16 July 1953 and were supported by workers from the private sector. They finally won: the relocation indemnity was suppressed, the indemnity for living away from France was retained and applied to all civil servants, and their salaries were increased (40% in Guadeloupe, French Guiana and Martinique, and 53% in Réunion). While this was a struggle for the equality of treatment, it led to unexpected and perverted consequences, due to the transformation of local economies into an economy of consumption. Being a civil servant meant financial security, which became more and more important in an economy where the industry

---

8 In Réunion, 95 per cent of civil servants struck from 18 to 25 May 1948, supported by workers from the private sector.

9 'La notion de "cadre local" est injuste, humiliante et discriminatoire [...] La notion de "cadre local" est une survivance contre laquelle doivent s'élever tous ceux qui, comme nous, sont partisans de la doctrine: à diplôme égal ou à travail égal, salaire égal' (Césaire, 1946). Translation: 'The notion of "local middle managers" is unjust, humiliating and discriminatory [...]. The notion of "local middle managers" is a throw-back against which all those, like us, who believe in the doctrine "equally qualified, equally paid" must rise up.'

10 Translation: 'If a European wants to maintain the authority that is vital for completing his work, then he must pay particular attention to his clothes; hence his greater expenses.'

11 Translation: 'the metropolitan forced to live in a tropical environment cannot, because of his habits and difficulties of adaptation, be expected to live with his family in a hut, this being the normal habitat for the vast majority of the population'.

of services with lower pay progressively replaced industrial jobs. But it also produced an assimilated middle class, who hung on to what became undue privileges and who imposed a way of life that justified higher market prices for the whole population. In the 1980s, they became a political force leading political parties and unions, and getting elected to local and national institutions, bringing with them an ideology of assimilation and consumption. They have slowly shaped demands and needs, and reinforced the dependency on France, since their privileges rest on the French government's will to maintain them.[12] It remains to be seen if their children, who despite their university diplomas cannot find jobs, will challenge a system that produces both privileges and discrimination to the middle class.

In the 1960s and 70s, the arrival of consumer society went along with the increased repression of political demands. Electoral frauds were common, as was the brutal repression of demonstrations and of activists. Riots in December 1959 in Fort de France in Martinique, in February 1962 in Saint Louis in Reunion, and in May 1967 in Pointe-à-Pitre in Guadeloupe were expressions of anger against the lack of progress in the overseas territories in terms of jobs and education. There were protests against the creation of the BUMIDOM, a governmental office whose mission was to organize the mass migration of young Antilleans, Guyanese and Reunionnese to mainland France to fill up low-paid jobs in hospitals, post offices and the industrial sector (Léonard-Maestri and Reinette, 2007). The Creole language was forbidden in public institutions and schools. Vernacular practices and expressions were ignored, if not repressed. The infamous 1960 Debré Ordinance, which gave power to the French State to expel at will any civil servant who was deemed a threat to public order, targeted those who had a leading role in political or

[12] Over the years, there have been several reports from the French National Assembly, the Senate and government agencies on the perverted consequences of the increased salaries of civil servants for similar positions as in metropolitan France. Already in 1958, less than ten years after the 1946 law, a report from the National Assembly pointed to these effects (Brard, 2007). A 2014 report from the Senate concluded along the same lines: 'Or, ces compléments de rémunération, en majorant de 40% le coût pour les budgets locaux des fonctionnaires territoriaux dans les Antilles et en Guyane et de 53% à La Réunion, jouent un rôle majeur dans le poids des dépenses de personnel pour l'ensemble des collectivités des DOM' (Doligé, 2009). Translation: 'Hence, these salary supplements, which increase local budgets by up to 40% in the Antilles and Guiana, and 53% in Reunion, play a major role in adding to the weight of personal expenditure for all of the overseas territories'. Economists' analysis of the overseas territories also underlined the fragility and precariousness of their economies (see for example Wasmer and David, 2012).

union activity.[13] It was within this context of struggle against postcolonial forms of repression that memories of colonial slavery emerged. It was also in a global context of increased struggle against imperialism and of the Cold War, in a context of new regional emergences – the Cuban Revolution in the Caribbean, the independence of Mauritius in the Indian Ocean, the struggle against apartheid in South Africa and the war of liberation in Mozambique – that the memories of colonial slavery became a terrain on which to express demands for emancipation and decolonization. The 1848 Abolition Act was retrospectively criticized for bringing in new forms of subjugation, thereby betraying the promise of equality (Vergès, 2001).

In post-slavery and postcolonial societies, the legacies of colonial slavery can be seen today in the unequal access to land, and thus to capital, and in the lingering inequalities in health, education and jobs. Colonial slavery and colonial status, followed by the integration of these societies into the European Community and the creation of new global markets, have weighed heavily on the populations. For memories of slavery to remain a source of subversive cultural and political expression, we need to remind ourselves of the cultural, social and economic objectives of slavery. It was based on an economy of predation, feeding from access to cheap goods, the racialization of a mobile and sexualized workforce, and the creation of legal codes that excluded the racialized workforce from rights. It was a regime of terror, of brutal and cruel punishments that hindered expressions of solidarity and, consequently, the creativity and determination of those who stood against and resisted its systems. To explore this further, let us now look in further detail at these two key aspects in which French post-slavery and postcolonial societies have been caught, namely predatory economics and the organization of a racialized and exploited workforce.

The pacification of the memories of slavery belongs to a strategy that seeks to transform colonial slavery into a history that does not lean on the present (although laments over new occurrences of enslavement always appear in official discourse). What is missing is an analysis of the racialized economics and politics of slavery. Though this was present in the 1960s and 70s, and to a certain extent in cultural history, in France a moralistic discourse has dominated. If the moral condemnation of slavery is not only a necessity, but also a political objective (that is, the principles around which a community agrees to constitute itself), the disappearance of explanations that consider economic, cultural and social interests serve an agenda where

13 In 1963, thirteen people from Réunion, three from Martinique, nine from Guadeloupe and one from Guyana were sent to the Hexagon (Nouvet, 2012; see also Marchal, 2010; Rousse, 1992; Céleste and Médéa, 2012).

politics are reduced to adhesion to abstract values that mask relations of power.[14] In other words, morals express a common social ethics; they lead to principles whose application means a condemnation not only in words but in acts, of acts and words that exclude groups and individuals from the community of equals. The community sets laws whose evolution testifies for the expansion of rights of groups and individuals. A victim of racism, xenophobia, anti-Semitism, homophobia or sexism can resort to the law to seek damages and compensation. Struggles for justice and equality found the morals of a community; morals are not abstract principles but principles grounded in the fight of minorities against discriminatory treatment. In the example we are exploring here, the long absence of the recognition of the slave trade and colonial slavery as defining moments for the construction of France, its cultural and social identity, its wealth, embodies a lack of respect for the lives of many, and insults the dignity of those who built the wealth of France. The first reparation is the moral recognition of the crime; then other forms of reparation can follow the acknowledged crime. Moralistic discourse is the empty version of morals. It condemns the crime but does not want to acknowledge its concrete legacies. Its genre is the top-down one, absolving the State from the crime, saying 'We, who know and who are righteous, condemn those who committed the crime. They belong to backwardness; they have not seen the light'. This discourse does not acknowledge the benefits enjoyed by *all* of an economic, social and cultural system based on exploitation.

The social organization of slavery is a process that requires breaking the spirit of the enslaved and imposing servility and submission through the constant threat of punishment and torture, which were always performed in public to impress upon other slaves the idea that the master was omnipotent and enjoyed total impunity.[15] Yet, slavery was not just about cruelty and sadism; it was also about the pleasures of consumption (sugar, tobacco, cotton, and so on) and gender (not only the constructions of the male or female enslaved body, but also the gendering of products: sugar was associated with the feminine and tobacco with the masculine), as well as profit, the fabrication of whiteness and blackness, geopolitics, hope, love and despair. The difficulty of seeing slavery in the context of a complex set

[14] Note that morals in this context do not mean moralistic thinking, a derivation of the Christian discourse where a human being is seen as a monad and where social and cultural contexts do not matter.

[15] See for instance the autobiographies of Frederick Douglass (1996), Solomon Northup (2014) and Mary Prince (1988), or contemporary testimonies at http://www.antislavery.org/english/.

of relations made up of multiple forces, determinations and contradictions, and as a contingent, complicated and challenging world, may explain why jumping to a condemnation of slavery without understanding the fabrication of consent to bondage is attractive. Otherwise, it is necessary to dive into a world where the worst of human beings is made visible.

In my own work, a return to the political dimension has meant looking at the slave and the indentured worker as political and historical agents – that is, as actors in the global struggle for rights, social justice and equality. Likewise, a return to the economic dimension has meant looking at global networks of exploitation, the role of consumption, the destruction of the environment and its links to the organization of labour, gender and poverty. It means freeing the history of slavery from a moralistic and/or an orthodox economic approach. Two actions must be taken: first, we must challenge a periodization in the history of colonization which too often creates a clear and clean rupture between slavery and post-slavery economies (even though numerous works have shown how and why practices of slavery were kept alive and emancipation hindered); and second, we must ask why, in post-slavery economies, forms of bonded work continue to exist. In the French case, we cannot dismiss the fact that, in 1848, slavery was abolished in the French colonies and Algeria (where the war of colonial conquest was ongoing) was transformed into three French departments so that it was no longer a colony, but part of France. Thus, it had to elaborate new codes of laws that would serve two different situations and in which colonial interests had to be preserved. Post-1848 colonial politics must be approached transversally by looking at the rivalry with France's old enemy, England, whose colonial empire was expanding. In other words, colonial slavery must be thought of as a form of global work organization and as a moment within the long history of European colonialism and imperialism and its racial cartography (Moulier-Boutang, 1998). A moralistic approach masks these aspects and tends to lead to a Manichean view where good is pitted against evil, and where slavery is condemned in righteous terms that disguise the history of economic interests, racialized discourses and the hierarchical organization of society. Rather, the condemnation of slavery should be posed as an ethical question – why does a consumerist economy need some form of bonded work and what can be done about it? – and should therefore open up debates on rights, equality, social justice and solidarity.

This then raises key questions. What do we understand by social justice and the 'common good'? What are the universal principles by which we abide? The orthodox economic approach implies a linear history of progress where slavery leads to serfdom, which leads to industrialization, which leads to post-Fordism, which leads today to the culture industry, which has commoditized and standardized culture and art, suffocating individuality and destroying critical thinking (Adorno, 2001; Hall, Morley and Chen, 1996), with each 'progressive' step erasing the one preceding it. This is, of course, a teleological illusion. Many economic forms can coexist; for example, a woman can be deprived of identity papers and be forced into bonded labour while still owning a cell phone. Karl Marx, despite suggesting that there would be a linear trajectory towards emancipation, understood this when he wrote that trafficking in human flesh was an important source of profit: 'Direct slavery is just as much the pivot of bourgeois industry as machinery, credits, etc. Without slavery you have no cotton; without cotton you have no modern industry. It is slavery that has given the colonies their value; it is the colonies that have created world trade, and it is world trade that is the pre-condition of large-scale industry. Thus slavery is an economic category of the greatest importance' (Marx, n.d.: 94–95).[16] Marx (1867) also acknowledged the possibility that diversity of forms of slavery could exist: 'Alongside the modern evils, a whole series of inherited evils oppress us, arising from the passive survival of antiquated modes of production, with their inevitable train of social and political anachronisms. We suffer not only from the living, but from the dead'. Arguments that assert either that slavery bequeathed the industrial revolution or that it had no impact on capitalism come to a dead end because both think in terms of national economies. In fact, using a variety of quantitative techniques, economic historians have been able to show that the slave plantation could be a profitable enterprise. For Eric Williams, the profits of the 'triangular trade' between Europe, Africa and the New World 'made an enormous contribution to Britain's industrial development' (1964: 19). This view was, and continues to be, controversial. Slavery is seen as a backward and unproductive system that could not therefore have produced sufficient profits to assist capitalist accumulation. The debate on the transition to capitalism has tended to focus on the internal economic and social changes, which were necessary for capitalist development, thereby ignoring or minimizing the role of external factors. Working on figures for 1770, Robin Blackburn (1997), for example, has argued that triangular trade profits may have provided anything between 20.9 per cent and 55 per cent of Britain's gross fixed capital formation. Studies have shown that profits from the slave trade allowed bankers, investors and slave traders to invest in property, vineyards, mansions and art, thus accumulating

16 Marx also wrote that 'The slave market maintains its supply of labor-power by war, piracy, etc., and this rape is not promoted by a process of circulation, but by the natural appropriation of the labor-power of others by physical force' (cited in Kakar, n.d.).

capital (Pétré-Grenouilleau, 2009). The predatory economy rests on the coming together of a diversity of interests: individuals and groups agree to share risks and profits, while none feels bonded to another.

As such, predatory economics links financial, cultural and political networks across borders, fabricating people who do not matter and whose living and working conditions are unimportant. It has a destructive force which must meet an organized counter-force because, as Machiavelli wrote, 'It is an illusion to believe that those who dominate would ever be satisfied with what they own, that their superiority warrants wisdom. The avidity of the powerful is limitless and is only contained by the resistance of others' (cited in Lefort, 1992: 198).

Slavery, indenture and forced labour belong to the history of predatory economics, which has involved the massive displacement of people to serve the interests of the few, a gendered division of labour, rape, kidnapping, exile and survival, the establishment of rules and laws that legitimate the violation of basic rights to constitute a cheap workforce, the destruction of the environment and the development of 'green imperialism', which decides what must be preserved and what can be destroyed. A study of the ways in which land was cleared, cities were built around the sugar economy and rivers were polluted offers a new direction in which to broaden our understanding of slavery.

French post-slavery and postcolonial societies were integrated into the global organization of a mobile workforce. It began with the enslaved people – the thirteen million Africans deported to European colonies – and continued with the indentured workers – the millions of Indians and Chinese, the hundreds of thousands of Malagasy and Africans who were moved from one colony to another to serve local economic interests (Emer, 1986; Lai, 2004). Javanese and Vietnamese workers were sent to New Caledonia to labour in the nickel mines, while French and colonial convicts and political exiles were sent to French Guiana to clear the tropical forests. These societies also merged with movements of migration produced by European imperialism in the nineteenth century, among them Muslims leaving the Gujarat to escape famine and poverty, who settled in Madagascar, Mauritius, Kenya, Réunion, and so forth. Colonies were also places to exile political fighters: for example, Algerians (Lallaoui, 1999; Rachid, 2011; Anonymous, 2010) and Vietnamese (Donet-Vincent, 2003, 2006) were sent to New Caledonia or French Guiana. In other words, French economic interests beyond the 1848 Abolition Act continued to need a mobile workforce whose access to rights was denied and which remained highly racialized and gendered (just as it had been under slavery, the ratio among indentured workers being two-thirds men to one-third women).

While the histories of bonded and indentured labour, and of racialized access to rights and property, have shaped popular memories, it has been the memories of slavery (despite their marginalization) that have served as the matrix for these later memories. Memories of slavery have thus dominated post-slavery forms of unfree labour, with colonial slavery serving as the central reference point to speak of colonialism, exploitation and racism before being transformed into an empty signifier in official commemorations. On 10 May 2013, François Hollande, president of the Republic, quoted Aimé Césaire and declared that 'Le premier, c'est l'impossible réparation. [...] Le seul choix possible, c'est celui de la mémoire, et c'est de la vigilence, et c'est la transmission'.[17] For Césaire, reparation was impossible since it would lead to victimization and leave the wounds of deportation and exile unhealed; however, he also followed this statement by speaking about France's debt towards African countries and post-slavery societies: 'les Européens ont des devoirs envers nous [...], mais plus encore à notre égard pour des maux dont ils sont la cause' (Vergès and Césaire, 2005: 40–41).[18] A public debate on reparation is therefore needed that goes beyond individual financial compensation and explores with the populations concerned what public policies could be developed.

Indeed, representations of the populations of those who reside in post-slavery and postcolonial overseas territories have long been negative. A Senate report (Doligé, 2009), for example, talked of rooted negative clichés in the Hexagon regarding the overseas territories. They are viewed as living on welfare, as biting the hand that feeds them and as ungrateful citizens, all of which serves to justify a sense of exasperation towards their claims. The cultural, social and political terrain upon which the return to slavery and anti-slavery has been occurring in recent decades is thus conflicted and tense, while memories remain fragmented and territorialized. This territorialization of memories marginalizes the transcontinental connections constructed by opponents of an economy of predation. Instead, colonial slavery should be inscribed as a *singular* event *within* the long history of brutal exploitation and predatory economics, thereby making visible its connection with other forms of forced migration and labour exploitation, such as indentured labour.

As we draw a cartography of predatory economics, so too a cartography of resistance emerges. Redrawing these maps requires going beyond the

[17] Translation: 'the first point is that reparation is impossible. [...] The only possible choice is memory, vigilance and transmission.'

[18] Translation: 'Europeans have certain duties towards us [...], even more so since they have been the cause of our sorrows.'

discourse of geopolitics that traces the roads and routes of power. A critical cartography resides in the small details and requires an approach attuned to actual practices. In drawing a cartography of predatory economics, my aim has thus been to highlight important correspondences that foreground global financial connections, itineraries of exile, transnational solidarity, the circulation of ideas, and a sense of common interest among people living in different places where they speak different languages and hold different beliefs. What is mapped is not a faithful rendition of roads, ports, cities, mountains and rivers, as can be found in military maps, but rather the nodes and contact zones where exchanges, encounters and conflicts occur. Such a cartography reveals the asymmetry of access to goods and basic needs, the existence of inequalities and the creation of 'grey zones'. It is a dynamic cartography subjected to mutations and transformations, such as the discovery of new riches and new areas of mining, and the emergence of wars that displace fortresses and shift borderlines. It is also a 'cartography of the unexpected', of a world built through resistance whose outcomes can never be fully foreseen. It is the tension between the rules elaborated to maintain an order necessary to pursue the objectives of predatory economics and the push and pull of movements seeking to contain its destructive forces that construct the terrain where the unexpected arises.

Some examples of this cartography are the routes of Creole languages and cultures, and the circulation of ideas, poetry, music, rituals, knowledge of plants and disease, and techniques that the African and Malagasy enslaved took with them to the colonies. The other key example is the anti-slavery transcontinental movement and the global impact of the Haitian Revolution. Since 1994, the UNESCO Slave Route project has been tracing the multiple routes of enslavement and resistance, insisting on the intangible heritages of the enslaved. In South America, the emergence of social and cultural movements of Afro-Colombians, Afro-Brazilians, Afro-Bolivians and Afro-Venezuelans (the use of a general category should not hide more culturally specific complexities) has been redrawing the cartography of the sub-continent. The terminology of 'black' or 'Afro-' is morally and politically charged. For instance, in Colombia, since the late 1980s, with increasing black politicization, the term 'Negro' has been more common, although reference to *Comunidades Negras* ['black communities'] has been institutionalized to some extent by a 1993 law that refers to them as such. People may avoid all reference to colour and instead use regional terms. In the department of Chocó in the Pacific region, black people often refer to themselves as *Libres* ['free people'], a usage dating back to colonial times. The term *Costeño* ['coastal dweller'] is often used to imply blackness, since many Afro-Colombians live in coastal regions. In the English-language literature, the terms 'black' (also 'Black') or 'black person' are more common than 'Afro-Colombian' (Cifuentes, 1986). Artists, associations and scholars are contributing to the elaboration of new cartographies that exceed the borders of the nation-state, as they insist upon a cartography of diasporic formations.

A certain French republican universalism often hides a practice of 'white' communalism. Two important steps thus need to be taken. The first is to 'emancipate' slavery from moralistic and economistic approaches. The former has transformed the enslaved into an object of suffering that needs to be pitied and protected, whereas the latter has encouraged a reading of economy that rigorously separates different economic stages from each other – antiquity gives way to slavery, which gives way to feudalism, which gives way to industry – none of which can explain why forms of slavery or feudalism continue to co-exist with recent technological discoveries and in spite of important progress in humanitarian law and technologies (Vergès, 2011). The second is to show the central role played by colonial slavery in the making of France, Europe and the world, including its anti-black racism, and how this inserts a colour line in the making of republican citizenship. This would mean bringing back the radicalism of anti-slavery politics, its transnational conceptualization, its global history, its humanitarian impulse and the battle of ideas it provoked around human rights, equality and humanity. It is the simple facts that need to be repeated by remembering the singularity of the enslaved and the extreme unevenness and diversity with which slavery was applied throughout the French colonies and the colonial world, in order to map the local, regional and global dimensions of colonial slavery and anti-slavery movements.

Works Cited

Adorno, Theodor. 2001. *The Culture Industry: Selected Essays on Mass Culture*. London: Routledge.

Anonymous. 2010. 'Les bagnards algériens de Guyane: A la recherche d'une mémoire enfouie'. *Le Soir d'Algérie* 18 August. Available at http://www.lesoird-algerie.com/articles/2010/08/18/article.php?sid=104738&cid=41 (consulted on 16 February 2014).

—. 2013. 'Départements d'outre-mer: Il y a 60 ans, la grève des fonctionnaires'. *Lutte ouvrière* 155. Available at http://www.lutte-ouvriere.org/documents/archives/la-revue-lutte-de-classe/serie-actuelle-1993/article/departements-d-outre-mer-il-y-a-60-ans (consulted on 9 December 2013).

Blackburn, Robin. 1997. *The Making of the New World Slavery: From the Baroque to the Modern, 1492–1800*. London: Verso.

Brard, Jean-Pierre. 2007. 'Rapport d'information relatif à l'amélioration de la transparence des règles applicables aux pensions de retraite et aux rémunérations outre-mer'. 13 March. Available at http://www.assemblee-nationale.fr/12/rap-info/i3780.asp#P2070_191764 (consulted on 10 March 2014).

Céleste, Fabrice, and Laurent Médéa. 2012. *Les muselés de la République*. TikTak Productions.

Césaire, Aimé. 1946. *Archives of the Assemblée nationale constituante* 26 February.

Cifuentes, Alexander (ed.). 1986. *La participación del negro en la formación de las sociedades latinoamericanas*. Bogota: Instituto Colombiano de Cultura; Instituto Colombiano de Antropología (ICAN).

Doligé, Eric. 2009. 'Les Dom, défi pour la République, chance pour la France, 100 propositions pour l'avenir'. 7 July. Available at http://www.senat.fr/notice-rapport/2008/r08-519-1-notice.html (consulted on 14 February 2014).

Donet-Vincent, Danielle. 2003. *De soleil et de silences: histoire des bagnes de Guyane*. Paris: La boutique de l'histoire.

—. 2006. 'Les "bagnes" des Indochinois en Guyane (1931–1963)'. *Criminocorpus: Les bagnes coloniaux*. Available at http://criminocorpus.revues.org/182 (consulted on 16 February 2014).

Douglass, Frederick. 1996. *Narrative of the Life of Frederick Douglass*. New York: Library of America.

Emer, P. C. (ed.). 1986. *Colonialism and Migration: Indentured Labour Before and After Slavery*. London: Springer.

Gramsci, Antonio. 1971. *Selections from the Prison Notebooks*. Ed. and trans. by Quintin Hoare and Geoffrey Nowell-Smith. London: Lawrence and Wishart.

Hall, Stuart, David Morley and Kuan-Hsing Chen. 1996. *Critical Dialogues in Cultural Studies*. London: Routledge.

Hollande, François. 2013. 'Intervention du président de la République à l'occasion de la Journée nationale des mémoires de la traite, de l'esclavage et de leurs abolitions'. 10 May. Available at www.elysee.fr/declarations/article/intervention-du-president-de-la-republique-a-l-occasion-de-la-journee-nationale-des-memoires-de-la-traite-de-l-esclavage-et-leurs-abolitions/ (consulted on 11 March 2014).

Institut d'Émission des Départements d'Outre-mer (IEDOM). Available at http://www.iedom.fr/iedom/ (consulted on 10 March 2014).

Institut national de la statistique et des études économiques (INSEE). 2006. 'Les inégalités de revenus entre les DOM et la métropole'. Available at http://www.insee.fr/fr/themes/document.asp?ref_id=ip1279 (consulted on 10 March 2014).

Kakar, Ashraf. N.d. 'Slavery in America, Material Culture and Archeology'. Available at http://www.academia.edu/190353/slavery_in_America_material_culture_and_archeology (consulted on 14 February 2014).

Lai, Walton Look. 2004. *Indentured Labor, Caribbean Sugar: Chinese and Indian Migrants to the British West Indies, 1838–1918*. Baltimore: Johns Hopkins University Press.

Lallaoui, Mehdi. 1999. *Les Kabyles du Pacifique*. Paris: Au nom de la mémoire.

Lefort, Claude. 1992. *Écrire à l'épreuve du politique*. Paris: Calmann-Lévy.

Léonard-Maestri, Antoine, and Michel Reinette. 2007. *L'Avenir est ailleurs*. Cinéma Public Film.

Levi, Primo. 2013 [1988]. *The Drowned and the Saved*. London: Abacus.

Loi no. 83-550 du 30 juin 1983 relative à la commémoration de l'abolution de l'esclavage. Available at http://www.legifrance.gouv.fr/jopdf/common/jo_pdf.jsp?numJO=0&dateJO=19830701&numTexte=01995&pageDebut=01995&pageFin= (consulted on 10 March 2014).

Marchal, Manuel. 2010. 'Hommage aux Réunionnais victimes de l'Ordonnance Debré'. *Témoignages* 15 October.

Marx, Karl. 1867. 'Preface to the German Edition'. In *Capital, Volume 1*. Available at http://www.marxists.org/archive/marx/works/1867-c1/p1.htm (consulted on 10 March 2014).

—. N.d. *The Poverty of Philosophy: A Reply to M. Proudhon's Philosophy of Poverty*. New York: International Publishers.

Moulier-Boutang, Yann. 1998. *De l'esclavage au salariat. Economie historique du salariat bridé*. Paris: PUF.

Northup, Solomon. 2014. *Twelve Years a Slave*. London: Penguin.

Nouvet, Fernand. 2012. 'L'ordonnance du 15 octobre 1960, une loi scélérate'. *L'Humanité* 20 January. Available at http://www.humanite.fr/monde/l%E2%80%99ordonnance-du-15-octobre-1960-un-texte-scelerat-488191 (consulted on 14 February 2014).

Pétré-Grenouilleau, Olivier. 2009. *L'Argent de la traite. Milieu négrier, capitalisme et développement, un modèle*. Paris: Éditions Aubier.

Prince, Mary. 1988. *The History of Mary Prince: A West Indian Slave*. New York: Oxford University Press.

Rachid, C. 2011. 'La déportation des Kabyles vers la Nouvelle-Calédonie (Kalidoune)'. 30 June. Available at http://www.kabyleuniversel.com/2011/06/30/la-deportation-des-kabyles-vers-la-nouvelle-caledonie-kalidoune/ (consulted on 11 March 2014).

Ross, Kristin. 1996. *Fast Cars, Clean Bodies: Decolonization and the Reordering of French Culture*. Cambridge, MA: MIT Press.

Rousse, Eugène. 1992. *Combat des Réunionnais pour la liberté, T 1&2*. Saint-Denis: Océan Éditions.

Schmidt, Nelly. 2009. *La France a-t-elle aboli l'esclavage? Guadeloupe, Martinique, Guyane (1830–1935)*. Paris: Perrin.

Shepard, Todd. 2006. *The Invention of Decolonization: The Algerian War and the Remaking of France*. Ithaca, NY: Cornell University Press.

Vergès, Françoise. 2001. *Abolir l'esclavage. Une utopie coloniale. Les ambiguïtés d'une politique humanitaire*. Paris: Albin Michel.

—. 2006. *La Mémoire enchaîné: Questions sur l'esclavage*. Paris: Hachette.

—. 2011. *L'Homme prédateur: Ce que nous enseigne l'esclavage sur notre temps*. Paris: Albin Michel.

Vergès, Françoise, and Aimé Césaire. 2005. *Nègre je suis, nègre je resterai: Entretiens avec Françoise Vergès*. Paris: Albin Michel.

Vergès, Françoise, and Jérôme Sesquin. 2011. *Maryse Condé. Une voix singulière*. France 5.

Wasmer, Etienne, and Quentin David. 2012. 'Rapport sur la situation économique de la Nouvelle Calédonie'. Available at http://www.ufcnouvellecaledonie.nc/wp-content/uploads/2013/12/situation-economique-de-la-nc.pdf (consulted on 10 March 2014).

Williams, Eric. 1964 [1944]. *Capitalism and Slavery*. London: Andre Deutsch.

Notes on Contributors

Christine Chivallon is an anthropologist and geographer, currently Director of Research at the CNRS (National Centre of Scientific Research) in France. Her research focuses on space and identity, mainly in Caribbean societies, Caribbean migration to Europe and the memory of slavery. Among her major works are *The Black Diaspora of the Americas. Experiences and Theories out of the Caribbean*, (Kingston: Ian Randle Publishers, 2011) and 'On the Registers of Caribbean Memory of Slavery', *Cultural Studies*, Vol. 22:6 (2008), 870-891. Her most recent book is *L'esclavage. Du souvenir à la mémoire (Paris: Karthala, 2012).* See: http://www.lam.sciencespobordeaux.fr/fr/users/christine-chivallon.

Ines Mrad Dali is a graduate of the École des Hautes Études en Sciences Sociales in Paris (2009). Her Ph.D. dissertation focused on the black minority in Tunisian society since the abolition of slavery. Her current research looks at slavery, dependency and abolition in North Africa and in the Arab-Muslim worlds; she is also interested in the identity claims of black minorities in these regions, particularly in twenty-first-century revolutionary and post-revolutionary contexts. She is currently Assistant Professor at the University of Sousse in Tunisia.

Charles Forsdick is James Barrow Professor of French at the University of Liverpool and AHRC Theme Leadership Fellow for 'Translating Cultures'.

He has published on travel writing, colonial history, postcolonial literature and the cultures of slavery. He is also a specialist on Haiti and the Haitian Revolution, and has written about representations of Toussaint Louverture. His publications include *Victor Segalen and the Aesthetics of Diversity* (Oxford University Press, 2000) and *Travel in Twentieth-Century French and Francophone Cultures* (Oxford University Press, 2005).

Nicola Frith is a Chancellor's Fellow and AHRC Leadership Fellow at the University of Edinburgh and is working on a project entitled 'Mapping Memories of Slavery: Commemoration, Community and Identity in Contemporary France', which is funded by the AHRC. She is specialist in slavery studies and Francophone postcolonial studies, and has written a number of articles and chapters on reparations and the politics of memories of slavery in contemporary France. She is the author of a monograph entitled *The French Colonial Imagination: Writing the Indian Uprisings, 1857–1858, from Second Empire to Third Republic* (2014).

Claire H Griffiths is Professor of French and Francophone Studies and Head of Modern Languages at the University of Chester, and formerly senior research fellow (now honorary fellow) at the WISE Institute for the Study of Slavery and Emancipation at the University of Hull. She has published a number of books on development and culture in former French African colonies. Her current project is focusing on visual discourses of development in the Francophone world.

Kate Hodgson is currently a Postdoctoral Research Fellow at the University of Liverpool and is working on a British Academy-funded project entitled 'Haiti and the International Politics of Anti-Slavery'. Recent articles include 'French Atlantic Appropriations: Montlinot, eighteenth-century colonial slavery, penal and forced labour schemes between Europe, Africa and the Americas', *Forum for Modern Language Studies* (2015) and '"Internal Harmony, Peace to the Outside World": Imagining Community in Nineteenth-Century Haiti', *Paragraph* 37:2 (2014).

Renaud Hourcade is a postdoctoral researcher with the Curapp-CNRS, University of Picardie (France). His PhD research on local memories of slavery in France and the UK was undertaken while a member of the IEP de Rennes, where he also taught sociology and politics. His work was published as a book by Dalloz in 2014, entitled *Les ports négriers face à leur passé. Politiques de la mémoire à Nantes, Bordeaux et Liverpool.*

Sotonye Omuku is a graduate of the University of Bristol in French and Music. She completed her PhD at UCL in 2013 on a project looking at representations of slavery and the slave trade in Francophone West African literature.

Srilata Ravi is Professor of French at the University of Alberta and Research Fellow in the School of Humanities at the University of Western Australia. Her research interests are in Comparative literary and cultural studies; Francophone postcolonial studies and Indian Ocean studies. She is the author of *Autour de l'œuvre de Gérard Bouchard. Histoire sociale, sociologie historique, imaginaires collectifs et politiques publiques* (2015 co-edited with Claude Couture); *Rethinking Global Mauritius: Critical Essays on Mauritian Literatures and Cultures* (2013); *Rainbow Colors-Literary Ethno-topographies of Mauritius* (2007); *Ecritures mauriciennes au féminin: penser l'altérité* (2011, co-edited with Véronique Bragard); *Asia in Europe, Europe in Asia* (2004 co-edited with Mario Rutten and Beng Lan Goh).

Catherine Reinhardt is a lecturer in the Department of World Languages and Culture at Chapman University, California. She is the author of a number of publications on slavery, race and memory in the Caribbean, including *Claims to Memory: Beyond Slavery and Emancipation in the French Caribbean* (New York: Berghahn Books, 2006) and 'Remembering and Imagining Slavery: Postcolonial Identities and the Memorial Landscape in the Eastern Caribbean', in Anna Scacchi's and Elisa Bordin's *Transatlantic Memories of Slavery: Reimagining the Past, Changing the Future* (Cambria Press, forthcoming).

Françoise Vergès holds the 'Global South(s)' Chair at the Collège d'études mondiales, Paris, is Consulting Professor at Goldsmiths College, London and works as an expert for the Memorial of the Abolition of Slavery of Nantes. She has published extensively on the memories of slavery, Frantz Fanon, Aimé Césaire, French republican colonialism, postcolonialism, feminist theory and the postcolonial museum. She is the author of films, works regularly with artists and has curated exhibitions for the Memorial of Nantes.

Index